POLAND 1945

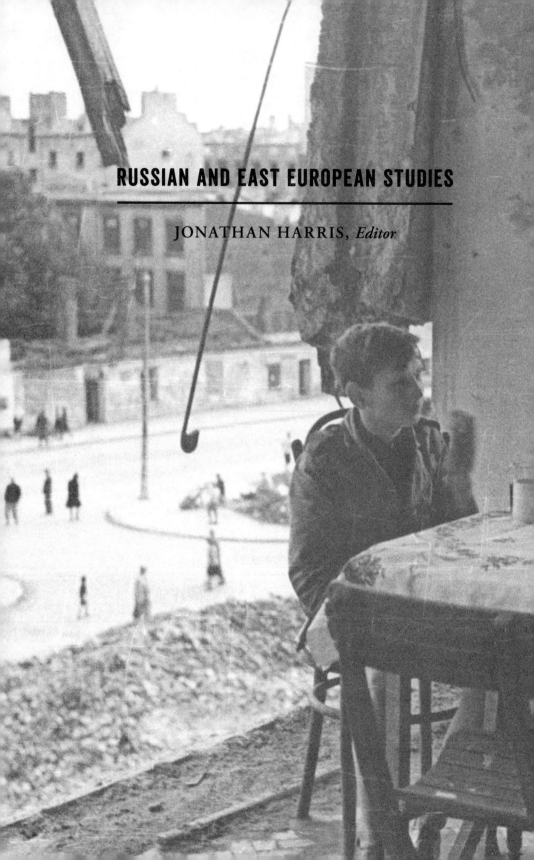

RUSSIAN AND EAST EUROPEAN STUDIES

JONATHAN HARRIS, *Editor*

POLAND 1945

WAR AND PEACE

MAGDALENA GRZEBAŁKOWSKA
TRANSLATED BY JOHN MARKOFF AND MAŁGORZATA MARKOFF

UNIVERSITY *of* PITTSBURGH PRESS

This publication has been supported by the
©POLAND Translation Program

Published by the University of Pittsburgh Press, Pittsburgh, Pa., 15260
Copyright © 2020, University of Pittsburgh Press
Manufactured in the United States of America
Printed on acid-free paper
10 9 8 7 6 5 4 3 2 1

Cataloging-in-Publication data is available from the Library of Congress

ISBN 13: 978-0-8229-4599-4
ISBN 10: 0-8229-4599-1

Cover photograph: A family meal in a destroyed building. Warsaw, September 1945.
Cover design: Alex Wolfe

To my grandmother Władysława Gawryluk,
who in 1945 was seventeen years old.

CONTENTS

POLAND 1945

JANUARY 1945

I will buy wall maps: Poland under the Piast dynasty, the Polish Commonwealth in 1771, Orbis terrarium antiqui.

—*Rzeczpospolita*, Jan. 1, 1945

• • • • • • • • • • • • • • • • • •

On January 3, 4, and 5 the Polish Army Theatre is again performing The Wedding by Stanisław Wyspiański after the interruption caused by Miss Kossobudzka's illness.

—*Rzeczpospolita*, Jan. 4, 1945

• • • • • • • • • • • • • • • • • •

Warsaw is free!

—*Życie Warszawy*, Jan. 17, 1945

• • • • • • • • • • • • • • • • • •

The City Commandant announces that on January 18 it is permitted to remain outdoors until 10 p.m. due to the liberation of Warsaw.

—*Życie Warszawy*, Jan. 18, 1945

• • • • • • • • • • • • • • • • • •

Journalists (columnists, reporters, technical personnel) as well as persons with skills and a passion for journalism will be hired. Apply at Administration, Życie Warszawy, 194 Grochowska Street.

—*Życie Warszawy*, Jan. 21, 1945

• • • • • • • • • • • • • • • • • •

We will base our Western border on the Oder and the Neisse.

—*Życie Warszawy*, Jan. 22, 1945

• • • • • • • • • • • • • • • • • •

Halina Hanczke-Świder is searching for Zofia Kozłowska, age 57, residing at 11 Słupecka Street, and Tadeusz Hanczke, a surveyor, age 37, residing at 62 Filtrowa Street.

—*Życie Warszawy*, Jan. 23, 1945

• • • • • • • • • • • • • • • • • •

I announce that the Municipal Abbatoirs are now open, specifically, at 1/2 Sierakowski Street where calves, sheep, goats, and pigs are slaughtered and at 48 Grenadierów Street, where horses are slaughtered. Unregistered slaughter is strictly forbidden and punishable by law.

—*Życie Warszawy*, Jan. 23, 1945

• • • • • • • • • • • • • • • • • •

In Warsaw the first teahouse has been opened in the courtyard of the demolished building at 71 Marszałkowska Street.

—*Rzeczpospolita*, Jan. 24, 1945

• • • • • • • • • • • • • • • • • •

I am searching for two seven-year-old girls, Jolanta Zielińska and Krystyna Zielińska, who had resided at 44 Grójecka Street before the events and were later sent to the Pruszków Transit Camp. They vanished without a trace. Leave a message at 44 Grójecka Street, Warsaw."

—*Życie Warszawy*, Jan. 24, 1945

• • • • • • • • • • • • • • • • • •

Today, on Jan. 25 at 4 p.m., Wanda Wasilewska will deliver a speech on Polish Radio.

—*Rzeczpospolita*, Jan. 25, 1945

• • • • • • • • • • • • • • • • • •

Frozen potatoes can be consumed. They only have to be peeled and blanched with hot water. As a result, they will lose their sweetish flavor. Holders of category V coupons may stock up on frozen potatoes. District Food Supply Offices.

—*Życie Warszawy*, Jan. 26, 1945

• • • • • • • • • • • • • • • • • • •

Proprietors of all tailor shops, registered and unregistered, who are not working for the army, are called on to report before Jan. 31 at the Industrial Department, Light Industry Section, at 306 Grochowska Street, room 9, in order to sign their contracts for military orders.

—*Życie Warszawy*, Jan. 30, 1945

• • • • • • • • • • • • • • • • • • •

The Polish Teachers' Association asks to be notified about vacant rooms for its members who lost their only homes due to wartime events.

—*Życie Warszawy*, Jan. 30, 1945

Figure 1.1. Riverfront, a Polish city. 1945. PAP (Polish Press Agency).

Remembering

My grandmother who was born in 1926 doesn't remember the end of the war.

"But how is this possible?" I'm surprised. "You don't remember how that sailor was kissing a nurse in Times Square?" I was born in 1972.

"My child," Grandma gives me a pitying look. "That was the *American* end of the war, in August 1945."

"But perhaps you remember fireworks in Warsaw on May 9? In the ruins of the Central Railway Station, the Soviets shot up the skies from the gun tractors of their 155 mm howitzers."

"Come on," says Grandma, "You know very well that I was not in Warsaw at that time."

On May 7, 1945, she certainly wasn't in Reims either, where Germans signed the act of surrender for the first time. Nor was she in Berlin a day later, where at the demand of Joseph Stalin they signed it again. She couldn't see the French representative General Jean de Lattre de Tassigny threatening to kill himself in the headquarters of Marshal Georgy Zhukov. The Americans, Russians, and British hadn't agreed to his signature on the act of surrender. Finally, after numerous hours of negotiations, they gave in. In Germany it was almost midnight on May 8. In Moscow it was already May 9, 1945.

"But you must remember the end of the war somehow." I don't give up: "I would remember."

Grandma searches her memory. Yes, now she remembers. It was in Weinsberg, in a transit camp surrounded by vineyards, designed for foreigners and protected by Americans. She ended up there after she had escaped from a labor camp in Mannheim, where for several years she made ammunition and spare tractor parts for the Germans.

"We were waiting for that day, though in fact we had been liberated for weeks," Grandma reminisces. "I remember standing on a huge square in a crowd of boys and girls—Poles, Lithuanians, Czechs, French, and others. Someone shouted, 'The war has ended right this moment! They signed!' We started to shout, soldiers were firing a salute, and we were kissing one another at random."

"You too, Grandma?"

"What do you think?" she asks. "When it's the end of the war, you don't care if someone is Polish, Russian, or American. You just kiss everyone."

My grandmother spent the entire year of 1945 and half the next one in Germany.

"Don't go back. The Communists will send you to Siberia right away," said the emissaries of the London government to scare the former forced laborers.

"Come back, we need your hands, we have to rebuild the country," said the envoys of the Polish government to convince them.

"Did you want to return?" I ask Grandma. "Did you know that Poland had changed shape? That your mother was transferred from Lwów to Gdańsk? Did you get the news that the Germans had to move to the West? Did you hear that Warsaw was turned into ruins?"

"I knew a little bit. My mama and I exchanged letters," she says. "And I was not going back. In Weinsberg I married your grandfather, whom I had met in a camp near Mannheim. Then I had a baby. We were planning to emigrate to Canada; my family was there."

But Grandma's baby died of meningitis, and after that nothing mattered to her. She was not afraid of anything—Communists, Siberia, ruins, or repatriation. She decided to go back to her mother, so one day she and Grandpa took a train to the new Poland. From Germany they brought a jar of candies and a little mutt. Grandma had taken pity on him after American soldiers had attached an Iron Cross to his neck and chased him through the streets of a German town.

Finally, in September 1946 my grandparents arrived in Gdańsk and knocked at the door of her old house on Bitwa Oliwska Street. The door was opened by Stefania, my great-grandmother, after whom I got my middle name. I'm curious.

"Do you remember what she said when she saw you?"

"She said nothing," says Grandma.

"You don't remember?" I ask.

"I remember very well. My mother began to cry. 'Why did you come back here, my child? What for?' She wept. 'It is horrible in this Poland.'"

FEBRUARY 1945

General Włodzimierz Nałęcz Gembicki is searching for his sister-in-law Maria Nałęcz Gembicka and her daughter Basia. Address: Sokołów Podlaski.

—*Życie Warszawy*, Feb. 2, 1945

• • • • • • • • • • • • • • • • • •

The Jewish Community of Warsaw announces that its activity in Warsaw has been resumed at a new office at 41 Targowa Street.

—*Życie Warszawy*, Feb. 2, 1945

• • • • • • • • • • • • • • • • • •

Bathroom mirrors, pocket mirrors. Wholesale. Granica Glassworks, 105 Grochowska Street.

—*Życie Warszawy*, Feb. 2, 1945

• • • • • • • • • • • • • • • • • •

The management of the clubhouse of the 24th District Civic Committee at 20 Piotr Skarga Street informs the residents of Targówek that the new clubhouse hosts a library. We are open every day and you can join anytime.

—*Życie Warszawy*, Feb. 3, 1945

• • • • • • • • • • • • • • • • • •

I will sell white and red cloth suitable for national flags. Information at 18 Kawęczyńska Street.

—*Życie Warszawy*, Feb. 3, 1945

• • • • • • • • • • • • • • • • • •

Attorney will buy judicial robes, copies of the civil code, and will rent a typewriter. 17 Wileńska Street.

—*Życie Warszawy*, Feb. 4, 1945

• • • • • • • • • • • • • • • • • •

The Administration of Post and Telegraphs is appealing to everyone to return furniture, equipment, and other office items illegally taken from its pillaged buildings at Warszawska Street and other places.

—*Dziennik Polski*, Feb. 6, 1945

• • • • • • • • • • • • • • • • • •

I will sell a large quantity of shoe polish. I am looking for a business partner. Information: 60 Kawcza Street.

—*Życie Warszawy*, Feb. 6, 1945

• • • • • • • • • • • • • • • • • •

I inform my parents Anna and Stanisław Orlikowski, residing in Włoszczowa at 21 Sienkiewicz Street, that we are alive. We are waiting, come get us. Marta Świderska, Warsaw-Praga, 6 Białostocka Street.

—*Życie Warszawy*, Feb. 6, 1945

• • • • • • • • • • • • • • • • • •

Ms. Grottowa is looking for her son, his name is Wiesław Grott, and he was one year and five months old when on August 7, 1944, on Chłodna Street, a German snatched him from his father and handed him to a stranger. Light hair, black eyes, dressed in two undershirts, a shirt with blue and white stripes, a navy blue sweater, long white underwear, a white coat, and a blue cap with a white rim. Praga, 51 Radzymińska Street, Władysława Grott.

—*Życie Warszawy*, Feb. 7, 1945

• • • • • • • • • • • • • • • • • •

The Food Rationing Department announces that it will be issuing a hundred grams of butter priced at 16.50 zlotys per kilo to any one holding extra coupons for children. The butter will be provided in installments, subject to new deliveries. The present supplies are enough for about eight thousand children.

—*Życie Warszawy*, Feb. 8, 1945

• • • • • • • • • • • • • • • • •

A brochure describing the trial of the Majdanek Camp criminals will be published soon in 150,000 copies. The trial took place in November last year in Lublin.

—*Dziennik Polski*, Krakow, Feb. 12, 1945

• • • • • • • • • • • • • • • • •

Polish Radio is about to begin special broadcasts for families searching for relatives. Submissions free, Polish Radio, 63 Targowa Street. All announcements submitted to Polish Radio are free of charge.

—*Życie Warszawy*, Feb. 15, 1945

• • • • • • • • • • • • • • • • •

On January 5, 1945 a green rucksack was lost on the way from Lublin to Garwolin. The rucksack contained a purse with the only photos of a child who died during wartime events. Please send the photos to: Colonel Wiktor Grosz, Włochy, 39 Moniuszko Street.

—*Życie Warszawy*, Feb. 15, 1945

• • • • • • • • • • • • • • • • •

At the moment there are twenty-four canteens in Warsaw dispensing over eight thousand meals a day. Five bakeries have been opened. Starting February 20, the number of working bakeries will significantly increase.

—*Życie Warszawy*, Feb. 20, 1945

• • • • • • • • • • • • • • • • •

Since the food factories are now in full operation, jam rations on coupons will be available this month. Soon we will be distributing frozen fish, half a kilo per person.

—*Dziennik Polski*, Krakow, Feb. 23, 1945

• • • • • • • • • • • • • • • • •

The Chief Municipal Administration of Warsaw-Praga has issued the ordinance that: (1) all dogs have to be tethered but dogs being walked have to be muzzled and on a leash. Stray dogs roaming the streets will be eliminated (killed) by the police and the army. (2) This ordinance is in force for three months throughout the district of Warsaw-Praga. Doctor Donat Grądzki, veterinarian.

—*Życie Warszawy*, Feb. 23, 1945

• • • • • • • • • • • • • • • • •

Polish fiscal authorities are returning to prewar legislation and call for timely payment of current taxes and payment of overdue bills. There are no war-related tax allowances.

—*Życie Warszawy*, Feb. 27, 1945

• • • • • • • • • • • • • • • • •

Today, Tuesday February 27, in the Artists' Café, Jan Sztaudynger will read his Poem about Paris, written partly in Lublin.

—*Gazeta Lubelska*, Feb. 27, 1945

Junk, or Loot

Initially, they picked a large brick house with a barn in back, a granary, and beehives in the garden. They came to the front entrance and, after dismounting slowly, relaxed their backs, aching after the long ride. Steamy breath was coming from the horses' muzzles, dusk was settling in, and the temperature was freezing. Ten sleighs, twenty people, including two women.

How did they enter the house? Perhaps quietly, as if they were entering a church, touching reverently the upholstery of leather armchairs, something never seen before in their lives? Perhaps stamping a foot, just to scare away "those people" if they were still around? Did they stand silent in the living room among sideboards, paintings, and china figurines, wondering how they would display them on the shelves in their own shacks? Or did they scatter immediately, touching everything with their fingers like children and shouting, "It's mine"?

Niusia remembers that the man in charge told them not to touch anything. "You can't take anything just for yourself. Right now, we're going to sleep and in the morning we'll depart as a group, and whatever we find, we'll share equally."

Late that evening they had dinner. "Those people" had left slightly stale bread in the kitchen but the newcomers were afraid to eat it. What if it had been poisoned? So they ate their own supplies. They brewed coffee. It was bitter. Someone went out to the orchard, broke open a beehive, and pulled out honeycombs full of sleepy bees. They sweetened the coffee with honey, spitting the drowned bees to the floor.

In the morning they went down to the basement. One man, the most important among them, was hitting the dirt floor with a stick. They heard a hollow sound and began to dig. Under a thin layer of dirt they found two large, heavy chests.

It was January 1945, maybe February. Niusia doesn't remember exactly any more.

A HORSE, SOME QUILTS, AND A PHOTO ALBUM

How does it feel when you pull out the drawers from someone's cupboard and decide that from now on the silverware with the strangers' initials will touch your lips, or when you slip your hand between the sheet beneath and the quilt above, where someone else slept not so long ago, or when you examine coats, slips, and dresses left in the closet by a former owner? How do you ask the kind elderly lady who is sitting on the sofa in her room, "Miss Niusia, did you feel any remorse because of that?" How will I be able to understand her response, I who have never lived through war?

For now, I just sit down at her table and listen. About her father, an organist, whose name was Kazimierz, and his second wife Justyna, and their only child Niusia born in 1927, spoiled, bratty, independent, and determined.

"I had anything I wanted. When I insisted on going with my parents to a party at our priest's, I would go. Or to a party at our Russian Orthodox friends', I would go, too. I was headstrong."

She talks about her childhood in Bakałarzewo, a little town near Suwałki, separated from East Prussia only by a lake. About the only German in town who right before the war went for a walk with his family and never came back because he fled to Prussia. About another German who used to come from the Prussian side to the Polish side and swam in the lake with his Alsatian dog. About the German military policemen who drank vodka in the Bakałarzewo tavern, and when they were going back, staggering, children would follow them, shouting, "Hitler! Hitler!"

I ask about the war. Were they taken by surprise? No, not all. In August 1939 there were too many Polish soldiers sitting in the church tower watching the Germans across the lake through their binoculars, and too many were digging trenches at the border. So Niusia knew something was up. Even before that fateful September her father had harnessed a horse, while her mother tossed quilts and a photo album on the wagon, and then with a cow tied to the carriage they rode east. On September 1, 1939, when the Germans invaded Poland, the family was already in Sztabin, beyond Suwałki, and a few days later they reached Majewo near Sokółka, where Kazimierz found work as an organist.

When they returned to their village two months later, the former Bakałarzewo was no more. At the beginning of the war it had been a site of heavy fighting. Wooden houses were burned down, the church and school were partially bombed, their home was occupied by the Germans, but it had been looted (someone had stolen the furniture, the piano, and Niusia's guitar), and the stored grain had been carried away. The local Jews had disappeared.

Nevertheless, they spent the entire occupation in Bakałarzewo. Niusia's father bought a wooden house in Aleksandrów from some Old Believers who were being resettled to Lithuania by the Germans, and relocated it near an old house that had burned down in September. There was no school for Polish children. Niusia was taking piano lessons from a man her father knew and she read the popular novel *The Deluge* about a Swedish invasion three centuries earlier. Together with her father she made copies of birth and death certificates for other villagers who needed them, she issued sugar coupons for the local community under German orders, and she worked in the field for a *bauer*, a German farmer on the Prussian side of the border. Eventually, by the fall of 1944 the battle front to the east of Bakałarzewo was getting closer.

"Dad decided to go to Suwałki. We stayed with our friends and spent Christmas Eve with them. One day the Russkis entered the house, each carrying almost a kilo of *tushonka*, American canned meat. Mom cooked some soup for them. And then they told us that Bakałarzewo was free," said Niusia

SHOES

I try to imagine the Niusia of almost seven decades ago. She is walking along the empty country road. It's the beginning of January 1945, snowy, freezing. The front is now somewhere to the west. It will be a long and harsh winter. Those who will fall into the sea from the ship *Gustloff* will freeze to death in a few minutes. The girl isn't wearing heavy clothes because she has twenty kilometers ahead of her and she doesn't want to become hot. She is walking back to Bakałarzewo by herself to check whether their house has survived.

And her parents let her go just like that? Niusia, now age eighty-six, nods from her sofa, "It's strange. I must have insisted. I was terribly foolish."

So Niusia, age eighteen, keeps walking. She is passed by Soviet soldiers and processions of civilian sleighs. Sometimes the drivers give her a lift but they don't say where they are going and for what. Later on Niusia will come to the conclusion that they were the first looters.

"Two kilometers before Bakałarzewo I wondered what was there, in the fields on both sides of the river. It was many dead Russians. Piles of bodies. And bare feet. People had already managed to take away their shoes. There were many rifles and pistols beside the corpses and I came closer to see them."

Once in Bakałarzewo, Niusia could see that their family house had survived.

"When Mom and Dad found out the place was liberated and our house unburned, we returned. There were no windows because the glass was shattered, so Dad and I went one kilometer to Prussia. We selected some windows and brought them to Poland. Do you want to know how we did it? We simply ripped the windows from the walls and took them. There was nobody at that German house anymore. We went inside. Clothes were hanging in the closets; quilts were piled on the beds. There was food, stale bread, lard, and cured meat in the cabinets. However, we didn't touch any of it. Dad and I framed those windows in our house and then we could live in it," related Niusia.

Not long after this, a neighbor and his wife paid a visit, sat down at the kitchen table, and asked if the organist, Niusia's father, wanted to ride with them.

"Where to?" he expressed his curiosity.

"To the Prussian side, for junk," the neighbor responded. (Niusia will learn the word *looting* later.)

The father didn't want to go. But his daughter did. She started to get ready.

"Wait a minute, Niusia, your parents let you go just like that? All by yourself, ten sleighs, twenty people, only two women?" I ask.

Today, sitting under a landscape painting Niusia wrinkles her nose and tries to remember.

"How did it go? My Dad may have agreed . . . but I would have gone anyway, even if he hadn't allowed me. As I said, I was headstrong."

So they harnessed Niusia's horse to a sleigh and pulled off. Earlier, the man in charge had said: "We pick the manors and houses of rich farmers. Poor shacks are a waste of time. Sleighs in front of the house are a sign that our people are already there, so we keep moving. We share everything equally. Let's go!"

They picked a large brick house with a barn in back, a granary, and beehives in the garden.

FELLOW COUNTRYMEN, WE IMPLORE YOU!

Looters or *szabrownicy*. They walk, rush, and ride across the entire country. On foot, with carts, on bicycles, sleighs, and wagons, or hitchhiking with Soviet drivers. Winter, spring, summer, fall. Anyone and everyone. The early bird gets the worm. People from the countryside and from the cities. From Bakałarzewo, Suwałki, from Białystok, from Warsaw, Rzeszów, and Krakow. All of Poland is looting. Poles plunder villages and cities, country shacks and manors, apartment houses and offices, churches and museums, warehouses and train stations.

Szabrować means "to loot" and is derived from criminal slang. Looters have their own unwritten code of honor. They don't kill and take only what is "nobody's." But when they encounter a German, a Mazur, a Kashub, or a Silesian they rob him because he is not one of them. The looted goods are sold, swapped, or kept for personal use.

Looters are not divided into social classes and no one puts on any airs. They are prewar criminals, the unemployed, workers, peasants, teachers, clerks, housewives and high-society ladies, Polish and Soviet soldiers.

How many are they? Thousands, hundreds of thousands, millions? No one has been able to come up with a number. Academics will tell us they were driven by curiosity, poverty, revenge on Germans, demoralization, an upset postwar equilibrium, a broken moral compass, avarice, and wit. And by tradition.

The historian Marcin Zaremba, author of *Wielka trwoga* [The great fear], writes that looting always occurs during a transitional period, when one authority is on the way out and the next one has not yet been established. This has always been a part of any crisis, all over Europe. During unsettled periods, peasants attacked manor houses, servants stole property left by the dead lord, and during riots in the cities, shops and warehouses were also ransacked.

During the great flood in Poland in 1934, looters even showed up in the regions under water. At the time of the September Campaign of 1939, they combed through the property left in the backwaters by people taking flight and they plundered factories and storehouses in Warsaw. They were immediately attracted by the liquidation of the Jewish ghettoes carried on extensively by the Germans from the first years of the war. On September 18, 1942, the *Information Bulletin* of the Home Army wrote that "on this memorable day of the liquidation of the Otwock ghetto," Polish residents of Otwock, Rembertów, and Miedzeszyn "arrived at night in their horse-wagons, just a few hours after that barbaric act, and began to loot Jewish property. Whatever they could lay a hand on, they took away. They ripped off doors and windows, shelves, floor planks, not to mention furniture, clothes, and underwear that were the first things ransacked. . . . In the name of the noblest laws of God and man we implore you, fellow countrymen, not to demean yourselves to the level of wild dogs."

THE POLISH COMMITTEE OF NATIONAL LIBERATION IS STANDING UP

But the greatest wave of looting comes with the liberation.

In Lublin people are already looting between July 21 and 24, 1944, while the Germans are fleeing and the Red Army is entering. They take away private and public property, equipment from the municipal abattoir and furniture from offices. As a result, the staff of the Polish Committee of National Liberation have nothing to sit on. In August, looters are in Lvov and in January, they are in Radom, Krakow, Łódź, and in any little town that is regarded as liberated. Most of all, they are looking for food in shops, storehouses, mills, distilleries, bakeries, and slaughterhouses, but at the same time they take away anything they can carry, and sometimes they even snatch shoes from dead soldiers and civilians.

The left bank of Warsaw, liberated by the Soviets on January 17, 1945, is attacked by the looters the very next day. A desolated sea of rubble is raided from local villages. Soon after, they are joined by residents of Praga who walk from the right bank across the frozen river.

On January 20 reporters from the newspaper *Życie Warszawy* raise the alarm: "Hordes of plunderers that appear out of the blue are prowling in abandoned buildings. They pilfer everything: clothes, bed sheets, covers, pots and pans, even furniture is taken away on carts and horse-wagons that have come from God knows where." At the beginning of February the journalists write, "You can see women burdened with household appliances, children carrying sacks of books, and men pulling carts filled with furniture. Soft armchairs are thrown from the windows, falling right into the arms of thieves." In June 1945, the columnists of *Życie Warszawy* blame the looters for delays in rebuilding the capital: "Thousands of looters are still removing enormous quantities of windows, doors, gates, all kinds of fittings, locks, fixtures, all sorts of equipment, sheet metal, electric and telephone cables. From buildings that even right from the beginning were already livable or that needed only small repairs. In the market there is a vast quantity of looted objects."

But the looters will find their true El Dorado in the territories that not so long ago belonged to the German Reich. Later on Polish propaganda will call them the Recovered Territories.

A TUREEN WITH A GOLDEN RIM

They pulled the chests from the ground. One was full of dinner plates and bowls, teacups, jugs, saucers, and pots. And each object was white with a golden rim, made from porcelain so delicate that light could pass through. Twenty-four pieces of each. The second chest was filled with cut crystal glassware and ornamental bowls. "A plate for you, this one for you, for you a cup, and a jug for you." The man in charge was handing things out equally, even to someone who was caught at night in the granary, surreptitiously carrying out sacks of grain for himself. But somebody moved his ladder away, causing his fall. He was lucky. Nothing happened to him at that point. Later, punished by the group, he would be at the head of a convoy of sleighs through the frozen, mined marshlands.

Niusia took away a tureen with a golden rim, a white plate decorated with golden lilies, a crystal basket with a handle, and crystal salt and pepper shakers set on a sculptured base. She was convinced that the place had been inhabited by rich Germans.

They were packing the loot on the sleighs. Strong men were loading furniture and ornamented chests, Niusia was stowing crystal, porcelain, and a painting of Jesus knocking at the door. If they felt like it, they would tie quilts and covers with a rope. When they wanted to, they would roll the carpets from the floors and remove chandeliers from the ceiling, and they would load the beds on the sleighs as they pleased. Everyone was stuffing sacks of grain. The grain was not good for humans because before their departure "those people" poured kerosene on it. But it was all right for pigs and horses.

The man in charge wanted to grab a standing clock but its glass pane was broken and the hands were bent. Niusia was dreaming of a piano but it had been dragged into the courtyard, soaking wet, with a gap in its keys. It was a sign that before them someone else had been looking for junk.

Niusia's parents were happy on her return and liked all the things she brought.

Niusia now admits: "Looting seduced me."

A CUPBOARD AND A MOUSETRAP

"You ask me what it's like to enter someone else's home and take things arbitrarily? I'll tell you. It's better than in the fairy tales when you enter a room with an enchanted treasure chest because you are not allowed to take anything from it. Because here you come in and take what you want. You see hanging drapes? You take them, if you want to. If not, you don't. And you keep going. You ask me if I was afraid, or anxious, to set foot in a stranger's home? Well, no. At that time people were to some extent insatiable. And curious about how others lived, how they settled in.

"And it was all German. During the war I didn't experience anything bad from the Germans, but I remember their commander riding into the church on a horse. No, plundering their homes I didn't feel like a thief. After all, at that time the stuff belonged to no one. Yet I probably never would have entered Polish homes. Are you curious about how to distinguish a German house from a Polish one? German houses were made of brick, ours were made of wood. They had distinctive windows and in the kitchen their dinner sets differed from ours. We never met any owners there. But I know that sometimes they were hiding in the barns. It was dangerous, yet we didn't think about it. They were hiding horses, cows, and pigs from us. In the barns they built special cages and covered them with straw, so the animals wouldn't be visible. When our people found the cages, they would take them away, too.

"Later, I would go, too. Ten times perhaps. There was a high turnover of people in the bands. They would go in a couple of wagons, or a dozen, no one dared go alone. Everyone was going, anyone who felt like it. On wagons or on foot. Those who rushed there first opened the closets and picked the linen. No, not panties or undergarments but pillowcases, sheets, and covers. Right away, people were furnishing their homes fantastically! Oh my, what a great opportunity that looting was.

"We would go from one village to another, looking for grain. What was most important was to feed the pigs, to have fodder for the cows and oats for the horses. Everything else was just a chance opportunity. We would ride out no more than fifteen kilometers. Olecko was the farthest destination. Some of ours were venturing even to Giżycko, but I was never there. The bridge had collapsed. So it was mostly in the winter when the lake near Bakałarzewo was frozen that junk was moved around. When the ice broke, many people drowned, with horses and wagons. Not everyone managed to ride away from the lake up the steep slope. So people threw the loads off the sleighs. There were piles of chests, furniture, everything.

"I never found any valuable objects. Maybe the Germans took them away, maybe looters had found them before me. Looters left traces—burned holes in the living room floors, charred ceilings, and broken glass.

"Once I felt like taking a cupboard but our sleighs were already full and it wouldn't fit. I concocted a plan to unscrew its little doors, so without them it would be uninteresting to others. Then I went there for a second time to pick it up. It was pretty, white, more modern, and large. It even had an hourglass for cooking eggs. And many drawers. It separated our kitchen from a small room.

"Later, I brought a credenza with beautiful semicircular crystal sides. I also took a pair of light-colored beds and two matching nightstands with two little lamps. No one had grabbed them earlier because they were attached to the stands. And lovely mattresses. You know, we didn't take just anything. If we didn't like it in one place, we kept going. In this way I furnished my entire apartment. Because I was not going to get junk in order to trade it, but just for myself.

"Once Dad and I went to get a piano. Someone informed us that he had seen the instrument in one of the manors in Königsruh, now Dąbrowskie, halfway between Olecko and Bakałarzewo. On a whim we headed there, without any weapons. Together we lowered the piano from the second floor with a small pulley. The piano was black, ornamented, with brass candlesticks on the sides.

"Dad and I were in Olecko, too. We entered a shop, looked around, and saw little houses. Many of them. They were thirty centimeters high and forty centimeters wide. Wooden, made of planks, with a canopy and two stories. I took one. I didn't know what for. At home Dad and I had a closer look and it turned out to be a mousetrap!

"Looting was over in 1946 because people had arrived from all over the country and took over the houses. But even earlier the police were detaining the looters and seizing whatever they could find. Only instead of returning the stuff to the state, they would keep it for themselves. This way one policeman confiscated five cows and brought two of them to our pigpen. As soon as my Dad found out how they were obtained, he told him to take them back. He had no intention of dealing with a thief who was robbing people."

CABLES, PIPES, TRAIN TRACKS, AND BICYCLES

Looters' paradise: the Recovered Territories, that is, the previously German provinces that from now on will belong to Poland. The former inhabitants are gone and the new authority has not yet been consolidated. Some Germans have been able to flee to the already nonexistent Third Reich and those who stayed are waiting for a way out and mercy from the victors.

First come the Russians. They steal because they can, because they deserve it. This looting is official, almost bureaucratic. Special units are formed within the Red Army to manage the confiscation of property. Wherever they show up, they wreak havoc. They have power, authority, and transportation at their disposal. They take away entire factories. If a machine is too big to pass through a factory gate, they drag it through the wall. They take away 4,835 tons of equipment from the steam engine repair factory in Oleśnica. They dismantle clocks from the church towers. They rip up train tracks together with their foundations. They take away 866 kilometers of narrow-gauge railroad track from Silesia and Pomerania. In Wrocław they order newly arrived Polish civilians to move out from certain neighborhoods, so no one will disturb them while looting. They remove nineteen turbines from the Silesian power plants and in Gliwice they steal equipment from the factories, the hospitals, the pumping station, and the slaughterhouse. They burn books to warm themselves and drink pure alcohol from specimen jars looted from library halls, medical academies, and hospitals. They load knobs and heaters onto train wagons, they pull cables, pipes, and bathroom fixtures from the buildings. They drive herds of captured cattle. But they don't only loot the Recovered Territories. They grab anything that falls into their hands, for example in Łódź or Poznań.

It happens occasionally that some goods are damaged during dismantling. Or, put aside and forgotten, they rust in the rain and no one comes back for them. But if the Russians aren't able to steal something, they generally destroy it. On Hitler's birthday, April 20, 1945, they set Eylau on fire, a city that survived the war intact. On Victory Day they burn the historic center of Leignitz. In March 1945 the Provisional Government of National Unity (the Lublin-based pro-Soviet Poles) signs an agreement with the commanders of the Soviet army under which the Russians can freely dispose of German property, including property on the territories awarded to Poland. From that moment on the Russians act under cover of law.

Only on August 16, 1945, will the Soviet Union sign an agreement with the Provisional Government about German reparations for damages and renounce its claims to German property throughout the entire territory of Poland. But Red Army soldiers will ignore the law and continue to loot extensively.

In 1947 the Russians will estimate that up to August 2, 1945, on the territories acquired by Poland from Germany, the value of dismantled equipment and materials totaled $235.5 million. The value of equipment and materials taken away from Soviet-occupied Germany was assessed at $79.1 million.

A PRETTY COW AT THE ROADSIDE

Soviet soldiers, permanently drunk, are also looting all on their own. They are like children in a toy store without adults. They like a bicycle ridden by someone on a road? They take the bicycle. A cow at the roadside is pretty? It will be theirs. Polish homes, German homes, it doesn't matter. They enter as if the houses were their own, they aim their rifles at the owners and rummage in the drawers, search the pantries, and look under the mattresses. A bracelet, a jar of preserves, or a nightgown have the same value for them. Sometimes, as their way of saying good-bye, they rape the lady of the house and kill her husband.

Looted objects are traded for alcohol or sent home. Starting in December 1944 Soviet privates are permitted to ship a five-kilo parcel every month, and for officers the allowance is doubled.

Poles who were robbed complain to the police. Police officers try to go after the soldiers. In June 1945 police officers from Gdańsk file a report: "Unknown perpetrators from the Red Army assaulted the residence of the Wejherowo village police chief. After stealing food and clothing they fled. The perpetrators haven't been apprehended and the incident has been reported to the Red Army commandant who launched an investigation." In June the police raise the alarm: "Eight Soviet soldiers who had been rampaging through the area and stealing were caught. When police officers demanded their IDs they responded by shooting." In October they reveal: "During military movements numerous robberies committed by Soviet soldiers were reported."

Polish authorities are helpless. They can't officially condemn the army of the victors. Russian looters would then have to be called deserters and marauders. So the reports documenting their crimes become confidential. The Soviet military authorities are not consistent; sometimes an apprehended looter will get a one-day jail sentence, sometimes it will be the death penalty.

KHOROSHIYE SAPOGI—GOOD SHOES

I advertise in *Gazeta Wyborcza* that I am looking for memoirs from 1945. I get a reply from Ewa Prussak. She is keeping the memoirs written by her father, Wiktor Kaźmierowicz, in a clothbound volume. She lends it to me for a while.

In 1945 Kaźmierowicz, a Home Army soldier, had just graduated from high school and he was taking the train from central Poland to Wrocław to attend university. Many years after this journey he wrote: "The train was barely moving. Suddenly near the tracks, in the air, we noticed sparks that were coming closer to us very fast. The sparks turned out to be the glowing cigarettes of Soviet soldiers. They were on their way to loot. One of them was climbing awkwardly from the ground to the buffer. He grabbed my leg and started feeling my shoes. I heard, 'Khoroshiye sapogi, davai' (in other words, "good shoes, give them to me"). I kicked him with my other foot. The *boytsy*—brawlers—spread all over the train like worms. If they couldn't get inside, they would scurry around on the roofs. In their free hands they were lugging suitcases and bundles seized from the passengers.

Figure 2.1. Poster, 1946: "Looting, bribery, and theft don't pay." Archive

We could hear them swearing in Russian. The train was gaining speed and rushing into the dark night. The cries of the robbed passengers were getting louder and louder. The situation was really dangerous. But in an instant everything went silent. We were approaching some station. It was Kalisz. The train stopped. We looked out at the illuminated platform and we saw a few armed railwaymen and a large unit of the political police, the NKVD. They surrounded the train and began hunting for the night robbers. Most of them were caught. We got off the train and watched the passing scene. NKVD officers were leading the seized and disarmed fighters, who were walking like sheep, heads down, lugging their stolen booty. They were ordered to form a line and put the spoils down before them. There were a few dozen of them. They were surrounded by a crowd of angry plundered people. Many had no shoes or jackets. They were searching for their own belongings. Then some vans appeared and the NKVD officers started to shove their captives in. Some went in obediently, without making trouble. Others were resisting, struggling, and literally digging in their heels. I asked a railroad guard next to me why they were trying so hard to free themselves. It turned out that one out of every ten or so of them would be executed behind the station at random, as an example, and the railway guards would later have to dispose of their bodies."

THE LOOTERS' UNION

Following the Russians, a large wave of Polish looters moves to the Recovered Territories. Propaganda portrays Lower Silesia and former Prussia as a land of milk and honey, where fully furnished mansions are waiting for everyone, and the streets are covered with treasures abandoned by the Germans. In June 1945 *Życie Warszawy* reported: "The courtyards, streets, and squares of Olsztyn and Elbląg are covered with dozens of usable items. There are parts of mechanized vehicles and huge quantities of clothing abandoned in the ruins. They are not very damaged, but for a looter pursuing quick gains they are no longer valuable. And what can we say about demolished furniture, kitchen pots, household appliances, and piles of down filling lingering in the staircases?"

The majority of the looters are retailers. They go to the Recovered Territories even a dozen times but they only bring back what they are able to carry and sell themselves. Some of them are moving around the country by the Orbis bus, nicknamed "the lootbus."

Some looters, however, turn into wholesalers and begin to specialize in a single type of item for which there is demand. As a result, there are experts in coffeemakers, grinders, and household appliances for coffee shops and restaurants, as well as plates and cups that end up in Warsaw restaurants and cafés from Gdańsk and Wrocław. There are specialists in medicines who penetrate the abandoned pharmacies and later sell the drugs they find at markets all over the country. There are looters of books, paintings and sculptures, and car parts. A group of employees from the Post and Telegraphs Management plunders telecommunications equipment.

One Wrocław apartment was turned into a storehouse of household goods. Joanna Konopińska, who settled in Wrocław in 1945, writes in her memoirs, "The floor in this apartment was covered with a thick layer of carpets, one upon the other. Along the wall there were paintings of varied value, hanging and standing clocks, and wrist and pocket watches. The adjacent room was filled with several pianos." She adds, "There are many people—looters—who come here; they gather what they can and then they set off. . . . A quip circulates: 'The union was new, but how it grew! The Union of Looters.'"

Looting is a profitable moneymaking operation for office workers as well as senior officers of the Polish Army and the Office of Public Security, who are all sent to the Recovered Territories to maintain order. Those working for starvation wages often quit their jobs and turn to looting. Some find ways to keep changing their officially assigned, post-German apartments, in order to create an opportunity: while they are moving into their new homes, they clean out the old ones. Some make a fortune from looting. Lieutenant Colonel Faustyn Grzybkowski, the chief of the Regional Office of Public Security in Wrocław, steals a tiara with cut diamonds, a 24-carat gold bar, twenty-four German gold coins, several gold brooches with diamonds, and sixty-five other items made of gold. He also steals antique furniture, fur coats, and clothing. He shares the plundered assets with his supervisors, of course.

Kazimierz Brandys describes his trip to Silesia and his meeting with an official looter, a top manager, Z., in city C., who welcomed him with the declaration that it was only love for this place that was making him stay and sacrifice himself. "Signet rings on his fingers and his custom-made suit of English wool made me suspicious. In the house, or rather the mansion, he was occupying I saw marvels of luxury. His millions stared at the me from

Figure 2.2. Wrocław, Grunwald Square. The most famous looters' square in the Recovered Territories. City Museum of Wrocław.

each wall or each corner. . . . By accident, I found out that they called him the king of looting."

Szaberplac, or Looters' Square, becomes the most prominent spot in Wrocław. Originally, this was located at Mathias Platz (later Św. Maciej Square) and later it moved to Grunwald Square. Only barter transactions are in force. "Money has no value," notes Konopińska.

Here Germans barter their remaining property, mainly for food. Russian soldiers trade watches. Former forced laborers from Yugoslavia, France, or Greece, who haven't returned to their countries yet, swap silverware for paintings, mirrors for vases, and gramophones for fox collars. Live cats, rabbits, and chickens fetch high prices. But the most visible people are Poles. Among them are those who came to Wrocław for good and are dealing in objects found in rubble and ruins. But there are also those who commute by "the lootbus" or by train. For them it doesn't pay to carry off sewing machines and typewriters, bathroom tubs, gas heaters, and sacral figures ripped from historic altars, so they exchange them for more convenient objects. The Polish mathematician Hugo Steinhaus from Lvov will describe the "szaberplac" in Wrocław as "the largest gathering of panhandlers sitting on the largest pile of bricks and debris in Europe."

DOES WARSAW REALLY LACK FOR BRICKS?

Wrocław becomes the city of official looting. Nobody believes that the Recovered Territories will stay in Polish hands forever. So people would rather grab whatever they can, whatever they can take away, while there is still time. The authorities in Wrocław are flooded with requests from all over the country to donate badly needed items.

There is no furniture at the universities in Warsaw? Let's bring it from Wrocław.

A new national slogan: *The entire nation builds its capital*. Really? Then headed to Warsaw are bricks from demolished buildings, twenty-five wagons, thirty-five streetcars, gas lamps, even medical specimens, all shipped from Wrocław. Konopińska notes in her diary: "Does Warsaw really lack bricks from its own demolished buildings so badly that they have to be imported from this far away? . . . Railroad tracks were laid down on Wrocław's Oławska Street to make it easier to cart stuff away and now bricks cleaned of mortar are shipped off in freight cars." At the same time some buildings that could have easily been preserved are taken apart, and the ornamental elements from historic monuments in Wrocław are delivered to Warsaw for the future reconstruction of its Old Town.

The Music Academy in Krakow doesn't have any pianos? Wrocław has them, so it should give them away. In the future Wrocław will publish newspapers and books, but in the meantime its rotary printing presses are on the way to the capital. They will be used to print *Express Wieczorny*. In October 1945 *Pionier*, a Wrocław daily, informs its readers that this is a gift from Wrocław to Warsaw.

The furnishings of museums and churches from Lower Silesia are scattered all over the country. The principal recipient of the historic artifacts is Warsaw, but Poznań, Krakow, or Gdańsk are not fussing either. All of Poland hopes to enrich its collections with "gifts" from the Recovered Territories. The sword of justice from Świdnica turns up in the National

Museum in Kielce, and a collection of tiles from Ząbkowice Śląskie appears in Malbork Castle. A plate from the Bakers Guild in Dzierżoniów goes to Słupsk, and the artwork and historic furniture from the Reuss palace in Staniszów travel to museums in Warsaw and Krakow. Twenty-eight freight cars and 118 trucks filled with art collections will leave Lower Silesia and Opolian Silesia for good. Seventy years later Silesia will try to get them back, in vain.

Animals from the Wrocław Zoo, the three hundred that survived the war, also become "recovered property." Joanna Konopińska writes: "Recently, there are rumors that the rescued animals will be sent to the Poznań Zoo." Moritz the chimp goes to Łódź, Lola the bear goes to Krakow, Bärbel the giraffe and Lorbas the hippo travel to Poznań, and Beste the bison will end up first in Łódź and then in Białowieża Forest.

NECESSARY EVIL

During the first months after liberation Polish authorities turn a blind eye to looting. They are not capable of feeding, clothing, and housing all the Poles. So when people try to take care of themselves, the authorities regard it as a necessary evil. The newspapers are still condemning the looters, but they are also able to justify them. Even when they do reproach them, they do so with humor. In May 1945 the magazine *Przekrój* publishes Karol Szpalski's anecdote, "About the Looters": "This morning I met a guy who introduced the term 'looting' to the market. 'Where did you get this wonderful word from?' I asked. 'From where? I've looted it,' he responded, winking at me." In July Gwidon Miklaszewski's cartoons appear. In one cartoon two characters look astonished. "You have so many things here," says the first. "Oh, yes," says a stout woman in a green dress. "My husband is taking charge of the house as much as he can! Whatever was interesting in Wrocław, Sir, you will find here!"

But the mood is changing. In mid-November 1945 the government officially proclaims looting a crime. At the end of the month, Edward Osóbka-Morawski, prime minister of the Provisional Government of National Unity, issues a circular in which he condemns looting in the western territories as pillage detrimental to the settlers, and outlaws it rigorously. From now on only President Bolesław Bierut personally can issue a permit allowing the removal of anything from the western territories. All other permits from the central offices are no longer valid.

Figure 2.3. Police officer confiscating a looted mirror. 1947. Jerzy Baranowski, PAP

The wave of looting doesn't cease immediately but it is slowly brought to an end. Yet it still happens that plundered goods are taken away, hidden among the official things, even in hearses—between the coffins. Looting fever on a large scale will finally end in the summer of 1946. More and more often the authorities organize roundups at the train stations or confiscate looted items from the markets and squares. Occasionally, they seize plundered furniture and valuable objects directly from apartments. They will be returned to their lawful owners if they can prove that they owned them before the war.

Some of the looters who are caught are arrested and some sent to forced labor in debris removal or road repairs. It is more and more difficult to find vacant apartments and houses. The Recovered Territories are filling up.

THE FIRE

On the day the war ends, during a walk near Bakałarzewo, Niusia's father will step on a mine and die on the spot. For the next few years Niusia will replace him as the local organist. Soon she will get married. Fifty-six years later she will become a widow.

In the late 1960s, a fire will break out in Niusia's wooden house, the one that had been bought by her father from some Old Believers in Aleksandrów. The fire will consume the more modern, white cupboard and the credenza with its beautiful semicircular sides, the pair of beds, the cut crystal baskets, the piano that had been lowered down from the manor in Königsruh, and the painting of Jesus knocking at the door. The only item rescued by Niusia from the fire will be the white tureen with the golden rim that on one freezing day in 1945 was pulled from the ground in the basement of the large brick house with the barn, the granary, and the beehives in the garden.

MARCH 1945

Sunday, March 4, 1945, is a day dedicated to the rebuilding of Warsaw. All of us are showing up for this work.
—*Życie Warszawy*, Mar. 3, 1945

• • • • • • • • • • • • • • • • • •

The Grochów Sports Club, the capital's two-time champion, is resuming its activity in Warsaw. On Sunday, March 4, at 12 p.m. two teams, the Grochów Sports Club and TUR Okęcie, will play their first soccer game at the Podskarbińska Street stadium.
—*Życie Warszawy*, Mar. 3, 1945

• • • • • • • • • • • • • • • • • •

The Music Department of Polish Radio will buy musical scores of chamber, choral, and orchestra music. Please leave your offers in the Information Department of Polish Radio, 63 Targowa Street.
—*Życie Warszawy*, Mar. 3, 1945

• • • • • • • • • • • • • • • • • •

Warsaw awaits your effort.
—*Życie Warszawy*, Mar. 4, 1945

• • • • • • • • • • • • • • • • • •

Lists of people who were in Auschwitz, with notations indicating where they have been sent, can be found at the office of the Warsaw Committee for Social Care at 326 Grochowska Street. The lists can be reviewed daily from 9 to 11 a.m.
—*Życie Warszawy*, Mar. 5, 1945

• • • • • • • • • • • • • • • • • •

We call upon anyone who witnessed German crimes in Warsaw during the occupation . . .

to present written or oral testimony at the Secretariat of the Commission for Investigation of German Crimes in Warsaw, 3 Otwocka Street. In addition, the Secretariat asks for any documents illustrating and confirming German bestiality, for example, jottings, notes, diaries, memoirs, lists of executed victims, photographs, sketches, etc.
—*Życie Warszawy*, Mar. 7, 1945

• • • • • • • • • • • • • • • • • •

Warsaw City Theater, 20 Zamojski Street. On Monday, March 12, 1945, at 5 p.m. there will be a special premiere performance of Aleksander Fredro's play Maidens' Vows for invited guests and the press.
—*Życie Warszawy*, Mar. 9, 1945

• • • • • • • • • • • • • • • • • •

The Vistula Sports Society has suspended the membership rights of four athletes, namely, Rupa, Mordarski, Seralin, and Bieniek, under suspicion of playing under the colors of a German team during the occupation. A special commission named by the club will investigate the veracity of the accusations.
—*Dziennik Polski*, Krakow, Mar. 10, 1945

• • • • • • • • • • • • • • • • • •

Understanding the crucial needs of Warsaw, the Department of Cinematication at the Ministry of Information and Propaganda has issued a directive to add a tax of 50 groszy to the price of movie tickets. This tax has been collected since March 3 and will benefit the rebuilding of Warsaw.
—*Życie Warszawy*, Mar. 12, 1945

• • • • • • • • • • • • • • • • • •

I remind the residents of Warsaw that the regulations and directives regarding passive antiaircraft defense, including meticulous covering of lights from dusk to dawn, are still in force. On behalf of the Mayor of Warsaw, Lieutenant Colonel J. Kotwica-Skrzypek, Deputy Mayor.

—*Życie Warszawy*, Mar. 12, 1945

. . . .

Today at 1 p.m., for the first time in five and a half years, Warsaw will hear Wiech's humorous vignette 'On My Own.' It will be read into the microphone by Henryk Ładosz on the radio show The Merry Wave.

—*Życie Warszawy*, Mar. 18, 1945

. . . .

The retail system is expanding on the left bank of Warsaw. There are already 99 grocery stores (including 23 cooperatives), 17 butcher shops, and 12 soap shops.

—*Życie Warszawy*, Mar. 19, 1945

. . . .

All domestic animals in the District of Western Warsaw (horses, cattle, pigs, sheep, goats, and dogs) have to be registered at the Veterinary Department, 70 Bem Street, before March 31, 1945.

—*Życie Warszawy*, Mar. 21, 1945

. . . .

A mother with a few-weeks-old baby has been robbed of all her undergarments and clothing. She is asking for any lingerie and a dress. Aniela Otłowińska, 8 Bankowy Square.

—*Słowo Pomorskie*, Toruń, Mar. 22, 1945

. . . .

Needed: hammers and pitchforks for removing debris, crowbars, grapnels, field forges, railway tracks and trolleys, ladders, scaffolds, many kinds of wheelbarrow and debris carriers. Send offers to Warsaw Rebuilding Office, 33 Chocimska Street. Department of Clearing Warsaw Roads.

—*Życie Warszawy*, Mar. 29, 1945

. . . .

The Office of Information and Propaganda, Krakow Voivodeship, is asking all former concentration camp prisoners to recount their tragic experience, as well as the experience of their comrades. All documents, eyewitness stories, songs, poems, martyrs' diaries, letters, testimony, photographs, death certificates, etc. will be published so society can see how much suffering and anguish Poles were exposed to in the concentration camps.

—*Dziennik Polski*, Krakow, Mar. 30, 1945

3

Ice

"**H**ilfe! *Hilfeeeee*! Stop! Help! Somebody" A skinny boy, all bundled up, runs toward the four-horse wagon. His wooden-soled shoes skid on the ice. "The ice is breaking and our wagon is sinking. The horses are drowning. My whole family is on the wagon! Lend me two horses, just for a moment, so they can pull them out."

"These days it's every man for himself!" The man on the wagon laughs at the boy, whipping his horses. He sets off at full speed.

And then splash. The man goes right into a hole in the ice. The water gurgles. The coachman disappears together with his laughter, his wagon, his wife and children, all his possessions, and his four horses. Silence. It's snowing. The skinny German boy, all bundled up, feels his tears freeze on his cheeks. He turns around and runs to help his family.

I don't know if I have any right to all this. To pretend I know what it was like. I argue with myself that, after all, everyone is able to imagine bitter cold. But have I ever felt so cold that my nose, my ears, and my fingertips would turn white and get hard like plaster? Or have I ever experienced any freezing temperatures in which babies, though wrapped in quilts, turn into lumps of ice, and older children, three- or four-year-olds, in their similar bundles, slowly die of exposure? You walk a few kilometers with them and their body temperature will drop by several degrees. You walk a few dozen kilometers and you find a little dead body in the quilt. You have to leave it at the roadside. You are not going to drag it with you, are you?

So, no. I don't know this kind of cold.

But everyone is familiar with snow, I try to convince myself. You can imagine snow thick like sour cream, so heavy that if you take your eyes off the lamp swinging on the wagon in front of you, you are finished because you get lost. And you must have seen water frozen so thick that even horses and wagons could cross it. Hundreds, thousands of wagons and sleighs. Even tanks and trucks.

Perhaps I know this kind of snow and ice. But I have never wailed in grief over the ice-hole that has just swallowed my children. So I don't know if I have any right to say that I can imagine the winter of 1945.

But for a moment the bitter cold and snow have to wait. It was 1929, when the world was immersed in the economic crisis that would eventually elevate the Austrian Nazi Adolf Hitler to the top, and in the Henseleit family a tiny baby with a heart problem was born. He was named Werner.

Werner's mother was called Elisa Helena and she was the best mom in the world. Much later, she died of typhus in a hospital in Gotenhafen, now Gdynia. But at that moment she was cuddling her little son, praying for his health every day. She was a very pious Lutheran, so no meal, no important event at home could take place without God. She used to be a factory worker but when the babies started coming into this world she became a *Hausfrau*, as Germans call a homemaker.

Werner's father, Heinrich Adolf, would give the world to his nearest and dearest ones. He worked beyond human endurance in a factory, carrying heavy objects until his back hurt. He loved to surprise his wife and children. One day he sent a baker's boy home with a bag full of fresh rolls. Sometimes he would take them to the movies or to the merry-go-round. It would be a while before he would have to tell his children to hold hands and jump into a well.

This all happened in Mülheim in the Ruhr. As a matter of fact, wealthy Elisa and penniless Heinrich were from East Prussia, but their parents wouldn't allow them to marry. So the loving couple eloped to western Germany, where they had relatives, and got married in 1927. Werner was their second child. They already had an older son Karlheinz, born in 1927. Some time would pass before two pairs of twins were born to the Henseleits.

It was 1933. Adolf Hitler shook President Hindenburg's hand and became German chancellor, the Reichstag was on fire, and Werner was four years old. Together with his brother he watched the street through the window. Some people were running, chased by the police. One could hear shots fired and cries: "*Halt*!" Their parents pulled them away from the window and told them to lie on the floor. Werner could hear his father say that bad times had come and that in the rushing crowd he had noticed his brother Otton who didn't support the new regime. A day later Uncle Otton came with a bunch of books and his father hid them at the bottom of the closet.

Apart from that, Werner was a happy child. He visited his grandmother in East Prussia twice. She gave him many toys and sweets. Werner loved Christmas, when at night his parents decorated a tree for their children and placed presents underneath. He liked going to school, where after recess his teacher called the students: "Dear children! Classes are beginning!" He was a good student. He mastered the difficult art of bicycle riding. His father gave him a hug and told his mother how proud he was of his little son.

Winters happened to be cold and it snowed there, but so feebly that nobody cared.

Werner's father was not going to work in the factory anymore. He told his family he would die soon because he was so tired.

"Time to return to East Prussia," he announced.

The boys packed their toys, the parents packed their belongings, and together they boarded a train that would go through Danzig to a small station in Insterburg, now Chernyakhovsk. Their neighbors, relatives, and friends said good-bye, and many cried. When the train with the Henseleits passed through Poland, the parents explained to their children that it was a country of people just like Germans, some were good, some bad.

This all happened in 1937 when the world was absorbed in the disaster of the airship *Hindenburg* that had burst into flames, and as Adolf Hitler schemed about how to gain more *Lebensraum*, living space for the *Herrenvolk*, the master race. When two years later Hitler unleashed his colossal war, it was also the year in which two little girls were born to Elisa and Heinrich Henseleit, Inge and Ursula.

Times might have been harder for the Henseleits in East Prussia than they were in Mülheim but they didn't complain. They lived in Klein Baum village, district Labiau, near Kurisches Haff. Their house belonged to Mr. Grigolet, an estate owner who employed Werner's parents. His father woke up at four in the morning to feed and groom the horses he worked with in the fields. He didn't talk about dying anymore. From time to time he sighed with pleasure and praised the beneficial effects of the country air. He earned 30 reichsmarks a month, received six liters of milk every day, and occasionally got a sack of flour. Werner's mother also worked on the farm and in the field. Near the house she built a coop for twelve hens and four geese, and a sty for two pigs. Each of the Henseleit's animals had its proper name. The pigs were called Maxim and Ulrich. The family also had a small garden with its vegetable section.

The boys' school was in Gross Baum. At first Werner and his brother Karlheinz had some problems. Both the teacher and the students told them they were not Germans because nobody could understand them. How was this possible? Here's how. In East Prussia people spoke Plattdeutsch, which sounded different from the German spoken in the Rhineland. For example, for "I buy" the boys used to say *Ich kaufe* but now they should say *Ik kööp*. In the Rhineland, "He runs" was *Er läuft*, but in East Prussia it was pronounced *He löpt*. But after a few months the Henseleit boys picked up the new dialect.

For the first time, the real snow and the bitter cold appeared for the children. For a while the effects of harsh weather could be held at bay by using the skates that the boys had gotten for Christmas. When they eventually lost feeling in their toes and noses, they just went home and sat near the warm stove.

The war had been going on for a few years Millions of people had died at the various fronts and in the concentration camps. They lost their minds, their homes, and those near and dear. But the Henseleits were hardly touched by it. To be sure, Heinrich became familiar with the war because he served for a short time as a soldier, hauling ammunition on his horse-wagon far from home, but he had returned to civilian life very quickly. Mr. Grigolet was able to bring him back to Klein Baum as an indispensable worker on his estate.

Elisa and Heinrich Henseleit experienced a personal tragedy in 1942. Elisa gave birth to another pair of twins, Gerda and Gisele, but a month later one of the girls died. Werner carved a cross for her grave.

The next to last year of the war was without hope for Hitler who was losing on every front and could only count on the *Wunderwaffe*, the miracle weapon that would help him regain control over the world. And it was without hope also for the Henseleits: Karlheinz was drafted and sent to the front. Elisa suffered from gallstones but the doctor said there could be no operation because the patient's heart was too weak. She didn't leave her bed and the pain persisted. Every day the family would pray for her health.

Heinrich and fifteen-year-old Werner took care of the farm and the children. In the evening Heinrich peeled potatoes and vegetables, and in the morning his son made some soup. Werner changed the baby, dressed the twins, washed them, fed them, and wiped them. He worked in the garden and cleaned the house. At noon he ran with lunch to his father working in the field. He went to school twice a week, because he couldn't go more often. He didn't go outside much and he didn't have time to play with his friends. Marianna K., an ethnic German, helped him with laundry and ironing.

For the Henseleits their last Christmas in East Prussia was sad. Elisa was in bed, Werner baked the cake, his brother didn't come home on leave from the army, and his father worked on the farm until late that night. There were no presents. It was December 1944.

Two months earlier, at the end of October, Soviet soldiers crossed the border and entered the Third Reich. One of their units attacked the village of Nemmersdorf, later Mayakovskoye, less than one hundred kilometers east of Klein Baum.

Ilya Grigoryevich Ehrenburg, the Russian writer and essayist, cheered on the Soviet soldiers with the following words: "Don't count the days, don't count the kilometers. Count only one thing, the number of Germans you have killed."

So the soldiers didn't count the days. They were aware that anything they seized in Germany would be theirs: forks, women, quilts, teenage girls, watches, old women, cut crystal, sometimes little girls. In Nemmersdorf, however, the Russians didn't have much time to seize property. Following

Figure 3.1. Nemmersdorf, East Prussia. Propaganda photo of Germans inspecting civilian corpses after the massacre supposedly committed by the Red Army. October 27, 1944. AFP, East News

a few hours of uninterrupted gunfire the Germans pushed them back, out of the village. But the world was about to hear of the slaughter the Soviets committed there. Already on November 2, in movie theaters all over the Reich, the German newsreel *Die Deutsche Wochenschau* showed the corpses of more than fifty raped women as well as children killed with a shot to the head. The newspapers reported that German women had been nailed to barn doors, that they had been raped on the altar. Hitler's propaganda minister, Joseph Goebbels, exploited the massacre in order to boost declining morale among German soldiers as well as civilians. The Volkssturm, a national militia established just one month earlier, recorded an increasing number of volunteers.

It was fifty-seven years after the war that the German journalist Michael Vogt found witnesses to these events. They admitted that the slaughter in Nemmersdorf had been faked. Most residents had managed to flee and the Russians shot thirteen of those who stayed. They had no time to do anything else. It was the Germans who brought the dead bodies to Nemmersdorf from other places. Before they took the pictures they pulled up the skirts of the murdered women and girls, and they removed their underwear to make them look like rape victims. This version of events was confirmed by one of the village residents, Gerda Meczulat, who had survived that day. No one ever attested to any crucifixions.

But soon the Soviet army flooded East Prussia and this time its soldiers had more opportunities to make Goebbels's propaganda come true. That was why people should have begun to bury their china sets under the apple trees, prepare their wagons, groom their horses, pack their quilts, climb on, and flee west.

But no civilian could leave East Prussia without permission. It was forbidden by Gauleiter Erich Koch, the East Prussian Oberpräsident. He had sworn to defend every meter of Prussia till the last drop of blood. And he was not going to spread any doubts about the power of the Third Reich by abandoning it like a rat. He kept sending telegrams to Hitler, promising him that he would stay there till the very end. Hitler was pleased. Two million people in East Prussia, Germans, Allied POWs (prisoners of war), and foreign forced laborers were at the mercy of this insanity. When at night people saw a red glow and heard gunfire, however, they were not going to wait around idly for the arrival of the front. Despite the ban, the roads of East Prussia were full of refugees.

Figure 3.2. East Prussia. Russian tanks attacking. January 1945. BE&W

Now the time had come for the snow and bitter cold. On January 4, 1945, Joseph Stalin received information from his meteorologists. In Leningrad the thermometers showed five degrees Fahrenheit and polar air from Finland was flowing into Europe. That meant the Masurian marshes and lakes would freeze and the Russian tanks wouldn't sink in them. Stalin set Friday, January 12, as the day of the offensive. So by then everything would be well frozen.

At the same time Klein Baum was crowded as never before. German soldiers, tanks, trucks, and field kitchens headed east. From the east, wounded soldiers and civilian refugees were coming in a continuous stream. There were Germans from Lithuania who had started leaving in June the year before and Prussians from the eastern border who dreamed of escaping far away from the Soviet army.

The civilians parked their wagons on the meadows around the village. They asked the locals for boiling water and a warm place for mothers and their children. The Henseleits couldn't take in anybody. Elisa was feeling much worse. Her fever hadn't gone down and only morphine could relieve

Figure 3.3. East Prussia. Germans fleeing the approaching Red Army. Spring 1945. AKG Images / BE&W

her stomach pain. But every day, father and son made a big pot of soup for the refugees. Every day they offered them tea and coffee.

Heinrich Henseleit didn't want to hear the sounds of firing that were coming nearer the village. He didn't run with the others to the forest to check the craters made by the Soviet bombs dropped the night before. He didn't pay any attention to his son covering the home windows at night so that, from the air, the enemy couldn't see the lights. One day he even declared that most certainly the Russians wouldn't enter Klein Baum. For this occasion, he prepared a feast and slaughtered two pigs. One was offered to the people who came on the wagons. And, sure, he buried chests with glasses and pots, and stored some supplies in the basement to avert starvation, but he did it halfheartedly, and only because his neighbors had done it.

When at the end of January an SS-man with an order for immediate evacuation showed up at Heinrich's home, Heinrich told him quietly that he was staying in Klein Baum. How could he and his family leave their home on such a night, with its bitter cold and snow? The SS-man put his gun to Heinrich Henseleit's head. Heinrich didn't know that already on January 15, Grand Admiral Karl Dönitz, commander of the German navy, had ordered a sea evacuation of the civilians and the military from the east Baltic regions. Gauleiter Koch didn't agree with this action. He still believed in the invincibility of the Third Reich. "It was a matter of honor," he told a journalist in 1986.

But the refugees from the east kept on coming. There was chaos on the roads and the train stations were swarming with thousands of homeless refugees. There was no more space in Pillau, now Baltiysk, where by Dönitz's orders ships were waiting to carry people across the Baltic Sea to western Germany. On January 21 the admiral lost patience and, without informing Adolf Hitler, gave the green light to the evacuation of civilians from East Prussia and Western Pomerania. The code name for this operation was "Hannibal."

But the SS-man was not going to explain the political complexities of the Third Reich to a peasant from Klein Baum. He kept holding the gun to Heinrich's head and remarked that everyone who wanted to stay was a spy and a traitor, so he had to die. Hearing this argument, Heinrich Henseleit got ready to flee.

Two strong horses.
    A big covered wagon.
    Three sacks of oats.
    Half a smoked pig.
    A bed.
    Blankets, pillows, quilts.
    Warm clothing.
    Family albums and documents.
    In a cardboard frame, Elisa's photo from the times when she was still in good health: a plump, cheerful woman with light-colored, kind eyes was looking peacefully into the camera. You could only guess that her long hair reached her knees.

Heinrich carried Elisa in his arms and put her on the bed in the wagon. Next to her, under the quilts, he hid three children. He attached two bicycles to the wagon but they were immediately knocked down by a military vehicle. He would drive and Werner was to walk alongside, to warm up. The boy wore wooden-soled leather shoes and he was never cold in them. In his breast pocket he carried Elisa's photo. There was a place at the back for Marianna K. and her husband, but soon they would get off to wait for the Red Army because suddenly they remembered they were Poles after all.

They set off. It was minus twenty-two degrees Fahrenheit. Snot froze in the nose, legs went numb and lost any feeling. Sometimes people would fall off the wagon like fruit shaken from a tree because they couldn't stretch their legs. They zigzagged. They should have headed west but the Soviet army formed a semicircle around East Prussia, so the Henseleits' wagon and other wagons often had to turn in the opposite direction. They stopped in villages that were full of refugees. The locals welcomed Elisa to their homes, put her to bed, cooked some soup, offered tea and coffee, and swore they were not leaving. The Russians would never reach them. Next day they, too, joined the procession of refugees.

On the way the Henseleits made friends with Frau Holzer and from now on they stuck together. For quite a while the woman had been traveling on her own with two sons: fifteen-year-old Hanz and six-year old Kurt. Her horse was hardly breathing.

One day Werner noticed a wonderful leather jacket in a ditch. It would be great for his father, he thought. He stretched his arm to get it and immediately tossed it away because there was a human hand in one sleeve. This was the first corpse (or rather body part) in his life. Another time he noticed a light carriage with two horses parked at the roadside. An elderly couple was napping inside, covered with a thin blanket. Werner ran to ask them if they needed any help, perhaps they had gotten lost. Then he realized they were dead. They had frozen. Later he would see more dead bodies. He would get used to the sight. He didn't know it yet but soon he would get a temporary job taking care of them.

Until mid-February the Henseleits' wagon, like thousands of other wagons, moved senselessly in East Prussia, now smaller and smaller and now totally surrounded by the Red Army. In fact, there was only one way for them to escape. You could get to the narrow Frische Nehrung, that is, the Vistula Spit, across the frozen waters of the Frisches Haff, or the Vistula Lagoon. From there you should try to reach Pillau in the east or Gotenhafen in the west. From both places there were ships taking the refugees to the ports that still belonged to the Third Reich.

Every refugee would surely be dreaming of leaving Gotenhafen on the magnificent, large, safe ship *Wilhelm Gustloff*. But since January 31, 1945, this dream had been out-of-date. The ship, sunk by a Soviet torpedo, was

Figure 3.4. A ship overloaded with East Prussian civilians leaving the port of Piława. March 1945. Ullstein/BE&W

sitting at the bottom of the sea with its more than six thousand refugees. Most passengers who fell into the water died immediately from hypothermia. Only twelve hundred people were rescued. But no one who went to the shore of the frozen lagoon knew this, as Goebbels had ordered this tragedy kept secret.

We could use some silence now. Just to hear the ice surface split under the hooves. Tiny cracks radiate with a crunch extremely unpleasant to the human ear. A person who heard it might have had time to jump out of the way. But there was no silence. The frozen lagoon was filled with noise, a cacophony of sighs, crying, moans, and shouts. The lagoon shores were already mostly occupied by the Soviets. You could get to the other side through one of the five passages between Balga and Frauenburg, now Frombork. Everywhere it was the same. The coachmen who reached the shore in the unending processions of wagons, shouted. The tired, petrified horses neighed. Someone tried to jump the line, the military trucks with priority honked, and the luxurious cars of dignitaries and church officials had no intention of waiting. Someone's mother died, someone had lost a child.

There were some police officers, screaming with all their might, striving to restore order. From the seven rows of wagons and sleighs they tried to form a single line that would enter the ice once the barrier was lifted. Before that, however, they had to search the refugees' wagons and issue instructions. Heavy items were not permitted. The ice had only so much resistance.

"Unload at least half, fatsos! Now you have an opportunity to see that this is war!"

The cabinets filled with preserves, the sacks of potatoes, the suitcases with family silverware, the Prussian dowry chests with embroidered tablecloths, the sewing machines, and the slabs of lard all landed on the shore.

"Horse hooves have to be wrapped with rags! Otherwise they won't be able to walk on the icy surface."

"Once on the ice, follow the trail marked by the little spruce trees that are placed in the frozen ice-holes! When it doesn't snow, there is fog. It's easy to get lost."

"Keep your wagons fifty to one hundred meters apart!"

"Watch out right before the spit!"

The icebreakers opened a fifteen-meter-wide water lane along the lagoon from Elbląg to Piława. You could get to the other side by crossing temporary

Figure 3.5 Evacuation of German civilians across the frozen Vistula Lagoon. February 1945. Ullstein / BE&W

footbridges over the lane. The barrier was up. Heinrich Henseleit brought the horses onto the ice. There was a ten-kilometer walk ahead of him, one meter of ice and three meters of water under him, Frau Holzer behind him, and Werner next to him. They set off. They would get to the other shore in two days and three nights.

They moved. They stopped. They dragged along for hours. They moved again. And again they stopped. They passed by hundreds of dead horses and human cadavers, and abandoned wagons frozen in ice like insects in amber. Werner thought that soon they would join the corpses. He no longer believed they would survive this. They heard the roar of the incoming planes and they hid under the wagons, although they knew this made no sense. Only Elisa was left alone on the wagon. The air-strike was short. There were splashing fountains of water around them. From their hiding place, the Henseleits could see entire fleets of wagons disappearing in the ice-holes made by the projectiles. People on the wagons waved their hands,

Figure 3.6. Evacuation of German civilians to the West. 1945. Süddeutsche Zeitung Photo / Forum

screamed something, and then they were gone. And it got quiet. The planes flew away. The already dead, people and animals, had been joined by the newly dead. Others moved forward.

It was already night when the right front wheel of the Henseleits' wagon suddenly sank into the water. In the darkness Heinrich didn't notice that the ice onto which he had just driven was thin as a healing wound. He was lucky because they were sinking very slowly, held up by two interlocked ice floes. But even their two strong horses wouldn't be able to pull the wagon out. Frau Holzer's horse refused to help. The horse stuck to his guns, standing a few dozen meters from them. He didn't want to come closer. Heinrich took Elisa and the children off his wagon and carried them to the Holzers' wagon. He went back to grab oats for the horses.

Werner, a skinny boy, all bundled up, could see a coachman and his four horses passing by. Werner ran toward him to ask for help. But the man refused to help, drove away laughing, and fell right into a hole in the ice. The water gurgled. The coachman disappeared into the water

Figure 3.7. Evacuation of Armored Division Grossdeutschland from Balga on the Vistula Lagoon. Soldiers are building rafts to flee. March 5, 1945. Albert Otto / Ullstein / BE&W

together with his wagon, his wife and children, all his possessions, and his four horses.

There was no solidarity on the ice of the Vistula Lagoon. People remembered a woman whose horses had given out. She cried for help. To no avail. Everyone just stared. They remembered the unfortunates who had fallen into the water. It would be enough to hand them a pole, a piece of rag, anything. But they were drowning quickly because nobody was going to hand them anything. After many years, Robert Krause, a mailman from Domnau, now Domnovo, told Egbert Kieser, a writer, about a young woman standing in the fog over the ice-hole. Wailing like an animal, she stirred the water with a long stick. No one could pull her away from the hole. She would threaten anyone who tried to approach her. Someone shouted from a passing wagon: "Push her into the water and let her soul finally find peace!"

Werner jumped into the water up to his knees and detached the horses from the sinking carriage. The Henseleits harnessed them to Frau Holzer's wagon, but her horse still refused to walk, so they left him behind. They set off but Heinrich remembered that he had forgotten to take the food from his wagon. He rushed off in its direction but what was left there was only a quiet ice-hole.

Finally, they reached some dry land. The shore was a bit steep and the horses struggled in the mud and slime. They joined the crowds on the spit. Police officers directed them westward.

The last of the refugees, immersed up to their knees in water from the ice melting in the spring sun, crossed the lagoon on March 4, 1945. Soon after, everything melted, swallowing the corpses of people and horses.

In 2010, in now-Polish Frombork, a monument was erected to commemorate the 450,000 refugees from East Prussia crossing the Vistula Lagoon.

Everything took forever. The freezing temperatures, the mud, the hunger. A procession of wagons traveled across the spit. I'd like Werner to warm up his frostbitten ears (we have to wait for the Red Army soldiers for help with this), to feel the warmth of the fires toward which he puts his frozen feet, or to eat his fill because he won't survive very long on leaves dug up from under the snow. What's more, I have bad news for him. If he ever thought that crossing the Vistula Lagoon was the worst thing in his life, he would be wrong. Worse was yet to come.

Right now I'm watching another episode of the newsreel *Die Deutsche Wochenshau* from March, starring Adolf Hitler. He ceremoniously awards the Iron Cross to young boys who have proved their exceptional heroism at the front. The Führer pats each piece of cannon fodder on a cheek that doesn't yet need shaving. He's delighted that children are ready to defend the Reich to the end that will come very soon.

It was already worse. First, Frau Holzer disappeared, back on the spit. She and her older son started walking toward the soldiers to beg for some food, just at the moment when police officers ordered everyone to rush westward, really fast.

"Get moving! Move it! The Russians are coming," they screamed.

Heinrich Henseleit pulled over to wait for Frau Holzer, but the soldiers commanded him to move. So he drove away in her wagon, taking Kurt with him. They would never see her again.

Then Elisa died. She had contracted typhus on the way. She had diarrhea.

She vomited and couldn't eat or drink. Werner changed her and cleaned her almost constantly. They got her to Gotenhafen. Police officers wanted to send the Henseleits' wagon to the port facilities. It was their last chance to escape by sea on one of the ships, fishing boats, or coal barges that still carried refugees and that regularly sunk with everybody on the deck, but the police officers didn't mention this. Heinrich refused to go. He wouldn't leave until his wife felt better. They were lodged in the apartment of some German woman, in a house on the way to Witomino. After a few days Elisa ended up in the hospital at General Litzmann Platz, now Kaszubski Square. When Werner visited her for the last time, she would whisper to him, "Stay together." They never saw each other again.

The German woman's house was hit by a bomb. The wall in the Henseleits' room collapsed but they were all right because they had hidden in the closet. The same bomb killed their horses. Heinrich let his neighbors slice them into cutlets, but he didn't touch a single piece himself.

Later Heinrich Henseleit, his two sons, two daughters, and little Kurt Holzer stepped down into a large bomb shelter. It was next to their destroyed house and had been designed for several hundred people. Some had settled in there quite well and even had their own beds. The Henseleits, however, slept on blankets. Their only food was a small pail of lard.

It was the end of March 1945. The Soviets entered the city. They ordered the shelter opened. They killed the German soldiers hiding inside. The civilians were chased away and were told to walk toward Witomino. Heinrich Henseleit and his children were among them. Tripping over dead bodies, they would soon get lost in the forest.

Now it's time for the good Russians.

They met the first of them in the forest. Although they stole Heinrich's watch and searched him, they let them go free. Werner understood them a little because he had learned some Russian from the slaves working on Mr. Grigolet's fields in Klein Baum.

The next Russian was even better. The Henseleits, wandering in the forest, had happened on a Russian camp. A Russian got out of his tent and told them not to be afraid because he was a doctor and had children himself. He checked Werner's frostbitten ears and, despite his father's protest, took him to the field hospital. There he injected some substance into his ears, stuck some pins into his earlobes, covered them with a thick layer of ointment, and wrapped them with a bandage. After two weeks another frontline doctor took the bandage off and the frostbite was gone; as a souvenir Werner had pin holes in his ears.

More good Russians, almost the last, encountered in the Kashubian village of Wiczlino, fed the Henseleits with potatoes and fat, after which the whole family suffered from diarrhea. The good Soviets showed them an abandoned house where they could stay. The house had no windows or door locks, but it was their best house in a long time. There was a deep well in the courtyard and Werner got his water there.

Now it's time for the bad Soviets.

"Where is Mama?! *Wo ist frau?*" Drunken Red Army soldiers rushed into the Henseleits' house.

"Not be here. Not live." Werner was murdering the Russian language.

They didn't believe him. They came back every day, every few hours, they searched the house, and aimed their guns at the children. They noticed a neighbor, a former owner of the house who had brought some potatoes for the Henseleits. Putting a gun to Werner's head they told him to show them where she lived. A dozen of them paid her a visit.

On April Fools' Day, April 1, 1945, the worst of them came to the house. Five young men and one a bit older, dressed in military caps and brown pants, worn in the past by SS men. They ordered Heinrich to get ready to go. The children stayed. Heinrich cried, begging them to let him stay. Who would take care of his little sons and daughters if he was not there? Who would feed them? Who would defend them? They had nobody here, just him. The older soldier wanted to say something and it looked as though he tried to defend the Henseleits but the others sent him to the car. Heinrich looked at Werner, Ursula, Inge, Gerd, and the little son of Frau Holzer for the last time.

"Hold hands and jump into the well," he told them, leaving.

Screaming, they ran after the car that had taken him away.

Five German children left alone in a house in a Kashubian village. The youngest was not even three years old, then there were the twin girls, age five, seven-year-old Kurt, and Werner, a teenager. He had to take care of them. In the field he found frozen potatoes. He sliced them, dried them on a heated steel plate, and gave them to the children. The meadows behind the house stretched to the forest. Covered with excavated trenches, they were filled with the corpses of German soldiers. Werner went through the pockets of the dead bodies, checked their rucksacks, and took out some moldy bread from the last provisions issued by the field kitchen. He dried the bread on the stove and offered it to the children.

Once, just for a moment, some more good Russians showed up. They promised to bring Heinrich back. But the next day they only brought bread and meat. Heinrich had not been found.

Was this the end of April? Did Adolf Hitler poison his dog, marry Eva Braun, and then shoot himself in the head, biting down on a cyanide capsule at the same time? Werner didn't know about any of this. How could he? Undoubtedly spring was here, because with the warming breeze from the fields came the deadly odor of decomposing bodies.

He had gotten a job. With no pay, of course. One day a man came from the village, a Pole, and he told Werner to go to the field and bury the rotting soldiers.

"This is an order, Kraut!" he screamed.

Kicking arms and legs, sometimes individual fingers, or corpses without heads down into the ditch was the easiest thing. The worst thing was when the corpses had faces. Then Werner poured sand over their eyes. So they stopped looking at him. Every now and then he went home to check whether the children were safe. He gave them water and dry bread, and returned to the bodies. In the evening he bathed the children in the well water. He didn't wash their clothes, just boiled them in the big pot on the stove.

In mid-May 1945 newspapers all over the world reported that Adolf Hitler might be alive, hiding somewhere in Europe, wearing a black beard. At the same time Werner Henseleit became a slave. A Kraut, a fascist, a louse, who was supposed to work for potato peels and leftover bones. Who could be kicked, punched, and whipped. For the war. For hunger. For fear. For suffering. For the concentration camps. For the fact that he didn't know Polish and instead of the straw that was demanded he brought a pitchfork. For the fact that he couldn't control the horses and a furrow in the field was crooked. Good God, how clumsy this German was. Let him die like a dog. Who cares?

It was the village head who decided the Henseleits needed some assistance. He sent Werner to one of the wealthiest and most respected landowners in one of the Kashubian villages. He was truly a pious man who liked to pray often and aloud. He was a new Polish settler. He had his own children and a wife who'd prefer to move to the city. She even tried to poison her husband's horses to get her own way.

Werner's sisters, Inge and Ursula, had been separated, ending up in different foster families. Kurt Holzer had become a hired hand in some other village. Werner could visit them every Sunday. Gerd, the youngest brother, could stay with Werner. When Werner worked in the field or on the farm, the child had to sit on a pile of sand all day. If he moved, he would be punished, too, this Kraut trash.

They slept on a filthy bed in the hallway. In the fall of 1945, when it got colder, Werner made a bed of straw in the cowshed. A pleasant warmth came from the cattle but on some freezing nights the tears on the boy's face would turn into painful icicles. Before going to sleep Werner told his brother they would be there only for a while, that their father would come soon to take them home. Sometimes he dreamed of his mother; she was worried and stroked his head. In the end some people took Gerd in. He was exhausted. The conditions were too harsh for a three-year-old, even a German.

Werner didn't know about the Red Cross. He didn't know that German orphans were being evacuated from Poland and that he had some rights. He thought that after the war all Germans had become slaves. His employer's neighbors could see how very badly he was treated. They encouraged him to run away or to work for them. But Werner was scared. After all, he belonged to his master. That was what he was told by the policemen who drank moonshine with his boss. Werner had to distill it in a shed.

"We'll shoot you, if you're not obedient." They were pointing their fingers at him.

1946

Werner's boss deferred to his wife. He sold his estate and moved to the city. He swapped his slave for a small carriage. Werner became a hired hand at some other farmer's. The new boss could see the human being in him. He fed him and offered a bed. He didn't yell and didn't beat him.

Werner would no longer be a German. In March, following the advice of someone from the village, he made out an application to the Municipal Court in Wejherowo that was typewritten by one of the clerks because

Werner still didn't know Polish: "I kindly request that Polish citizenship be granted to me. Despite my German nationality I feel I am of Polish blood. . . . I am an orphan and I do hope to serve for the sake of Democratic Poland." He was lying. He did not feel Polish, but he thought that this was the route to an easier life.

Gerd, who had stopped talking and was afraid of people, returned to his brother. They shared one bed. Werner talked to him gently. One day he heard his little brother sing a song. He was saved! On the other hand, Werner lost all contact with Kurt Holzer. He looked for him in the village where he used to work but nobody knew what had happened to this little German boy.

1950

The last German children were about to be evacuated from Poland. This time the head of the local community informed Werner, who in turn made contact with his siblings. They had received one-way tickets, and on a set day they were to meet at the Wejherowo train station. In Germany they would be sent to an orphanage. The German Red Cross would be looking for their relatives. Perhaps some of them were still alive?

Inge didn't show up at the station. Should they leave without her?

"We are staying!" said Werner. "We must stick together."

They returned to their Polish guardians.

1953

Werner was now a hired hand for his third farmer. He worked on the farm from dawn into the afternoon. After that he would climb onto the cargo bed of a pickup truck and travel to Gdynia for the night shift at Dalmor, a firm that dealt in fishing and fish processing. The fish he tossed on the table were gutted by women. One of them was a Kashub and her name was Janka. She had nine siblings and an exceptionally beautiful smile.

Her mother didn't mind that Werner was German. She received him at home and prepared a celebratory dinner, Werner's first good meal in Poland. She was only worried that her future son-in-law was so skinny that his pants were hanging loose on him.

1955

Werner and Janka got married. For Werner Henseleit this was the first year of freedom.

Figure 3.8. Wedding photo of the Henseleits. Werner and Joanna, also called Janka. 1955. Werner Henseleit's archive

Figure 3.9. The Henseleits. 2014. Werner Henseleit's archive

In the meantime, Heinrich Henseleit, or rather, his wreck, came back to Germany from Soviet captivity. He lived with a relative in Reinfeld. Before he died of exhaustion after three months, he was looking for his children through the German Red Cross. He managed to find Karlheinz, the oldest son, who had survived the war. But none of them had any hope of finding the remaining four children. Heinrich died, convinced that Werner, Ursula, Inge, and Gerd were dead.

Werner learned all this later from his brother, whom he found through the Red Cross.

THE 1970S AND 1980S

Werner Henseleit tried to leave for Germany. Once a newly found relative sent him an official invitation and some money for the tickets. But the Polish authorities denied him a passport. He was still working at Dalmor, as a crane operator. He was a highly valued specialist.

1995

Inge, Ursula, and Gerd made their lives in Poland. Karlheinz didn't feel right in Germany and emigrated to Canada. But pensioner Werner decided to leave Gdynia, where he lived, and move to Germany. He took his wife with him. Their daughters, grandchildren, and great-grandchildren would come to visit.

Werner and Janka live in a small cozy apartment on a quiet Hamburg street.

The skinny boy with a heart problem needed half a century to get home.

Winters here are exceptionally mild.

APRIL 1945

After partial cleaning of Wawel Castle, this most magnificent surviving monument of Poland is now open to the public. For the time being, visits are only permitted on Sundays and holidays.

—*Dziennik Polski*, Krakow, Apr. 5, 1945

• • • • • • • • • • • • • • • • • • •

The 15th District Civic Committee at 2 Kawęczyńska Street is organizing foreign language courses. Russian classes taught by Prof. Pietrov begin on April 15.

—*Życie Warszawy*, Apr. 8, 1945

• • • • • • • • • • • • • • • • • • •

The third offering of the Socio-Political Course for city and state workers organized by the Warsaw Office of Information and Propaganda begins on April 12. The course will last two weeks, from 8 a.m. to 2 p.m. in the Warsaw City Council Hall.

—*Życie Warszawy*, Apr. 10, 1945

• • • • • • • • • • • • • • • • • • •

The distinguished pianist Prof. Zbigniew Drzewiecki will appear on Polish radio in a special Chopin recital. It will be this great pianist's first performance on Polish Radio since 1939.

—*Życie Warszawy*, Apr. 10, 1945

• • • • • • • • • • • • • • • • • • •

The May 1 Celebration Committee in Warsaw appeals to all citizens who may own any collections of songs and compositions about this holiday to lend them for a short period of time. Report at 3 Otwocka Street, Room 30.

—*Życie Warszawy*, Apr. 12, 1945

• • • • • • • • • • • • • • • • • • •

Filling in craters and trenches, fixing paving slabs, and any sort of repair of road surfaces may only be performed after obtaining permission from the Department of Supervision and Government Contracts of the Warsaw Reconstruction Office.

—*Życie Warszawy*, Apr. 13, 1945

• • • • • • • • • • • • • • • • • • •

With regard to the reconstruction of Warsaw, all sculptors are requested to attend a meeting on April 14, 1945, at 11 a.m. at their Association Office in Saska Kępa at 19 Poselska Street.

—*Życie Warszawy*, Apr. 13, 1945

• • • • • • • • • • • • • • • • • • •

To stay healthy: Drink boiled water only, protect food products from flies, and burn garbage.

—*Życie Warszawy*, Apr. 14, 1945

• • • • • • • • • • • • • • • • • • •

Your land allotment will supply you with fresh vegetables and preserves for the winter.

—*Życie Warszawy*, Apr. 16, 1945

• • • • • • • • • • • • • • • • • • •

With regard to the distribution of cooking oil for April, the Food Rationing Department requests that all grocery stores prepare appropriate containers (barrels and churns) to collect and dispense oil.

—*Życie Warszawy*, Apr. 19, 1945

• • • • • • • • • • • • • • • • • • •

For a few weeks the print shop workers of Publishing Cooperative 'Book,' 12 Smolna

Street, have been devoting one hour longer every day to benefit the reconstruction of Warsaw.

—*Życie Warszawy*, Apr. 19, 1945

. . . .

The Warsaw School of Economics [WSE] is accepting student applications from people who live and work in Warsaw. More information at the WSE Secretariat in Warsaw, 6 Rakowiecka Street.

—*Życie Warszawy*, Apr. 21, 1945

. . . .

Applicants for working at exhumation sites will report at 8 a.m. with their own shovels at the following locations: in Żoliborz at 10 Lelewel Street, in Powiśle at the corner of Solec and Wilanowska Streets, in Śródmieście at 24 Koszykowa Street, in Mokotów at 8/10 Willowa Street, and in Czerniaków at 42 Stępińska Street. The wage is 10 zlotys per hour for 8 hours a day. After the job is completed, there will be bonuses.

—*Życie Warszawy*, Apr. 22, 1945

. . . .

An independent female battalion has been formed as a part of the Citizens' Police. Policewomen from the battalion are assigned to direct traffic and work in vice squads.

—*Życie Warszawy*, Apr. 24, 1945

. . . .

The Krakow Voivodeship Office reminds everyone about blackouts and covering lights. Violation of this ordinance will result in a fine of up to 500 zlotys, or will carry a sentence of up to 14 days in prison, or both.

—*Dziennik Polski*, Krakow, Apr. 25, 1945

. . . .

Between April 25 and April 28, caramels in the amount of 100 grams will be provided for the holders of Coupon No. 1 of the Children's Vouchers. Price: 50 zlotys/kilogram.

—*Życie Warszawy*, Apr. 25, 1945

. . . .

The Warsaw North Civic Committee in Żoliborz has finished setting up two soup kitchens in Żoliborz and in Bielany. Each of them can provide 250 meals a day. These establishments were repaired and new cauldrons and equipment were installed. These soup kitchens, designed for the poorest residents of the district, will be opened as soon as provisions from the Food Rationing Department are available.

—*Życie Warszawy*, Apr. 27, 1945

Why Did You Come Here?

It had hardly stopped raining when he appeared in the store. Although it was only early afternoon, he was drunk. He was swaying over the crate from which I was picking hard August apples.

"May I help you?" he asked, as he belched courteously in my direction, and leaned against the frozen foods counter, because all this was taking place in a small store in the middle of Będlino.

I ignored him. I was buying apples, first, because I like them, and second, because they were supposed to break the ice between me and the saleslady.

"Will I find any of the first settlers here? In the village? I mean the people who arrived in 1945?" I asked as I paid for the fruit.

In the countryside shopkeepers and village heads are the fundamental source of information. And local drunks, for sure.

"Go to Mrs. Halinka Borcuch." My self-appointed guide exhaled loudly and the woman behind the counter nodded her head. He continued, "Maybe you will drop in at my place? I have a lot of old photographs." He winked at me flirtatiously.

"Some other time," I answered.

He was beginning to tick me off.

"My husband and my kid are waiting. Outside," I added.

Figure 4.1. Repatriates from the East in the Western Territories. PAP

NEUHOF, THAT IS TO SAY, BĘDLINO—FOR THE FIRST BUT NOT THE LAST TIME

I went out to the muddy little square in front of the store. Puddles were drying up in the sun. Modest buildings were lined up along the road like beads on a string. A little mutt with an upright tail, dirty and wet, was barking behind the fence. I could make out among the trees the large brick building that had belonged to the prewar Forestry Department. A small village sandwiched between Złocieniec and Wałcz, in the bottom right corner of Drawsko Lake District. When I finally met Halina Borcuch, she would describe the village unambiguously to me, "Listen, lady, so what's here in this Będlino? No hope, no nothing. Just take a rifle and shoot it."

At the beginning of March 1945 there was fighting for control of the German defense line called the Pomeranian Wall in Będlino (at that time Neuhof). When the first Będlino village head, Stanisław Bania, arrived in the village a few days later, he encountered burned-out barns, stables, and houses. "There is not a single pane left in the windows," he noted. "The exit streets are mined and some village streets are barricaded. There are mines under all this. A few cows ripped apart by the mines lie in the streets. There is a lot of straw and human waste in the houses and apartments, and pig and cow intestines in the backyards. Many dead soldiers lie in the gardens; I buried twenty-eight of them. Some cows and pigs roam the fields. There is not a living soul in the village."

The first Polish settlers came to Będlino in the beginning of July 1945. Perhaps Halina Borcuch was among them. I had to find her.

I tossed the apples into our dated Peugeot minivan.

"Let's go. Quickly!" I called out to my husband and daughter who had gotten out of the car to stretch a bit. We had just finished the long drive from Stepnica.

But my inebriated chaperone was faster. He staggered in our direction together with his companions. (Where on earth did they come from?)

"You are from that Provident lending agency!" he accused me, and pointed his finger in my direction. His companions were unpleasantly silent. I neither confirmed nor denied it. We shut the doors and took off toward the house of the village's oldest living settler.

FEAR

At the end of June 1945, on a hot Warsaw afternoon, forty-nine-year-old
Wanda Melcer climbed onto a truck's cargo bed. Before the war she was
a popular poet, a writer of books, and a leftist journalist. What made her
famous was both her collection of articles, *Dark Continent, Warsaw* (1936),
illustrating the everyday life of the Warsaw Jewish community, and her
marriage to a famous athlete, Teodor Sztekker. They were both celebrities
in their time.

Seven men followed her onto the truck. Among them were journalists
and representatives of the Artists' Association, the Writers' Association, and
some of the repatriation organizations.

What was awaiting them was a journey through villages and cities that
were unknown to them in the southern portion of East Prussia, Western
Pomerania, Brandenburg up to the line of the Oder and Neisse rivers, and
Silesia. Those were places that just a moment ago had belonged to Germany,
and now were about to become Polish Varmia, Masuria, Pomerania, Lubusz
Land, and Silesia.

The truck and the passes were arranged by the Central Union for Resettlement. They were given a specific assignment: go, marvel, and then
encourage Poles to settle there in large numbers, because the resettling was
not going well.

They did not know what to expect, nor were they even sure if they
would find any food there. Just in case, they took with them a few baskets
of eggs. After three weeks they came back to Warsaw thoroughly hating
scrambled eggs.

Soon afterward the Social and Academic Library published a slim
20-zloty book, *Expedition to the Recovered Territories: Reportage*, written by
Wanda Melcer.

What was I supposed to call them? Recovered, Exploited, Piast Lands,
Claimed, Returning, Western Territories, or Wild West? None of these
names used after the war definitively labeled the formerly German lands
that were assigned to Poland.

In May 1945 *Życie Warszawy* reported on "our Western lands that until 1939 had been under German rule." A journalist whose byline was D.
wrote: "There are surely very few people who recognized that Schewidnitz

in Silesia is Świdnica, the former capital of the Piast Duchy, or who realized that Schwiebus is simply Świebodzin, the capital of Świebodzin Land under the Piasts . . . or that Frauenburg is Franbork, where our great fellow countryman Nicolaus Copernicus worked and died."

Among ordinary Poles, journalists, and officials, the term *Recovered Territories* became the most popular. In 1938 the Polish army annexed Zaolzie—disputed with Czechoslovakia—and this term was used, for the first time, by President Ignacy Mościcki in his decree "On the Unification of the Recovered Territories of Cieszyn Silesia with the Polish Republic."

To make things easier I have decided to stick to Recovered Territories.

In August 2014, on a cloudy morning, I followed the route of the truck that almost seventy years earlier had taken the group of journalists to the Recovered Territories. To feel safer, I took my husband Robert and my seven-year-old daughter Tosia. We had been traveling together for years and even her question, "Are we there yet?" asked a hundred times during the trip, seemed totally amusing.

We are descendants of settlers. After the war Robert's grandparents arrived in the small town of Jasień near Zielona Góra, from Łęczyca and from somewhere around Kielce. I am a granddaughter of repatriates who came from somewhere near Lvov and from Warsaw. I was born in the Recovered Territories twenty-seven years after the war. The houses in my city, the armchairs in my grandma's room, the landscape painting over her table, and her crystal carafe were all previously German. In our Sopot apartment the faucets were marked *kalt* and *warm*. Our relatives were buried in the Lutheran cemetery among tombstones with inscriptions in Schwabacher lettering. My first word of German, *Fleischermeister*, a master butcher, I learned from a tombstone.

As a child I worried that if something was previously German, one day it might become "previously Polish." In my genes I subconsciously adopted the fear of my settler ancestors that the place I live is given to me for only a moment.

I assumed that traveling across the Recovered Territories I would meet people who, like my grandparents, had to begin a new life in a foreign place. I was curious about whether the lands where they had arrived were still foreign to them. Did they leave their hearts in the places they were born?

Or, if they felt at home, since when? What are their descendants like? Did they rid themselves of that fear I still have in me?

AS IN AN AMERICAN MOVIE

"There is a lot of traffic on the roads," noted Wanda Melcer. "All kinds of vehicles are traveling westward. People on the vehicles are having fun. They are chattering, laughing, and singing. You recall American movies showing their settlers, their west-moving pioneers. Oh, here it is, a wagon straight from their movies. Its barrel-shaped frame is covered with canvas and its arc-shaped body on creaking wheels is drawn with dignity by a pair of spiral-horned oxen."

They left Warsaw and drove toward Olsztyn. They were bouncing on the hard benches of the truck. They passed wrecked tanks, destroyed houses, and the bloated corpses of people and animals. But decades later, we were speeding along on smooth asphalt, counting the trampolines in the gardens of the houses, and the cut-out swans made from old tires. *Signum temporis* 2014.

In Mława they were stopped by a military patrol. Before entering the Recovered Territories, they would need passes to continue. We realized we were in former East Prussia because the wooden houses disappeared and most buildings were made of red brick. Even stables and barns were made of stone.

CANDIEN, THAT IS TO SAY, KANIGOWO. I FIND A LITTLE GIRL

Where the hell is Hańkowo? I was infuriated, staring at the map of Poland. It was the first village on the route taken by Wanda Melcer and her companions. A little beyond Mława, four kilometers beyond the former border, already in East Prussia. "A large and affluent village," as she had described it, couldn't just totally disappear. But nothing. I reached for the dispatches of the *Życie Warszawy* journalist who had been on the same truck. But he was writing about a Kanikowo that for a few weeks had been inhabited by eighty settlers.

I would have problems with the names of villages and little towns until the end of my trip. In 1945 there was total naming chaos.

One of the settlers reminisced, "We immediately changed the names of the villages ourselves. For example, we changed Kleefeld into Klementów, because the village chief's name was Klemeński. Later that name was officially changed to Trzcinna Góra."

The Commission for the Determination of Place Names at the Ministry of Public Administration was just beginning its operations. Some places would regain their Slavic names (Breslau—Wrocław), other places would get old polonized names (Zoppot—Sopot), or newly polonized names (Hirschberg—Jelenia Góra), and in some cases completely new names would be assigned (Drengfurth—Srokowo, to honor a commission member, Professor Stanisław Srokowski).

That's why I sometimes wasn't able to guess which villages or little towns those journalists had in mind. But at that moment I got lucky. Moving my finger on the map from Mława to Olsztyn I guessed that Wanda Melcer's team might have made a stop in Kanigowo (German Candien) near Nidzica. We picked this village for our first stopover.

A strapping fellow, half-naked, and so sensitive. He was shaving when I knocked at the door. I asked him a question that he couldn't actually answer, because right away I could see he was too young, but we had to begin our friendship somehow.

"Do you remember the journalists' visit to Kanigowo in 1945?" I asked. He answered "yes."

"No, not personally," he added immediately, because he was born after the war. His now dead father, a blacksmith, arrived here from near Ciechanow in the spring of 1945. He ran a previously German forge until the taxes finished him off. And his mother, who had also died, sometimes recalled that strange group of journalists.

"They had come in a truck. Some of them were in uniforms whose caps bore eagles without a crown. They did shopping in my sister's store. They asked whether the Russkis were doing any damage in the village," he said.

And I could see clearly that this strapping fellow, Zbigniew Maciejak, Kanigowo's village head, was overcome with emotion at these past memories that were not even his own but his mother's.

They had just stopped when the entire village surrounded their truck. There was only one thing these people wanted from the Warsaw reporters: reassurance that they would definitely be able to stay there. "They ask very cautiously if we think that nothing will change anymore. That there won't be any new war, attacks, resettlements, and expulsions," noted Melcer. So they swore to the settlers that nothing would change, although the Potsdam Conference hadn't yet begun.

Freshly baked bread, potatoes, and milk appeared on the table. The hosts who welcomed the journalists, cartwright Jan Nowicki and his wife, had owned about two hectares of land in Poland. Here they received forty hectares. Their house in Kuklin (Przasnysz county) had burned down, and one of their children, a seven-week-old baby, had been killed by Germans shooting at her cradle.

The reporter was marveling at the farm they took over. She wrote: "Yes, this is a house, a large house, not like the shacks we are used to in the poor villages of our overpopulated counties. It is made of stone and covered with red roof tiles. It is sunlit through its large windows with double glass panes and has a city-style door and a stone-paved porch." The backyard was guarded by a small dog on a thick chain and a German woman was helping in the farmyard.

What the Germans left in the kitchen were pots and plates, mallets and strainers, and even an embroidered cloth praising the benefits of an early wake-up. There were German quilts and pillows in the rooms, agricultural tools in the shed, a concrete floor, and an automatic machine for cleaning the troughs in the cowshed.

I found the house of the cartwright Nowicki. It wasn't difficult. People in the village showed me the way. You just had to go straight ahead along the paved road, pass the previously German Lutheran church in which every Sunday, before the war started, 407 residents of Candien had prayed, and turn left. The house was at the corner. It was made of stone and covered with red roof tiles, just as described by Wanda Melcer, except for the new, smaller house that had been attached to its side. The farm was surrounded by a concrete fence, its stone-paved yard was swept, and there was a trampoline in the garden, a sign that children lived here.

The Nowicki family of 1945 had a daughter, too. Wanda Melcer wrote: "I stroke your hair, little Marianna. You are so brave, your black eyes are so fearless . . . you five-year-old settler, you feel at home here."

They must have seen me through the window of the new house, because a young woman with a Yorkie in her arms appeared on the porch. Right afterward she was joined by a second woman in an apron, a bit older. They talked eagerly. Both were related to the cartwright, who had died, like his hospitable wife. But they couldn't help me. They didn't know any of the history of their settler ancestors.

"And Marianna?" I asked. "The girl was born about 1940, and her sister was killed by the Germans. Do you know anything about her?"

"Aunt Maria!" they shouted like trained chorus girls. "She lives in the city, not far from here."

I grabbed my cell, we dialed the number, and she picked up right away. But she refused to meet. I insisted that I would come to her for half an hour, for fifteen minutes. That it was great luck for me as a reporter to meet that brave girl from the news story, to hear what she remembered from those first days in Kanigowo, that her generation was leaving, that this was the last moment, that it was about memory and the readers. But she asked me to leave her alone.

For a moment I stood in front of the house, admired so much by the journalists seventy years ago, and I felt like a child whose lollipop was taken away.

"They are tough people, those settlers in Hańkowo, and surely they will do well," wrote Wanda Melcer in the end. She was leaving Kanikowo in a better mood than I.

AND I AM TALKING TO YOU, FISHERMAN

I put Melcer's book into the car door compartment and all the way I kept checking to see if it was still there. I was unwittingly stroking its rough canvas cover and when I was holding it in my hands I smelled a delicate aroma of must. I had bought it online for 10 zlotys and on the third page I found it had been stamped by the Z. K. Wałbrzych factory library. I will never know for how many years it was sitting on a library shelf in that old coke plant with the number 4025/71. Did anyone read this pitiable book? If so, rather rarely. Although it was published in 1970 it was in mint condition.

I gave it a second life. This fat, clunky book of 659 pages, titled *Memoirs of the Settlers of the Recovered Territories*, edited by Zygmunt Dulczewski and Andrzej Kwilecki, became indispensable for my journey. I never parted with it, not even for a moment.

And all this because of Wanda Melcer's sloppiness. In the beginning I thought I would be able to follow in the tracks of her stories. From village to village, from town to town, I wanted to look for people she had talked to. Yet very quickly I realized that her book wasn't enough to guide me through the Recovered Territories. Because this prominent reporter was hired to write propaganda full of exclamation marks and excitement.

She was agitating from Masuria: "The fish are splashing in the sun, jumping over fine shiny waves. Sailor, athlete, tourist! This is for you! . . . And I am talking to you, fisherman, settle here!" She was reporting from Szczytno: "In the beginning of June the sawmills were not yet taken over. Foresters, sawmill workers! This is for you!" And from Olsztyn she was writing: "Polish doctor! Nurse! These lands long for you!"

But Melcer was skimping on details. She did not like to disclose place names and she did not reveal the names of her interlocutors. Probably with time that trip became tedious for her: "Now we look at these villages, cowsheds, and stables with indifference. We got used to them."

The newspapers from 1945 were no better. Reporters from all the Polish magazines went to the Recovered Territories, but they came back with personal impressions, and rarely with facts. How could they help me find the repatriates?

And at that point, the memoirs came in handy. Writing memoirs after the war became a craze. There were contests for housewives, engineers, teachers, and peasants. The Western Institute in Poznań announced a writing contest for settler memoirs and received 205 submissions. The most interesting were published in a book that went through several editions. Forty-four years later I bought the 1970 edition on the Internet. From this book with yellowish pages and a rough cover I selected ten fragments and marked them with colored Post-its. Finally, I knew where to go.

There was also a map. It was published in *Życie Warszawy* in 1945 and indicated the cities of the new Poland without much care, such as Lignica (the future Legnica) or Żegań (Żagań) along the Oder and the Nisa (the Neisse).

We couldn't follow that map because on it Poland looked like some crazy dream of Stalin's. It represented only half of Poland, the western part, as if after the war we had never received Varmia and Masuria and, in addition, had lost all territory east of the Vistula. The author of the map simply cut away half our country.

Maybe it was the fault of the editor who ordered a sketch of the new Poland? Maybe he didn't want to show the eastern territories? In order not to trouble readers over the new line dividing Poland and the USSR? After all, on the other side of the border we were leaving 178,800 square kilometers (Vilna, Nowogródek, Polesie, Wołyń, Tarnopol, and Stanisławów voivodeships, as well as parts of Białystok and Lvov voivodeships), and our beloved cities of Vilna and Lvov. It sounded much better that in return for the Eastern Borderlands we obtained the 101,000 square kilometers of the western territories: East Prussia (after the war, Olsztyn voivodeship), West Prussia, also known as Western Pomerania (Koszalin and Szczecin voivodeships), Lubush Land (Zielona Góra voivodeship), Lower Silesia (Wrocław voivodeship), and the German part of Upper Silesia and Opole Land (Katowice and Opole voivodeships).

Wanda Melcer was delighted: "Citizens, can you believe how many towns and cities we obtained along with these territories? No more and no less than 327 (mostly in Silesia), and that is half the total number of cities in Poland. . . . Yes, these cities are suitable for living in: modern, hygienic, excellently managed, and decorated with charm."

STALLE, THAT IS TO SAY, STALEWO—"LITTLE ANGELS, ARE YOUR ASSES WARM?"

She was coming from the direction of Malbork. Her feet were skidding on the cobblestones that had probably been laid there by Mennonites, Dutch Protestants escaping persecution, who had arrived in Pomerania in the sixteenth century and stayed there until the war. But Józefa didn't know that. Neither did she know that she had just passed their cemetery on the right. Later on, one of the settlers dragged a cemetery gate to the village and placed it in his front yard.

In a tiny trunk she was carrying bread, butter, fresh eggs, a pot, spoons, and a blanket. In Biała Podlaska, Józefa had seen an advertising kiosk with a poster calling for settlers. So she decided to leave her native village in the Lublin region, her widowed mother and five sisters, and their fields—four hectares—that had been partly covered with concrete for an airbase. "They didn't want to write 'settling' on my resettlement card because I was single. So they wrote 'visiting family' but I was definitely determined to settle," wrote Józefa Nogat in her memoirs for the Western Institute. In her pocket she was hiding a piece of newspaper and a letter from a male acquaintance. Twelve words: "Come immediately, train station Stare Pole, village Stalewo, community Tirgard, Gdańsk Lowlands." So she already had someone there.

Later on, she brought her mother and her aunt. She received ten hectares and raised pigs and cows, fought the mouse infestation (one cat from the head office cost 500 zlotys, the equivalent of a hundred kilograms of wheat), grew barley and clover. "We had no experience regarding what, when, and

Figure 4.2. Bolesławiec. The Gołębiowskis, repatriates from beyond the Bug River, and a Holstein cow, in front of their new home. Jerzy Baranowski, PAP

where to sow. Many a man sowed wheat or sugar beets for the first time, as I did, for example!"

But for now, she reached the village. She saw a Lutheran church made of wood and brick, with its steep roof and separate tower. Soon Poles dismantled the church piece by piece and only a part of the historic interior would be saved. Someone fired up the stove with a wooden angel from the baptismal font. People would say later that he was shouting, "Little angels, are your asses warm?"

She stopped by a house of a kind she had never seen before. It was large and white, with dark wooden beams and an arcade supported by eight pillars. One day she may have learned that it had been built in 1751 by the Mennonite Georg Poeck. She could live in it, if only she wanted. But she preferred to find a house with people in it. To be safe.

This happened on July 22, 1945. At least, that's what she wrote. We don't know if she gave the correct date. Soon, Józefa would become an activist, join the Peasants' Party (though preferring the Polish Workers'

Party), organize the farmers' wives' circle, become secretary of the Sugar Beet Growers' Association, and would join the commission for eradicating the pig plague. So perhaps July 22, the first anniversary of the Manifesto of the Polish Committee of National Liberation, suited her image? Anyway, her name "Nogat" was a pseudonym. She borrowed it from the river flowing near Stalewo.

We were in Stalewo. Tosia went to the store to scrounge something sweet from her father. I walked with the village head, who kept saying she was tired of this multiyear official job and was planning to quit. She pointed at the brick house of the Szwagierek family. She was sure they were settlers. I passed two green Audis with their buffed chrome-plated rims and with white ribbons here and there. They were ready for a wedding. I opened a small gate and walked toward the door. A little boy ran out from the house, shouting. In the hall, he dropped a potato pancake. I steered clear of the greasy stain on the floor, and following the aroma of the heated oil, I entered the kitchen. So many of them, I thought. They occupied all the chairs and stools, and the entire sofa. The oldest of them, Jan Szwagierek, was sitting near the kitchen cabinets. His wife Krystyna, with an elegant hairdo and wearing an apron, was sitting by the stove. The others were younger: daughters, sons, sons-in-law, and daughters-in-law. It was difficult to count them all. Seeing my surprised face, they burst into laughter.

"The wedding was on Friday," explained one of them. "Today is Sunday, so this is the continuation of the continuation of the party."

The little boy touched my recorder with his greasy finger and whispered reverently, "Smaltphone." And again he ran away, accompanied by his siblings and cousins.

I pressed the red button to record.

Jan Szwagierek was a real chatterbox. And he was so amusing. After each sentence I broke up with laughter. He remembered Józefa Nogat, why not? He said, "Her real name was Ziutka Rutka. She lived in the same house as my wife, but on the south side. She lived with some fellow, got pregnant, lost the baby. And then they moved to Jegłownik."

Szwagierek's wife, Krystyna, was more serious. She spoke very little and weighed her words. But it was she who interested me more because she had arrived here in August 1945. Her husband came three years later from near

Kielce. She recalled, "From our village, only we and the Szczygieł family came to Stalewo. Later came the Lendzion and the Kuc families. People settled wherever they wished. We were supposed to live where the Sawickis are living now, but my mother went over there, and she looked around, and she saw one dead German, and another dead German. 'I'm not going to live here,' she said, 'I'm leaving.' I remember the rat infestation. They were scurrying in the yard. My mother picked up her youngest child, and we all waited in front of the gate for our father to come. Those rats, they were like cats. We poisoned them.

She continued, "There was nothing German left in the house. When the *bauers* [farmers] were fleeing, they took whatever they could with them. Only the unfortunate fellows who used to work for them, were left, but they had nothing. Only once, glasses . . . no, we didn't find any glasses. The ground dipped beneath the cauldron used for cooking animal feed. We thought a German was buried there, we dug, and found two tubs full of cut crystal."

"Did the Russkis do any serious damage in the village?" I repeated the reporters' question from seventy years ago.

Jan Szwagierek burst into laughter, but his wife didn't. She replied, "When it was getting dark, all the German women would gather at our house. The Russkis were chasing German girls a lot."

Józefa Nogat remembered that those were hard times for Polish women, too. "Surprises were lurking everywhere, especially for women, regardless of their age. Once, when a lady friend went to buy cows, she came back without the cows, without the money, and as a woman she lost something else," she trailed off.

I walked to the Stalewo road. The monumental Żuławy house with its wooden beams and the arcades supported by eight pillars was still towering above the village. But where was the church? I asked a passerby. He shook his head. The church had not yet been rebuilt.

FOR WORK AND PROSPERITY

It was supposed to be a fairy tale. The internally displaced people, smiling and singing, should get on the clean trains and quickly reach their destinations. They were supposed to wait for no more than a week at the train stations to be taken to their new homes. By that point, the Germans should be far away, on their way to even farther west. But the Germans' furniture,

Figure 4.3. Ligota, near Katowice. July 1945. A nine-day stopover for repatriates from Stanisławów. Stanisław Bober / Collection of the Karta Center

jewelry, embroidered tablecloths, jam jars, horses, pigs, and cultivated fields were waiting for the Polish settlers. And all this was supposed to be controlled by the employees of the State Repatriation Office, the SRO. This office had already been created by the Polish Committee of National Liberation on October 7, 1945. Its job was to organize repatriation from the Eastern Borderlands and to supervise migration within the country, the return of Poles—those who had been expelled by the Germans—to their native regions, and the resettlement of people in the Recovered Territories. With time, however, the significance of the SRO diminished, and more organizations for resettlement were created, among others, the Central Resettlement Committee and the Office of the Plenipotentiary General for Repatriation.

Wanda Melcer described one of the SRO resettlement collection points with fascination: "Usually it is a large square outside the city but near the train station, fenced and with a few barracks. These barracks are wooden buildings with glass windows and covered with a roof that doesn't leak. . . .

Figure 4.4. Ligota, near Katowice. July 1945. A nine-day stopover for repatriates from Stanisławów. Stanisław Bober / Collection of the Karta Center

In the barracks there are wooden cots with straw mattresses and blankets, tables, benches and stools, basins and buckets. Internally Displaced Persons are then offered a comfortable space where they can sleep, eat, relax . . . receive information, visit a doctor, or get a job."

The overall objective was to persuade as many people as possible to move to the new west and the new north of the country. On the posters joyful images of peasants wearing folkloric hats, holding bindle sticks, and marching westward were chanting, "To the Oder River, to get the lands of our fathers, and prosperity."

Special events were planned in honor of the Recovered Territories. Toward the end of June, the Organizing Committee for Recovered Territories Week staged a commemoration in the Polonia movie theater in Warsaw. Edward Ochab, the plenipotentiary general for Recovered Territories, delivered a speech. In the artistic portion of the event, Władysław Szpilman played the piano.

Życie Warszawy kept making appeals for settlement: "In June alone at least one million people should be resettled in the West. It requires significant effort and large expenditures, but this is only an introduction to the great work of resettling a few million people in the West."

Wojciech Żukrowski was reporting to the weekly review *Przekrój* from Silesia: "Driving in the countryside I saw moving scenes, peasants praying at the thresholds of their new farms and carrying the image of Our Lady of Poczajów in the regained fields."

Mieczysław Wionczek from *Przekrój* was mocking Poles' fears of the Wild West: "Because the counselor's wife from the first floor said that it was very dangerous there. That at the Oder, Gestapo officers dressed in women's clothing were attacking the pioneers. And that you had to bring your own food because the Germans would offer you poisoned bread. And also that nothing was certain about the Oder and the Neisse. You go, she says, and later they will cut you off. . . . But actually no one wanted to attack us. In Opole the county chief was a bit surprised that there were so many morons in Krakow who were wasting their time telling far-fetched stories. In Opole I met my uncle from Stryj, my cousin from Tarnopol, and a friend of my first wife from Baranowicze. They are very satisfied with everything. They have never heard of any excesses or attacks. . . . I wept. The Wild West does not exist."

KÖSLIN, THAT IS TO SAY, KOSZALIN—"THIS BIZNESS TAKEN OVER BY REZIDENT OF GNIEZNO"

This meeting was especially important to me, because Ryszard Janusz Szyndler was the only author of a memoir about Koszalin that I managed to find there. Others had died or had left and all traces of them were gone. This oldest of the living Koszalin settlers was waiting for me with a smile. In his garden he showed us his plum tree full of purple fruit, and the retired camper in which he and his wife had visited all of Europe. And then we sat down in his room, I in an armchair and eighty-eight-year-old Ryszard Szyndler and his cat on the sofa, under a German painting seized in 1945 to decorate the wall.

His father, a prewar postal worker from Warsaw, was the first to come to the Wild West. The main square in Koszalin was still burning when he and his colleagues took over the surviving building of the main post office. It

was March 28, 1945. The Soviet army was stationed in the city, the roughly
five thousand Germans who hadn't managed to flee were slinking along
the walls, fearfully, and the number of Poles in the city equaled the number
of fingers in a few pairs of gloves. Telephones, telegraphs, and transportation weren't working. No one could send anything, nothing was reaching
Koszalin, there was no regular transportation in the country, no one had
Polish money and German money was invalid, but during office hours the
post office window was open. An old Polish postal worker, one of seven
who arrived from Warsaw, used to say, "What kind of post office is this
without an open window that has a clear sign indicating working hours?"

Ryszard's mother came from Warsaw right after his father. In May they
were joined by their son, nineteen-year-old Ryszard Janusz Szyndler. He
had fought in the Warsaw Uprising and was released from a labor camp in
the Berlin suburbs just a month earlier. He came to Koszalin to meet his
parents. He decided to stay a bit longer. His first job was at the post office
window that no one would come to.

Later in his memoir Ryszard Szyndler would call these first dozen days "the
time of the Koszalin Republic in the Wild West." "I was wandering in the
abandoned homes and warehouses for hours, looking with curiosity at old
stuff and rusted mementos. In some apartments everything was left as if
their residents had just gone for a short trip. . . . In one apartment a clock
of unusual appearance on a credenza attracted my attention, but when I
went inside the apartment I saw the bared teeth of a dead old woman who
had hanged herself on the doorknob," he wrote.

In August 2014 Szyndler added, "I was curious about how people had
lived, how they had furnished their apartments. Before the war, Koszalin
was a part of the Reich's hinterland, a city off the beaten track, well-kept,
clean, but a bit provincial. As my residence I chose a very nice house on
Ogrodowa Street. Later on it was given to a large family."

Because at the post office window one could be bored to death, after
six days Ryszard Szyndler joined a two-person group that was supplying
postal workers with food.

He continued, "We had two horses and we would go to the countryside
to hunt pigs roaming the fields. One of the postal workers was familiar with
butchering. One day the Russians showed up. We had good relations with
them. They asked me to take them to the pigs because I knew where to go.

After we loaded two pigs onto the wagon, they picked a bigger one. 'Listen, Ryszard, it's because we are the victors,' they explained."

Szyndler went on, "Another group of postal workers was in charge of securing the material goods in the city. Every day they would bring typewriters, mechanical calculators, radios, motorcycles, fabrics, paintings, and furniture. We didn't take anything from apartments, only from warehouses. Everything was then registered."

"For myself I took two paintings to decorate some walls in my new house, but nothing more. When we notified the head office in Poznań that we had those things, we were told that some people would come to pick them up. And so they did, but afterward we heard the unpleasant news that unknown perpetrators had attacked the escorts and had stolen everything. Later on, I met one of the transportation supervisors. He was leading a comfortable life," recalled Ryszard Janusz Szyndler, and paused.

He wrote in his memoir: "We were living in clover and we had everything. Some kind of primeval, patriarchal, and family unity was created among us. . . . I note one more important aspect of our existence at that time: an almost total lack of money. . . . During our evening conversations more and more often we would express our fears that the imminent normalization of conditions, or in other words 'civilization,' would bring our 'Koszalin Republic' to an end."

The end of the Republic arrived at the Koszalin station by train in June. It got off the railway cars together with a group of several hundred residents of Gniezno. They were the first settlers who right away began to take over private accommodations and shops.

Szyndler wrote: "It looked like the Klondike Gold Rush and a murderous race to the gold-bearing areas. In practice it was like this: the settlers who were only scouting were equipped with chalk. And on every store, apartment, or house they would write a short announcement that they were taking possession of a given building. Repeatedly. I remember one inscription, the most frequent: 'This bizness taken over by rezident of Gniezno.'"

In 2014 Szyndler told me, "I am a bit ashamed of the way I wrote about them. Most of them were decent people with great commercial or artisanal skills."

He also recalled that the greater the number of people who came from all over the country, the more difficult it was to communicate. Varsovians were annoyed by the accented "shpeech" of people from Vilna and regarded them as backward, unsubtle, and primitive. Mazovians, on the other hand, were called "barefooted Tonys from Russian Poland" and they were distrusted as unintelligent sly dogs who had come to loot. People from Greater Poland, nicknamed by others "Poznań spuds," were putting on airs, claiming to represent a higher civilization. In 1947 all those people were united by their fear of the Ukrainians and Lemkos resettled in the Recovered Territories by Operation Vistula. People would whisper among themselves: "They will murder us, they are Ukrainian fascists—*Banderites.*"

Ryszard Janusz Szyndler took a sip of coffee, placed his hand on his cat's head, and told me that Koszalin was his city 100 percent. He had visited his son in America and traveled to many cities. They are too big. He goes even to Warsaw less frequently. Here, you could walk to the opera or to the movies. You could stroll through the whole city in a single day. He added that he was aging well in this town still permeated with the spirit of the Prussian province. He wouldn't exchange it for anything else. It didn't matter to him that it had been built by the Germans.

GROSS PANKNIN, THAT IS TO SAY, PĘKANINO—THE STRANGE SENSATION OF BEING IN A FOREIGN PLACE

I found citizen Kazimierz Szkolniak's letter in *Życie Warszawy.* "On May 29, 1945, I left for the West together with my neighbors. . . . We wanted to see what was there and check it out. People tell different stories. That there are attacks, that Poles are being expelled, that there is no land, that the livestock and the buildings are destroyed. . . . We reported at the SRO station. They directed us to the village of Duży Pankin, three kilometers outside the city. . . . The buildings here are very nice, like little boxes. Everything is made of brick, electricity and plumbing are everywhere, and there are electric machines for chopping straw, threshing, and even cutting wood."

The village he was describing was on our route.

It was ugly. Sad and gray. Residents of Pękanino should skip this chapter, because if they love their village, it will break their hearts.

We felt like shouting, "Settlers! What have you done to Gross Panknin? Where are those nice buildings like little boxes that once fascinated the peasant from near Warsaw? Where are those fifteen farms that in 1939 housed sixty-four people? (Nowadays there are just a few more.) Your village didn't suffer during the war. The local cemetery and a small factory for plastic bags, why are they the best maintained places in Pękanino? The three remaining formerly German farms made of stone, huge as fortified castles, surrounded on both sides with a large barn and a cowshed, and with a gate big enough for a hay wagon, why do they look as if they were about to collapse?"

We parked our car at the edge of the road.

The man was standing on the crumbling steps of a prewar brick house that in its size and beauty resembled a Polish country manor. He didn't see me because, leaning over a crate, he was sorting out cucumbers. The branches of the big tree were very low. It was as if they wanted to stroke his back. A front yard surrounded by tall and neglected brick farm buildings was separating my family and me from the street. We felt we were standing in a castle courtyard.

I cleared my throat. He straightened up and smiled.

"No, the Szkolniak family doesn't live in this village," he said. "No, I haven't been living here since the war ended," he added.

He had bought the farm at the end of the 1970s from some settler's children who didn't want to stay there. He was living in it with his wife and two grown-up children.

He invited me to his house and seated me at the kitchen table. On the wall shelf I noticed a Polish edition of *A Theory of Justice* by the American philosopher John Rawls. He sat down at the other side of the table. His name was Stanisław Kubic. He noticed I was looking around. He explained that a German family, the Buttkes, had lived here. They were different from the rest of the village. When the whole village was baking cakes to celebrate the conquests of its army, they didn't participate. Kubic knew this from a Polish slave who was forced to work for them during the war. They treated him like a household member. When fortunes changed and the Russians entered the village, the Buttkes were taken to the transit camp in Białogard, and the former slave brought them food. Whether they had liked Hitler or not, they had to leave their native land when it became Poland. Once, someone from the Buttke family visited Stanisław Kubic. Kubic then returned to him the rotted clothing and chipped plates that he had found in a storage place when he was renovating the basement. There were also books, probably religious, but Kubic put them away and couldn't find them later.

"What's it like to live in someone else's shoes, custom-made in a different size?" I asked. "To open a door that someone else made for his family, every day, or to walk on stairs built for other people?"

"Weird," he replied. "I have the strange sensation of being in a foreign place. I come from Zakopane. I was born in 1940, but nine years later my parents moved to a place near Krakow. Yet I felt at home there. People are connected by tradition. Here, we are strangers to one another and we don't have common roots."

As a farewell gift he gave me a few cucumbers for my daughter. She wanted to thank him in person, so we went back to his front yard. Then I had to gather some courage to ask him why those three post-German farms looked like they were about to collapse. Was this from some fear that Germans would come back and take what was theirs before the war, so it wouldn't make sense to take care of them?

He smiled. "Not at all. We simply can't afford to fix them." He shrugged his shoulders slightly.

BUCHHORST, THAT IS TO SAY, ŻELIMUCHA—A GLASS OF MILK FOR A TEACHER

Huckleberries for half the price. That was the only thing we found in Żelimucha, a village located thirty minutes outside Koszalin. We were sitting on a boulder next to our car and we were devouring the little navy blue berries from a plastic box that I had just bought from a local grower.

Fifteen minutes earlier the owner of this patch of land, one hectare or so, immersed in his huckleberry bushes, waved his blue hand in an unspecified direction.

"There is no one left from that time. Those who used to be here have died or have sold their homes and have gone back where they came from," he said.

The owner's mother emerged from under a bush. "Right now we are the oldest family here. We arrived in Żelimucha in 1960," she commented.

"Did the school survive?" I tried to outshout the tractor's radio that was playing music at full volume. It was a modern tractor.

"Yes! But now it is a private house. You have to go in this direction!" He stretched out his arm and disappeared into the bushes.

He didn't want to teach there. The building had been destroyed and the benches were turned upside down. There was no glass in the windows, or hinges in the doors. Someone had ripped off the metal stove doors. And the blackboard was hanging on one hook. Władysław Stachurski decided to look for a different school. A few years later, when the Western Institute called for settlers' memoirs, he responded.

The deputy village head asked him to stay. He invited him for a glass of milk but instead poured something homemade and alcoholic, and offered him scrambled eggs. Stachurski insisted he wouldn't stay. The deputy village head's neighbor whispered into his ear that there was a large number of settlers' children. September was coming but they didn't have a teacher. Stachurski replied that he had to go back. The deputy village head was trying to entice him, promising him a good life. He added that Stachurski could stay in the local policeman's house because it was spacious, and that the entire village would feed and clothe him. If Stachurski decided to take a farm, the villagers would plow, sow, and harvest his field. Then the village head showed up and poured more "milk" into Stachurski's glass. In the evening Władysław Stachurski made up his mind to stay in the village and accept the teaching position.

He was twenty-six, came from Garwolin, and before the war had completed only the first year of high school. During the war he was a forced laborer in Germany. After the war he came up with the idea of becoming a teacher in the Recovered Territories. For the school superintendent in Białogard, Western Pomerania (earlier Belgard, Pommern), he was like the most precious of treasures. Settling was advancing very rapidly but the settlers' children were left without teachers. If the superintendent only could, he would pull down the heavens for people like this courageous fellow. Gaps in your own education? You will catch up. Lesson plans? You will get them. But where am I supposed to teach? Here are the names of four villages near Białogard. Please visit them and pick one.

And that's how Stachurski ended up in Żelimucha.

"I am registering the children," he made a note on August 30, 1945. "At the same time I am learning about the milieu and the backgrounds of the settlers. . . . What a diverse mix! People from the regions of Łódź, Krakow, Kuyavia, and Łowicz. From beyond the Bug. All of Poland! . . . Different levels of intellectual development among children the same age, different habits and views, both among the children and their parents, different cultures. . . . I have thirty-four children."

He spent all his days at school. In the fall, due to the lack of window panes, he temporarily moved the school to a private house. He spent his evenings alone at home. His domestic help was a German woman, Gertrude. "I don't have any social life," he wrote. Sometimes he would visit a teacher who lived alone in a nearby village but more often he was visiting his students' parents. He divided them into three groups.

Those in the first group were called the true pioneers. Hardworking people, they kept their farms clean, and they were in the minority. One of them confessed to Stachurski that the others treated him like the village idiot. "He says no one visits him because he doesn't serve vodka."

Those in the second group, who mostly arrived from beyond the Bug, were criticized by him for being messy, but he tried to understand them. Stachurski wrote about one of them: "According to what he told me, since he had a farm there, quite good, he did not come of his own free will, he had to come. What was he supposed to do when they moved the border? . . . It is often hard for them, mainly because they don't know how to operate machines, electricity, etc. It is not surprising, since they did not have them where they came from. I noticed that his farm was an eyesore."

Those in the third group in Żelimucha were drunks and rogues who made their wives and children cry. He counted ten of them. And for them he had no excuse.

All winter he was studying for his high school finals. At the end of April 1946 he finished the school year, distributed report cards among his students, and informed the village head that he was going to college and that one day he would return to the Recovered Territories. He must have been successful because the publisher of *Memoirs of the Settlers of the Recovered Territories* made a note next to Stachurski's name: profession—researcher, address—Koszalin voivodeship.

GROSS STEPENITZ, THAT IS TO SAY, STEPNICA—STAŚ, WHERE ARE YOU TAKING US?

A dark cloud like a dirty quilt was hanging low above the Bay of Szczecin. The storm was coming from the direction of Germany. A large dog with no leash was running on the beach. Two tourists rolled up their beach screen and then were running toward their rented room. We could hear the monotonous hissing of the pressure washers used by the fishermen and their women to clean the seaweed from the nets. Tosia was enjoying herself on a swing, but I was rushing her. Before it started to rain I had to find someone who knew Eugeniusz Szmigiel, one of the authors of the *Memoirs*.

If it's true that all people on this planet are separated by only six handshakes, I was close. Someone from the local municipality office sent me to the restaurant in the port. From the restaurant to the fisherman's home. The fisherman's wife showed me where her husband was cleaning the nets. The fisherman told me to go to the chairman of the Rybak company. Skidding on the fish scales, I went to greet the chairman. He pointed to his daughter Dagmara, a history major, who in turn was to take me to her grandmother, Teresa Jałukowicz.

Right after the first handshake with Mrs. Jałukowicz, I found out that Szmigiel was dead and that his family had left for Sweden. He was from Łódź. He spent the war in Gross Stepenitz as a forced laborer at the local miller's. When the war ended, he stayed in the village as its first settler. He managed to restore electricity and to turn on the mill that had been damaged during the war. Soviet and Polish officers stationed in Stepnica with their armies were ecstatic. "When I showed them the flour they were flabbergasted. . . . They swung me in their arms, shouting 'our hero boy' in Russian, *geroy malchik*."

Of all of the authors in the book with the rough cover, Eugeniusz Szmigiel reached the farthest point beyond Szczecin, almost to the new German border. Only a small piece of land and a bay separated him from it.

Teresa Jałukowicz née Wawrzyńczak offered me coffee and went to the kitchen to boil some water. I could hear the monotonous buzzing of the refrigerator. She walked back through the long hall, sat down, adjusted a little vase on the table, and started talking. In her story it was September 1945, and a lonely horse wagon had been moving for two days. Their journey started in Białogard and was to end in Stobnica, changed a year later by bureaucrats to Stepnica. The passengers, although guarded by two armed policemen, were fed up with their traveling. Grandmother kept calling her son-in-law: "Staś, where are you taking us? To the end of the world!" But Teresa at age eleven—Tereska—was afraid of the trip through a dense forest. She had never seen anything like it in her native Błoń near Warsaw. And she was afraid of the robbers, because she had heard that they were attacking the settlers just like them, the Wawrzyńczak family—parents and their three children—stealing the life possessions they were taking to the Recovered Territories. Grandmother was only accompanying them to help out with the move. They had sold what they could, and they took all the necessities. Now they were tired, bouncing among their pots and quilts, with no end to the road in sight.

Teresa had to stop her recollections for a moment because the water in the kitchen was boiling. She made some coffee, brought some cookies, placed an ornamental mat under the cup, and picked up the thread of our conversation.

Her father was a forced laborer near Gross Stepenitz. After the war he was supposed to come back to Błoń and restart his life, the life that had been interrupted in September 1939 when he left to fight. The family wasn't dreaming about any Recovered Territories.

She knocked an invisible speck of dust off the polished table top and said, "When the war was over, my father miraculously found himself in Stepnica and somehow, also miraculously, he was recruited by the police. He wanted to return home but they seized his documents, and told him: 'You will stay here to build Stepnica.' I don't know exactly how it was. When I was a little girl I wasn't interested and I didn't ask."

Tereska's mother didn't want to go. She was tired and recovering from typhus. But her husband, Staś, was encouraging them, claiming the place was like a little town, and that he had found a house in the middle of the village, close to the police station and the church. It was completely furnished, abandoned by the Germans. There was even a piano there. He added that four Polish families already lived there, so they wouldn't be lonely. That there was a bay, so in the summer they would swim there. That soon there would be a school for Tereska. That he had been promoted to deputy police commander, so his salary would be higher. Yet he didn't mention to his wife that occasionally there were shootings between the police and the Soviet army. Neither did he say that the Polish army hated the Polish police, and vice versa. (On Easter day, 1946, these two groups exchanged fire and several people were killed). He didn't disclose that one had to be very careful at village festivals. That it was easy to lose one's life when quarreling settlers were reaching for their handguns or rifles, so abundant everywhere.

In Stepnica, Tereska was looking for dolls, her first in the post-German houses. Instead, she found Christmas decorations. She didn't remember her first Christmas Eve. What did they eat? Did she have a Christmas tree? She's forgotten. On December 31, 1945, she didn't attend the first New Year's Eve party at the local government office at the riverside. It was for adults only and fifty settlers were invited.

When we were saying good-bye to each other, she shouted unexpectedly, "I used to know Szmigiel. He was cool, very cool."

NEUHOF, THAT IS TO SAY BĘDLINO, FOR THE SECOND TIME, AND LAST

The house stood almost outside the village. Modest, simple, with a slanted roof. We arrived there and Halina Borcuch appeared on the doorstep, followed by a grown son. A woman peeked out from a house next door. (It will turn out later that she was Halina's daughter.) The drunk from the store must have used a shortcut because he entered the hallway right after us. "Watch out, Halina! They are from that Provident company," he yelled, and slumped on the chair.

Halina Borcuch was fragile and tiny. She could buy her clothing in the children's department. Her grandchildren called her Little Grandma. Her chestnut hair, freshly colored, was curly, freshly permed. There was the dignity of the English Queen about her. She didn't even bother to look at the drunk. She leaned over a narrow table toward me and answered the question I asked her. "I knew Stanisław Bania. He was a blacksmith and our village head. He ruled over everyone. He took that large brick house, the former Forestry Department. But then he moved out."

The drunk lifted his head and belched. "He was a ringleader and an auxiliary policeman. That's what he was!"

Stanisław Bania, the first Będlino village head, recalled the beginnings in his memoirs: "The night has come. There are neither lamps nor candles. One can still hear the booming of cannon and the planes flying over. Dogs have started to howl. I am sitting with a loaded rifle by the stove and grenades are on the chair next to me."

He was a son of smallholders who emigrated for bread to the other side of the ocean. He was born in America in 1899. He returned with his family to the homeland. He took care of geese and cows, worked at a country manor, and starved. In 1935 he completed the seventh grade of primary school as a home-schooled student. "I had to read a lot of books." He spent the war in German slavery, working as a blacksmith in the village of Neuhof. "Five years of moral suffering, humiliation, beaten by the police, and treated like a slave." In March 1945, along with the Germans, he was evacuated westward. Then he was liberated by a Soviet patrol. On his way back, together with other liberated Poles, he found himself in Falkenburg (Złocieniec) near Neuhof, or Będlino. He was appointed village chief of Będlino by a Soviet officer. To refuse, this was not a good idea.

He was a skilled organizer. He divided the work among the 267 Germans who hadn't escaped to the West. When the military front moved past the village, they left their hiding places and returned to their homes. They removed the debris in two weeks and began renovations. The grain, horses, and cattle were collected in one place and Bania appointed special units to guard all this. Other units were sent to work in the fields. They obeyed him because he was backed by the Soviet army. He rewarded good work with strong alcohol and better food. But he knew that in the neighboring villages the commanders, as the village heads were called at that time, were occasionally killed by unknown perpetrators. "There were some Germans in the village, who hoped that some foreign countries, like the USA or England, wouldn't allow these territories to be Polish."

He never parted with his weapons. And he waited for the Poles who were about to come. They showed up at the beginning of July 1945. "Sixteen families, all destitute. There were some who had never worked in the fields, and some who in their native village had had half a hectare or less. They lived six or eight people in one room with a clay floor. They came from Kutno county."

Halina Borcuch began her story, "I regret coming here. My husband used to kick himself, too. The Kordek family, from my native village, came here first. When they returned, they kept talking about the beautiful place with a lot of land, farms. People could take whatever they wanted. When I arrived here I got scared because I had no place to sleep. There were Germans everywhere. Was I supposed to enter their home? So we went to the Buczyńskis, who had come earlier, and we stayed with them until the officials allocated us a house.

"I am eighty-eight and I spent my childhood twenty kilometers outside Warsaw. I was fifteen when I was rounded up by the Germans. Until the end of the war I was making ammunition for them in one of the factories in the West. I was in charge of three large machines and was making cartridges sixteen hours a day. Since I was tiny they gave me a stool to stand on. On Saturdays the Germans organized festivities for us, I can't deny it. Forced laborers from the village were allowed to come. That's how I met Kazik, who worked for a *bauer*.

"In June 1945 we went back to Poland through Lignica. The first three weeks we spent in Łódź with Kazik's family. Then we went to my part of the world. We got married in July. In autumn we packed clothes and other things, and together with my parents we got on the train from Warsaw to Szczecin. We were accompanied by some other friends. Someone picked us up in Szczecin and brought us on horse-wagons to Będlino. The weather was nice, I remember this. I had a little belly because I was three months pregnant. Later on we were assigned a house. And we received the necessary documents.

"My dear, I went to my house with those documents, and Germans were still living there. They hadn't been expelled yet because they were needed by the forestry department. This room was occupied, that room was occupied, and there was a couple living upstairs. There were also some people with an older, sick sister. I sat down in the kitchen corner and started crying. But there was one particular German woman who stroked my hair, hugged me, and kissed me. She fried a lot of fish so we could fill our stomachs. We communicated through hand gestures since I didn't know German. I kept crying. I was greatly upset. I asked my husband: 'Honey, where have you brought me? Let's go to Łódź, to your family. We'll get jobs in some factory.' But he insisted. They persuaded him, so we stayed.

"The German woman vacated one room in the front part of the house, took away the furniture, and told us to move in. She had a daughter. Her son had disappeared at the front without a trace. She knew I was pregnant. I can't deny that she helped me and was kind to me. She cooked a lot of food and asked us to sit at her table. Dinners, breakfasts, I can't deny it. I was a bit concerned, but she hugged me again, stroked my hair, and told me not to be afraid, there wouldn't be any poison.

"When she moved out in 1946, she left me a complete set of baby linen. The other Germans had left the furniture but they had taken their clothing and sheets. I kept telling them: 'Please, take everything, this is all yours, I will buy these things for myself.' But they didn't want to. What they left behind was salt, sugar, and flour containers with wooden covers. Made of porcelain with blue inscriptions. And a hanging pepper mill. Oh, here on

the door frame, it has left a mark. But now we have none of their possessions. My cousin took the mill, and with time their things were replaced
with new things.

"At the beginning, it was quite safe here. But one time some people came
from the forest, with covered faces, armed, and on horses. They stopped at
the front door and the German woman started to shout. I went out, and she
called me, '*Frau, Frau.*' Four armed men with bandoliers. I felt like crying. I
thought, 'I had made those cartridges and now I was about to be shot.' The
German woman stepped forward, pushed me behind her, and said that *die
Frau* would have *ein Kind*. They stood there for a while, jibber-jabbered a
bit in German, and went away.

"The son of that German woman was found after she had left. After
many years he paid us a visit. He walked from one room to another, telling
us where the bed had been, or the table. He left us some German marks.

"At the beginning the atmosphere in the village was fine. The village
head, Bania, organized farmers' circles. Generally, if someone needed help,
people would help. We would go from house to house, asking if there was
something to be done. And no one cared if the neighbor was from the
Łódź region, or from central Poland, or from somewhere near Łęczyca. The
Zalewskis came from beyond the Bug, but they were helping, too. At that
time people were united. But later some left and went back to their native
regions. Something wasn't working for them."

Halina Borcuch and I hugged each other and we posed for a farewell
photo under the apple tree.

We were getting into the car when my village suitor came to say
good-bye.

"So you are not from Provident," he admitted. "Just in case, remember,
I have a lot of old photos at home," he reminded me and winked.

TO CLEAN AFTER A THOUSAND FILTHY PEOPLE

This was not a fairy tale. Did Wanda Melcer make up her description of
the SRO resettlement collection point? Probably not. In all likelihood, the
site was fixed up especially for the journalists' visit. In reality, the entire
resettling process was characterized by enormous chaos that was concealed
from the people.

Poles from the Eastern Borderlands who suddenly found themselves in
the Soviet Union had the difficult choice between staying on their land and

Figure 4.5. Warsaw, 1945. Repatriates from beyond the Bug River are waiting for a train that will take them to the Recovered Territories. PAP

facing attack from Ukrainian nationalists and from the next wave of Soviet collectivization or journeying into the unknown with their life possessions. As a result, people in Galicia and Volhynia were stuck at the train stations for months, waiting for trains heading west.

In May 1945 the government's Plenipotentiary for Resettlement reported from Czortków in the former Tarnopol voivodeship. "For three months now, and surrounded by constant promises, these people have been waiting for railway cars, so they could at least save their lives and with their work-loving hands seize the land awaiting them in the Poznań region. And that is their right. They have the grain they scavenged to start their new, well-deserved life in the Recovered Territories but have been unable to move. . . . Not one of these people believes that the only reason Poland cannot take care of them is because it doesn't have railway cars or that the mighty Soviet Union is not able to provide for them. These people keep saying sarcastically: 'Those who escaped the Banderite ax, let them starve to death.'"

Figure 4.6 Ligota, near Katowice. July 1945. A nine-day stopover for repatriates from Stanisławów. Stanisław Bober/collection of the Karta Center

   Displacing people from Lvov was moving very slowly because the residents boycotted the appeals to leave. Although displacing people from Belarus and Lithuania was going more smoothly, many Poles didn't want to leave Vilna. Before July 1, 1946, only 20 percent of those in this city registered for repatriation. Poles from Vilna would be immigrating to Poland into the 1960s.

   The State Repatriation Office accepted the principle that people from the northern part of the Eastern Borderlands would be moved to Varmia, Mazuria, Pomerania, and the Poznań region. Residents of Volhynia and Eastern Galicia would be transferred to Upper and Lower Silesia, and Lubusz Land. In reality, the repatriates were transported all over the country and dumped wherever there were vacancies. Most often, however, there were no immediate vacancies. The best the settlers could do was to live together with the Germans on their farms, or to camp at train stations for weeks. In July 1945 thousands of homeless repatriates were living at the Opole train station, in horrific conditions, with no water, food, and medicine. They were sick, they died, they were born.

Życie Warszawy reported: "Due to the lack of transportation, 20,000 repatriates are now being held in Opole and 10,000 in Koźle. For six or seven weeks, 30,000 people have been camping along the railway tracks, for kilometers. Under open skies, suffering from hunger and ill-treatment. Thirty thousand people! That is the population of an average provincial town! There are children among them, livestock, and, as a warning signal, there have been cases of infectious diseases. . . . In the face of these problems, the SRO is completely helpless."

The lack of hygiene at the resettlement collection points must have been severe because in June 1945 *Życie Warszawy* announced that the first public baths in Lublin were opened for repatriates. The idea came from the Special Headquarters for Fighting Epidemics. "The baths have been supplied with a new type of disinfecting machine," reported the newspaper.

Wanda Melcer was preaching: "The settlers have to remember that cleanliness and tidiness at the collection points are their responsibility. There are not enough workers who could clean up after a thousand filthy people every day. Every evening the settlers themselves have to organize a group that would help the staff."

People who were disappointed with the organization of settling wrote to the newspapers. At the end of May 1945 *Życie Warszawy* published a letter by the citizen Zenon Remiszowski: "I am a Varsovian whose house has been burned down. I have only a part-time job and I want to go west with my family. In mid-April I joined the Polish Western Association . . . I have been waiting for five weeks, pointlessly. The management of the Association is unable to provide any information, or point to any place of settlement. They advise me to go on my own."

Józef Patek from the village of Głęboka: "The unbelievable attitude of the SRO worker from Lignica. When he was asked how long we were supposed to wait for the allocation of the farms, he responded 'Why did you come here?'"

What the journalists were bringing back from their trips to the Recovered Territories were not only expressions of delight. In July 1945 a *Życie Warszawy* correspondent anonymously went with the settlers to Varmia: "After three hours of lessons in patience, the train moves on. Sitting in the so-called cattle car (dirty, without seats!) we make friends with our fellow travelers. . . . We have spent twice as much time traveling than indicated in the timetable. Finally, at two in the morning, in the middle of the dark night, we arrive in Olsztyn. . . . The organization of food supplies for the settlers, and of other things, is really bad. Apparently, there is food in some towns, but hundreds of kilometers away from Olsztyn."

SCHÖNBRUNN, THAT IS TO SAY, JABŁONÓW—"IN A MONTH, OR TWO, WE WILL NOT BE HERE"

Tosia and I were standing on the porch. A bit nervous, she was squeezing my hand because I had promised her that we would do the next interview together. But we were refused.

"I have nothing to say. I came here much later." An elderly woman leaned out from behind the curtain made of colorful plastic tassels hanging in the open door. She looked like a shaman woman. "My husband, he came in 1945. And he remembered everything. But he won't tell you anything because he had a stroke."

The tassels crackled and a slim gentleman appeared on the porch.

He smiled. "What don't I remember?"

"1945. You had a stroke," explained his wife.

"I remember everything about that year and I am happy to talk," he protested gently.

"You don't. You had a stroke." She wouldn't give up.

I interrupted the dispute. "Let's talk. If it doesn't work, we will go away."

The woman was stubborn. "It doesn't make sense, he had a stroke . . ."

Then I reached for my secret weapon. "Tosia, make a face!"

My daughter frowned, looked up, and pursed her lips. She looked like Shrek's cat. Janina Winiarska, Roman's wife, burst into laughter and gave up.

We were sitting in front of his house, in the village of Jabłonów, Żagań county, Lubusz Land. He was talking about his first teacher, Wilhelmina Trylowska, whose memoir I had marked with a colored Post-it note in my book with the rough cover.

They both came from near Lvov. She was from Stryj, he from Gliniany. Before the war they lived a few hours apart by horse cart. They didn't know each other, of course. He was a child born in 1937, she was a grown woman born in 1904.

Figure 4.7. Wałbrzych, 1947. Workers' settlement named God Bless, 80% of whose residents were Polish miners returned from France. The apartment of Józef Małecki, a miner from the Mieszko mine. In the photo, a family meal. From left: Józef Małecki, his daughters Lidia (age 13) and Stefania (age 14), and his wife Antonia. PAP

She came here first. One of her legs was shorter than the other. In the summer of 1944, she, her husband, and her son were shipped to Germany for forced labor. After liberation, together with a large group of Poles, they moved eastward, and in July they reached Żagań.

She wrote: "Here we found out there won't be any more transportation because the bridges are broken and we have to . . . settle in the Recovered Territories."

At the local government office, her family and some other Poles with children were ordered to move to Jabłonowo, "a wealthy village, they told us." She moved into the house across from the settler Horoszkiewicz's farm. She learned how to milk a cow and work in the fields. Her husband, also a teacher, refused, claiming this wasn't for him.

She furnished her home, collecting the furniture from post-German houses, cleaned and secured the school (this time her husband was helpful), and started to register children for the new school year. There were many

Figure 4.8. Wrocław, 1945. Repatriation of Germans from Wrocław and Lower Silesia. Waiting for a transport to Germany. FoKa / Forum

students and only two teachers, she and her husband, so they decided to consolidate the classes. At that point they didn't know they were establishing Żagań county's first Polish school.

She resigned herself to living for a while with an elderly German couple, the previous owners of her farm. "I could appreciate their loss because, having abandoned my own patrimony, I missed it," she wrote years later in her memoirs. It didn't work well for the German couple. "They had to live in one room. They were Heinrich and Elisabeth Gimpel. He, age seventy-two, seemed like an honest man, but she was very nasty. She always grumbled and called us names, swearing in her own manner."

Wilhelmina Trylowska, together with other women from Jablonowo, founded a farmers' wives' circle. The village was dirty but she learned how to make soap from fat and soda, and molasses from sugar beets. She also brought in a military doctor who checked all the Polish settlers (leg ulcerations in children and skin diseases in women) and the Germans (venereal diseases, mainly in women).

She wrote: "The doctor shrugged and said, 'I'm helpless, because these diseases are very common after any war.'"

The German Gimpels with whom she was living left Jabłonowo on December 9, 1945. They had been packing all night. Wilhelmina Trylowska baked cookies for them, offered them some butter, sugar, and fifty-four zlotys. "I knew the wandering life, so in this way I wanted to ease their suffering," she recalled in her memoirs. The German woman left her son's fur coat for the Polish woman. He hadn't come back from the war.

Three days later the Winiarski family from Gliniany arrived in the village.

Roman Winiarski was lost in thought. He was taking a trip down memory lane and remembered his family home made of wood and clay. That house was so warm in winter that from December to spring all the local children used to sleep at their place.

"My brother and I would sleep on the bread oven and others on the straw bundles, quilts, and blankets spread on the clay floor." His slight singsong eastern accent gave away his roots. "My father had a tiny plot and he also used to dig canals. It was hard work. He was a foreman. We didn't want to flee but the Russians came and told us either to accept Soviet citizenship or to leave the country and go to the Recovered Territories. They gave us all the documents and put us on a freight train. We had sold our cow and horse earlier. We packed grain, food, a bed, and my mother's dowry chest. I don't have this chest anymore. I took it apart, but I salvaged the metal fittings. There were five other families in our freight car. A *liddle* tight but we managed. We left in the autumn and arrived here in December."

This village was different from the ones they had known before. Four clubhouses, two bakeries, two roadside inns, a shop selling electric appliances, and a sheep farm that had been built by the German village head right before the war. Together with the family of a friend of his father they took one house. The former German owners of the farm were still living in one room.

"Our Germans were leaving in the third wave," recalled Roman Winiarski. "Their mother was crying. She asked us not to touch anything, not to demolish anything, just leave it as it was, because they would come back. We were waiting for them even under Bierut. We didn't do anything for a long time. Why would we do anything if they might expel us, just like we expelled them? That's how many people thought. My father kept saying, 'In month, or two, we will not be here, we will be going back to Gliniany.'"

The repatriates' fears about the provisional borders were alleviated by the newspapers. In June 1945 *Życie Warszawy* wrote, "The Soviet Government, without waiting for any treaties or conferences, gave these lands, won with the blood of its soldiers, over to the sovereign possession of the Polish Nation. . . . So our right to these lands is generally recognized. It will be formally recognized at the peace conference at which we will be able to count on the full support of the Soviet Union and other allied countries."

"Only after we received the documents that said this house was our property, as compensation for the one we lost in the east, did we feel we were at home," said Roman Winiarski. "But my parents always missed our old house. And my father used to say, 'If they only let me go back, I'd leave everything here and go immediately.' He never got used to the new place. He died forty-five years ago."

In December 1945 Roman Winiarski became a student of Wilhelmina Trylowska and her husband. She played the piano for her pupils and taught them to read music.

She made a remark in her memoir: "Teaching was full of obstacles. There was a shortage of books, notebooks, and pencils. I was teaching the students how to read with the very few textbooks they had. Instead of notebooks they used a variety of old printed materials and those in the first grade made use of little tablets and graphite sticks. . . . At that moment ink was not available, so they wrote their essays with pencils or crayons."

"Once, during the children's first communion, the teachers and their students were photographed in front of the school. This picture must be somewhere," said Winiarski.

"It isn't here," his wife interrupted him. "You don't know, you had a stroke."

After a few years the Trylowskis left Jabłonowo.

Barns we passed, churches that last. I was rhyming when we were leaving Jabłonowo, heading toward Wrocław. Enormous, made of brick, with eroded old roofs. And these cowsheds, masterpieces of prewar architecture.

Some standing on a foundation made of boulders brought from the fields, others made of brick from the very ground. Big, multifloored houses, more typical of a small town than a village.

Over there some devastated brick building, old trees along the road, and in the middle of them a granite monument. It was shaped like a prism with a cone on top, a German helmet on one side, and the inscription *Ihrem im Weltkrieg gefallenen helden. Gewidmet von dem Gemeinde Schönbrunn* (To the heroes fallen in the World War. Donated by the Schönbrunn community). The names of soldiers fallen in World War I were chiseled on both sides of the monument. A wooden cross, two votive candles, and artificial daffodils in a plastic pot were standing near the monument. Some woman was walking along the road. We stopped the car.

"Has this monument been here forever?! And so well cared-for?" we shouted through a half-open window.

"It has been placed here only recently!" she shouted back. "People took it apart after the war and tossed the pieces around. A few years ago they were found on the premises of the former state collective farm, cleaned, and put back together. Let it stand here. Does it bother anyone?"

MONDSCHÜTZ, THAT IS TO SAY, MOJĘCICE—"PLACED ON AN OPEN WAGON TO TEND THE COWS"

Bronia's grandmother made it very clear from the beginning that she wouldn't leave her place forever. As soon as the front moved forward, they would go back to Ponikowice right away. In Ponikowice, ninety kilometers from Lvov, she had her house, barn, and a small plot, all to be inherited after her death by her daughter and granddaughter.

But Joseph Stalin had different plans for the old woman. While she was tending and milking her cows, in December 1941 he threw a banquet in the Kremlin. It was a strange moment for a party since the Wehrmacht was already only eighteen kilometers outside Moscow. Yet Joseph Dzhugashvili enjoyed the risk. At the end of the party he took the Polish prime minister in exile Władysław Sikorski aside and asked him if he would mind a small correction of the postwar eastern border of Poland. Stalin added that after the war he wouldn't oppose Poland moving its western border beyond the Oder. Sikorski refused categorically. Stalin wasn't bothered at all. If after the war Poland took control of part of Germany, his legitimate annexation of the Polish Eastern Borderlands would be facilitated.

Even if his name was Joseph, some Stalin person taking away the Eastern Borderlands from Poland, together with Lvov, her village, and her cows?

"No way," Bronia's grandmother would say, if anyone had wanted to listen to her.

But no one listened to her and Stalin got his own way. In 1943 in Teheran he convinced the U.S. president Franklin Delano Roosevelt and the British prime minister Winston Churchill to discuss a new eastern border of Poland along the Curzon line. He was less precise about the western border.

In September 1944 the Polish Committee of National Liberation, established on Stalin's orders, signed treaties about resettlement with the authorities of the republics of Lithuania, Belarus, and Ukraine. The first repatriates from Ukraine reached Lublin as early as December 1944.

All winter Bronia's grandmother was visited by official agitators who tried to persuade her to go west.

"Russia is going to be here," they said.

Grandmother didn't believe it. But when her son-in-law, a miller, was killed by a Ukrainian, she didn't feel safe in her village. So she registered to leave, but she was planning to come back just as soon as everything had calmed down.

At the beginning of 1945 they showed up at the train station in Brody. A single old woman, grandmother; her daughter (whose husband, the miller, had died) with children; and Bronia, age eighteen, her semi-orphaned granddaughter (Bronia's father was in the war). They had two cows, including Bronia's raised from a calf, and some bundles with their possessions, among them flaxseed oil in one-liter bottles. During their journey they swapped the oil for food. They also had some evacuation cards that in the future were supposed to prove that Bronia would inherit half a barn and half of some plot of land left beyond the Bug.

They were never to come back to their native land, but they didn't know that yet. In February 1945 at the Yalta Conference, when the resolutions from the Teheran Conference were confirmed, their fate was sealed. Yet the exact line of the western border was not indicated. There were many proposals: the border was to go along the Oder with Wrocław and Szczecin split in half, or these two cities were to remain on the German side, or they were to become Polish. In 1945 Szczecin changed hands twice before it was decided that it would be a Polish city.

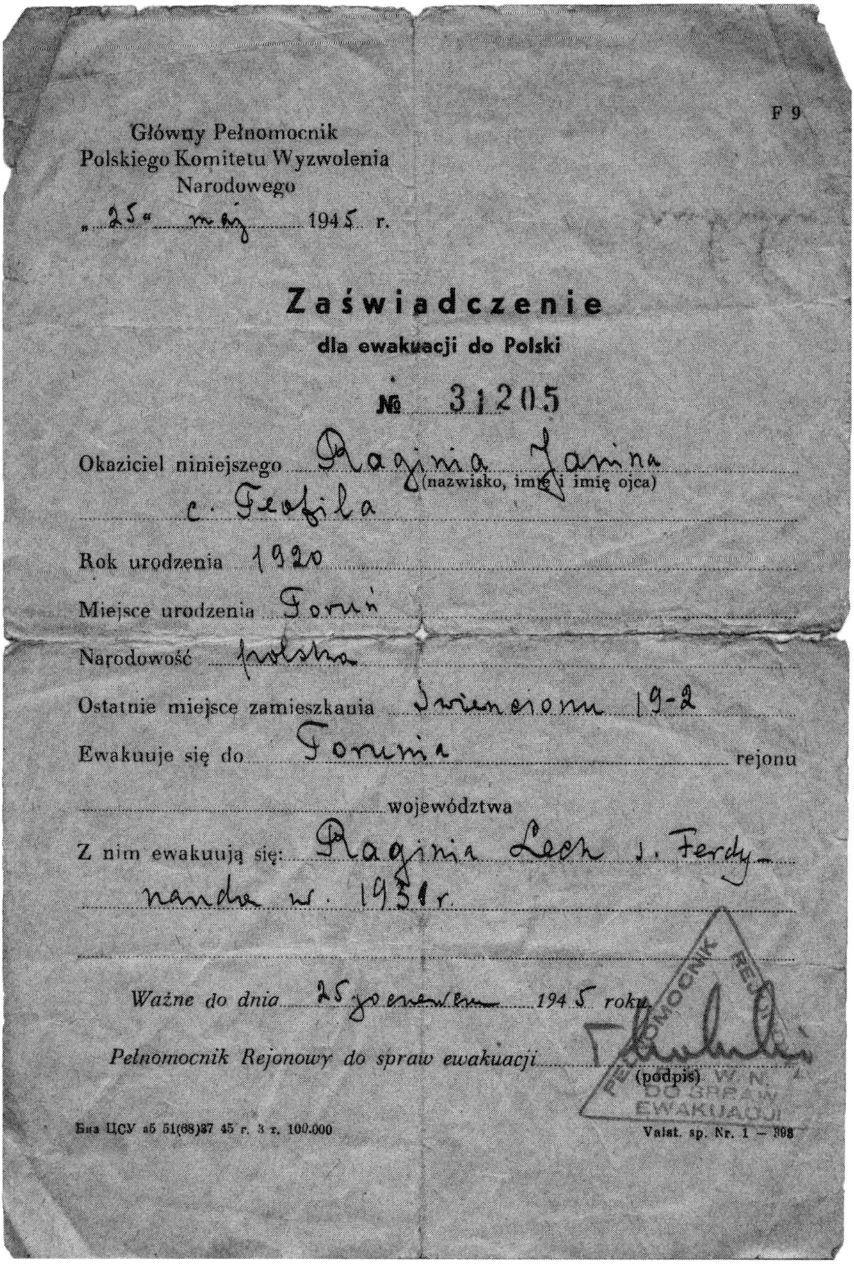

Główny Pełnomocnik
Polskiego Komitetu Wyzwolenia
Narodowego

„25" maj 1945 r.

F 9

Zaświadczenie
dla ewakuacji do Polski

№ 31205

Okaziciel niniejszego _Raginia Janina_
(nazwisko, imię i imię ojca)
c. Teofila

Rok urodzenia _1920_

Miejsce urodzenia _Toruń_

Narodowość _polska_

Ostatnie miejsce zamieszkania _Świeciorow 19-2_

Ewakuuje się do _Torunia_ rejonu

_____ województwa

Z nim ewakuują się: _Raginia Lech i Ferdy-_
nanda w. 1931 r.

Ważne do dnia _25 października_ 1945 roku

Pełnomocnik Rejonowy do spraw ewakuacji _____
(podpis)

Виз ЦСУ а5 51(68)37 45 г. 3 т. 100.000

Valst. sp. Nr. 1 — 393

Figure 4.9. A certificate of evacuation to Poland for Janina Raginia, daughter of Teofil, born 1920 in Toruń, of Polish nationality, destination Toruń. FoKa / Forum

In July and August 1945 new Polish borders were finally given legal form in Potsdam. Immediately, on August 16, 1945, the Polish Government of National Unity, recognized by the West, signed the Border Agreement with the Soviet Union.

Bronia's grandmother would speak less and less about returning, but she never stopped being surprised when the new authorities tried to convince her that she had been born in the Soviet Union.

One month after Bronia and her grandmother left, two hundred kilometers away, somewhere near Stryj, some shouting was heard in the house of a retired office worker, his wife, and their two children, Izabela, age nineteen, and Adaś, age ten. What was more important? Wedding porcelain or old family documents? Crystal and tablecloths or old school mementoes? What to take for the rest of your life and what to leave behind? In this family no one had any illusions of returning to the native land.

In *Memoirs of the Settlers of the Recovered Territories*, Izabela Grdeń reminisced: "Bombing in the memorable year 1939 merged with recollections of Banderite attacks, farms on fire, and the screaming of women and children murdered by them. Now it was possible to leave. . . . To escape and forget."

Their evacuation card was filled out by local officials, who also appraised their farm in prewar currency. In May 1945 they left their home with their life possessions locked in their chests, a cow, and a small stove. "One last look at the house, the orchard, and the lilacs in front of the house. The wretched horse decorated with lilac branches and harnessed to the cart moves forward. An indifferent Ukrainian man stands at the doorstep but you can't see him through your tears."

A bit later they showed up at the train station in Stryj. And only then did they realize they had forgotten to take Bryś, their beloved dog. It was impossible to soothe Adaś's pain but they couldn't go back for the animal. The train heading west could come at any moment.

The resettlement plan was supposed to include millions of people. By 1947, alongside Izabela Grdeń's family and Bronia's grandmother, over 1.5 million Poles from beyond the Bug were to have moved to the Western Territories. About 1.6 million people were coming from the concentration camps, prisoner-of-war camps, and forced labor in Western Europe. Some decided to come back from the prewar emigration. Some 250,000 Poles and Jews, deported to Siberia and Kazakhstan in 1940, were to leave the Soviet

Figure 4.10. Repatriates from the Eastern Borderlands on their way to the Recovered Territories. 1945. FoKa / Forum

Union. There were 2 million people from Central and Southern Poland who had lost their homes and property during the war and were hoping for a better life in the West and the North of the new Poland. Three and a half million Germans were to be expelled from the Recovered Territories. Earlier, a similar number had fled the Red Army.

We don't know if they knew each other. They must have run into each other in Mojęcice outside Wrocław, they must have met on the way to church, or store, or field. But Izabela Grdeń never wrote about it. And Bronisława Tworzowska didn't remember.

Once again I met a fragile woman, as if the prewar generation had been made of porcelain. Bronisława Tworzowska spoke very fast and moved with the speed of light so I could hardly follow her. She mixed crying with laughter, and her stories with prayers. She seated me at a long table. During holidays there was enough space for everyone in her large family. She ran to the kitchen to bring a sweet roll for my daughter, and right away she squatted at the kitchen cabinet looking for almond cookies. Then for a second she darted away for a wedding photo, and then for an instant sat down at the other side of the table, burst into tears, and then dried them with a smile.

"At the train station in Brody they placed me in an open wagon, a freight car with no roof, so I could tend the cows. Others were traveling in a freight car with a roof," she said. "Three weeks we traveled. We stopped for a long time in Katowice and I know—now—they had no idea where to take us because the war wasn't over yet. We got soaking wet when it rained. We had food because I milked the cows and swapped the flaxseed oil. And one day the train stopped in Wołowo, and we were told to get off."

A similar journey was awaiting Izabela Grdeń. "At the train station in Stryj we waited for three weeks under the open sky. . . . It was raining and the boxes were leaking. We tried to cover them as best we could with tarpaulins, tin sheets found at the station, and junk lying around. Our cow lost weight and its hair stood on end. Chickens with spiky feathers were sitting in cages, and it was raining and raining, tormenting people and animals."

A bribe collected among the exhausted settlers and handed to the stationmaster was helpful. The very next day a train was provided. As Izabela Grdeń recalled, "we were flabbergasted. The freight cars had no roofs. They were just ordinary coal wagons, higher and lower." But they got in and the journey began. It was to last six weeks.

When they reached their destination, they found out at the repatriation point there was no place for them. They were sent farther. When they stopped near Krakow, they had enough time to cut clover for the hungry cows. "Suddenly and unexpectedly, we were attacked by some peasants who were bashing us with sticks. . . . We couldn't understand why it was different there. We were going to our country because we had been attacked by Banderites . . . but we were met with cold reserve. We weren't prepared for this."

There were no places near Bydgoszcz, either. The post-German farms had already been taken by Poles who used to live closer to the German border. So they headed west. They stopped in Piła. And moved again. Outside Stargard, at the railway siding in the field, the railwaymen finally disconnected the locomotive. But the repatriates didn't like it there. "That village was not yet inhabited, therefore it wasn't safe for us. There were plenty of marauders and looters around, so we begged the train driver and the transportation supervisor to take us to Wrocław voivodeship."

In mid-June Izabela Grdeń's family got off at the train station in Wołowo.

Izabela with her parents and brother were immediately directed to Mojęcice. They lived on a small farm together with the German former owner. They worked the fields with Józiek, a half-Arabian horse that had served in the army during the war. But they were dreaming of moving to the city.

Bronisława, her grandmother, aunt, and children, weren't that lucky. "In Wołowo we were sitting on the bare ground, among the bundles, for three weeks. They didn't want us anywhere. It wasn't like that for everyone, just for families whose only adults were women."

Wanda Melcer wrote in her report from the Recovered Territories: "Another serious problem is the problem posed by typically 'weak' vs. 'strong' families. Strong is a family that consists of a man in his prime and able to work, children who don't need too much care, and a young and healthy woman. Weak is a family of a single woman with two children, and sometimes an aging father and sick mother. How can this wretched creature take care of a farm, where will she go, what will she do, who will take care of them?"

Bronisława Tworzowska said, "My aunt was walking from village to village but everything was already taken. Finally, she got to Mojęcice. There was an empty house, though earlier there had been horses in the kitchen, but we liked it, so we took it. We returned in the morning and cleaned the place all day long. Out of the blue, a guy who came home from the war, showed up in the evening and seized our house. He deserved it, but he wanted to move right away into a clean place. No one cared that we were there first. We had to keep looking. In the end, we found a small room by the barn. What mattered most was that there was a place for a cow."

After a few years Izabela and her family will move to Szprotawa. Bronia and her near ones will stay in Mojęcice forever. With time they will get a bigger house. In January 1946 Bronia will get married, and sixty-nine years later she will become a widow. She will educate her children. Her daughters will be teachers. She will contact her family, beyond the Bug, who have never left. And she will visit them regularly.

"My grandma had a son who was a cavalryman and who was captured by the Germans," said Bronisława Tworzowska when we were about to say good-bye. "When he was released, he somehow found out about us and came to Mojęcice. He wanted to stay, since he couldn't go back to Lvov. But when he realized that this land had been German, he said he would move to the real Poland, and he settled outside Gdańsk.

"He didn't know that those lands had been German, too?" I was surprised.

"He thought that was Poland over there because it took him so long to travel to," she laughed.

BOROWIAN, THAT IS TO SAY, BOROWIANY—"WHY WOULD THIS CHILD NEED THE POLISH LANGUAGE?"

I was looking over the fence of some Silesian woman in the village of Borowiany (Wielowieś district, Gliwice county, Silesia voivodeship). It just crossed my mind that if all the little dogs that were barking at me were cobbled together, we would probably get one Polish Tatra Sheepdog. It was supposed to be the last place on our route in the Recovered Territories.

In 1945 the eighteen-year-old repatriate Maria Balińska came here. On April 30 she was resettled from the village of Rodatycze in Lvov voivodeship. She had traveled with her mother and little daughter Magdalena. She was a teacher. She was assigned by the authorities to establish a Polish school in Borowiany. The pack of little barking dogs was protecting the house of a woman who might have known Balińska. At least that's what the village head told me.

Maria Balińska was the first settler in the village. She opened the school right away, in May 1945. Seventy-nine students enrolled. After years had gone by, she recalled in her memoir: "The girls kept asking me why we came to Silesia, why we didn't stay in Poland. I replied that their speech was perfect evidence that Silesia *was* Poland. I asked them if a native Berliner would understand their language as I did. Their stated consensus was no."

In 1921, during the plebiscite in Upper Silesia, 148 residents of Borowiany were in favor of affiliation with Poland, and 166 preferred Germany; before the war, therefore, the village belonged to Germany. Balińska noticed that in 1945 in Borowiany the peasants and some workers considered themselves Polish. "In contrast, some workers' families that had earlier been privileged by the Germans thought of themselves as superior. This group was very skeptical about me, and about Poland."

She started to polonize the children by teaching them folk songs. She lamented that the required reading list was limited. She needed *The Deluge* and novels by Kraszewski to present the former greatness of Poland. Instead, she had at her disposal *Antek* and *The Outpost* by Bolesław Prus, and some of Maria Konopnicka's novellas. "Personally, I am a big admirer of Konopnicka, but studying her works with the children, I was fostering the image of a poor and wretched Poland. That image, in combination with local opinion about Polish settlers, was not conducive to evoking national pride."

It had never occurred to her that even after sixty-nine years she would be remembered in the village. And not because she was the first Polish teacher here. People remembered Maria Balińska, the young woman who once got off her bicycle and was seriously amazed. "How is it possible that when I bicycle down from the hilltop, I don't have to pedal?"

The owner of the noisy little mutts threw her hands up. She had not been here in 1945. Years later, she followed her husband. But her friend, Augustyna Niedworok, was born here. ("She lives at the end of this road, you have to walk past the houses and then you are right there.") The woman behind the fence was speaking to me beautifully. She was composing her sentences in Polish, Silesian, and German at the same time.

In contrast, Augustyna Niedworok's dog didn't bark at all. He was lying on a little blanket spread over the bench in front of the house and in the fading light was watching a badminton match between Tosia and her father.

We were sitting by the kitchen window. The kitchen was cleaned as if Christmas were coming. Augustyna Niedworok (born in 1931) supported her face with her hands.

Her parents and grandparents were from here. Her father's last name was Heilisch and before the war he spoke with his wife in Silesian, but with his children only in German. When Augustyna was seven, she went to a German school. When the war broke out, her three brothers went to the front. All three survived. She didn't have any sisters.

"It was hard when the Russkis came to the village," she recalled. "It was January or February 1945. One morning I was in the woods with my friend. We were chasing each other in the snow when we heard shooting. We darted back home. Soon after, the Russkis came to our house. All officers, and fat. They wanted a heated room. But we didn't have any heating. So they left to look somewhere else. My mom got so scared, she was spitting blood. All over the village they were chasing young women. They would go from house to house, and if they felt like it, they would rape someone. One of them, who was in charge of the entire village, was fixated on some dark-haired girl. She spent three days sitting on the beam under the barn roof. Her parents brought her food and she was freezing. But he didn't capture her. The Russkis came to our home, too. They took the horses, shot the cows for meat, and searched the drawers. They didn't take much since we had nothing of value. I wasn't raped. Maybe because, despite being fourteen, I was so thin that I looked like a child?"

Augustyna's parents decided that it made no sense to send her to the Polish school established by Maria Balińska. "Why would this child need the Polish language?" they asked. They believed what other people in the village were saying: "The English will come soon, they will put Poland in order, and in a year, or two, Poles will not be here."

"We were Germans, we felt German, but we were turned into Poles by force," said Augustyna Niedworok. "I was little, I don't know, but my father must have signed some papers and we could stay. Poles who came to our village didn't expel us from our farms. But they took over the houses left by German settlers who had arrived here under Hitler and later fled west."

Maria Balińska was proud of her work among the local population but she was embarrassed by the settlers. They didn't know how to work in the fields like Germans, and they didn't want to. They didn't care about their farms because they hoped to go back to their native villages. Their houses and sheds were filthy. Balińska noted: "The local people have affluent homes and they take care of them. If you compare them with the homes of the Polish settlers, the difference is striking, and to the disadvantage of the Poles. Our women became the laughingstock of the Silesians, because they were always shabbily dressed. Even on Sunday they would walk barefoot while the local women dressed in city clothes, and always wore shoes. . . . The settlers were rarely called Poles. Instead they were they called Ukrainians or *chadziajs*, in other words, peasants from beyond the Bug. . . . The insults *Kraut* and *chadziaj* were part of everyday speech."

Augustyna Niedworok looked at me.

"You won't be angry if I say something?" she asked. "It is all true, what that teacher wrote. We were making fun of the Poles. I don't know who told us about *chadziajs*, but when one person used the word, another would burst into laughter. Their women were very sloppy. Theeeze days, they are flashy ladies. Our own women were always elegant. That was the difference between us. Some Poles took care of their farms, others didn't. But earlier, there was no drunkenness in the village. Our guys learned how to drink from the Polaks."

And later, I asked Augustyna Niedworok who she was after so many years living in Poland.

"German," she replied. "I have nothing against Poland. When others were leaving for Germany, my husband and I stayed. We are from here, our home is here, it is our land."

And then Augustyna Niedworok asked me why, exactly, did so many Poles come to Silesia in 1945.

"Most of them didn't have any choice. Their land was taken away from them," I responded.

"Who took it away?" she was astonished.

"Roosevelt, Churchill, but mainly Stalin." I was surprised she didn't know this. "He took a bit of Poland from the Poles, and a bit of Germany from the Germans. He moved most Germans to Germany, and brought Poles in their place."

"Ah, that's what it was all about!" Augustyna Niedworok burst out in August 2014, sixty-nine years after the war.

MAY 1945

Notice to Residents of Warsaw! The day of defeating Berlin, the day of conquering the lair of the Nazi beast, is the day of triumph for all free nations of the world. This is our great holiday. When germans destroyed and burned Warsaw, we dreamed of the fall of Berlin. Those who are not here anymore, those who died under the ruins of Warsaw, believed that this day would come. Today at noon at Theater Square there will be a major rally of Warsaw residents celebrating the capitulation of Berlin. Everyone to the rally!

—Życie Warszawy, May 4, 1945

The Organizing Committee of the Society to Fight Alcoholism (124 Grochowska Street) is calling on all representatives of the boards of Anti-Alcohol Associations to contact the Committee in order to organize a national congress of teetotalers.

—Życie Warszawy, May 4, 1945

The Department of Social Welfare is resuming child care with foster families. Foster families should apply at the Department Office, 10 Bagatela Street, as soon as possible.

—Życie Warszawy, May 5, 1945

On Sunday, May 13, at 10 a.m. there will be a solemn prayer service at the synagogue at Miodowa Street to commemorate the victory over germany.

—Dziennik Polski, Krakow, May 6, 1945

The outpatients' clinic for those ill from venereal and skin diseases is already open at 82 Koszykowa Street.

—Życie Warszawy, May 6, 1945

The Traffic Unit at the Headquarters of the Warsaw Citizen's Police seeks female applicants for directing street traffic. Apply at the Traffic Unit Office, 15 Kępna Street, Apt. 11.

—Życie Warszawy, May 7, 1945

The pontoon bridge was opened yesterday for two-way pedestrian traffic. Horse-drawn carriages are still permitted to cross, reversing direction every half hour. In this way, one of our urban traffic maladies—the pedestrian traffic jams on both sides of the Vistula—has been resolved.

—Życie Warszawy, May 10, 1945

A 60-ton supply of medical drugs and surgical instruments—an American gift to the Polish Red Cross—has arrived in Murmansk. From there it will come to Warsaw by train.

—Życie Warszawy, May 12, 1945

As we know, the labor brigades are cleaning bricks from the demolished buildings and collecting them in large containers (1,000 in each). It has been observed many times that some dishonest individuals are stealing the bricks for purely private purposes.

—Życie Warszawy, May 13, 1945

Recently, there have been cases of stores and stalls using documents from the Polish Red Cross archives as wrapping paper. This fact refutes our initial assumption that the archives were totally incinerated in August 1944. Some documents were probably removed from the building at Smolna Street by people who did not appreciate their value, especially with regard to war victims— the fallen, the dead, the prisoners of war, the disabled war veterans, etc. The Polish Red Cross is earnestly appealing to Warsaw residents to help recover these documents.

—*Życie Warszawy*, May 15, 1945

• • • • • • • • • • • • • • • • • •

Keep your city clean by burning garbage and any kind of waste found near your residential buildings and then burying it at least one meter deep. Do not drink unboiled water.

—*Dziennik Bałtycki*, May 20, 1945

• • • • • • • • • • • • • • • • • •

Since it is necessary to rescue the priceless national property that was severely damaged by the war, such as books, the Ministry of Education has opened the Center for Book Purchases (Władysław Gutry, director, Education Department, Warsaw School District, 6 Marszałkowska Street). Everyone who wants to sell books at market prices and make sure they reach public libraries should contact the Center Depository between 1 p.m. and 3 p.m., 7 Lwowska Street.

—*Życie Warszawy*, May 25, 1945

• • • • • • • • • • • • • • • • • •

After May 25, a half kilo of marmalade will be provided for the holders of Coupon No. 4 of the April Children's Vouchers. Price: 13 zlotys/kilogram.

—*Życie Warszawy*, May 25, 1945

• • • • • • • • • • • • • • • • • •

The exhumations at 4 Szpitalna Street (in the courtyard) will take place on Tuesday, May 29. The exhumations on the premises of the State Securities Printing House (Wybrzeże Gdańskie Boulevard) will take place on Wednesday, May 30.

—*Życie Warszawy*, May 25, 1945

• • • • • • • • • • • • • • • • • •

On May 6 at 11 Listopada Street a military medal 'For Defending Stalingrad' was lost. Please return to Second Lieutenant Michał Ryży, 6 Środkowa Street.

—*Życie Warszawy*, May 28, 1945

Figure 5.1. Stanisław Szroeder in 1943 or 1944. Stanisław Szroeder's archive

5

Deserter

"My name is Stanisław Szroeder. I'm a Kashub. In January 1945 I deserted from the Wehrmacht.

"You are one of us? No. So I'll speak Polish.

"First, take a look here. This is a *Wehrpass*, my military passbook. Here they wrote *Grösse in Zentimetern*, that is, height in German (158 centimeters). Not even one meter sixty. And here *Körperbau*, or body type: *schlank* (slim). *Augenfarbe* means eye color (light) and *Haarfarbe*, hair color (blond). I was simply a *knôp*, that is, a boy in Kashubian. Nevertheless, in November 1944 the gentlemen from the Military Board in Stolp, that is to say, Słupsk, evaluated me as fit for military duty and classified me as category 1. They immediately sent me for six weeks training in a battalion of the Reich Labor Service, or RAD, in Deutsch Krone, now Wałcz. I marched there, I crawled. I fired weapons. And in the middle of December I managed to pledge allegiance to the Führer.

"They sent me home for Christmas. They supplied me with a gas mask and a Wehrmacht conscription card. They told me to wait for a telegram. Because they were to call me to the front by telegram."

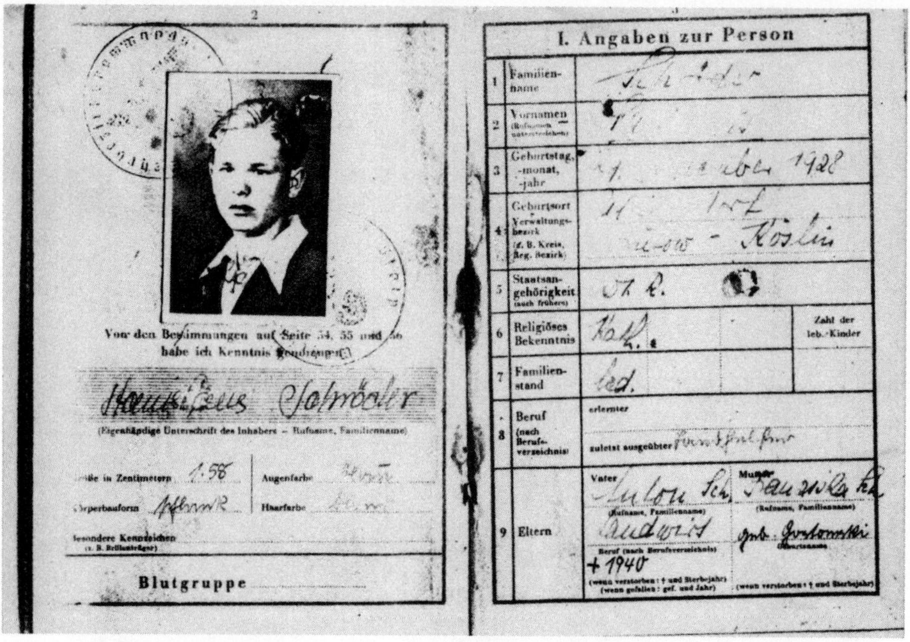

2

Von den Bestimmungen auf Seite 54, 55 und 56 habe ich Kenntnis genommen

(Eigenhändige Unterschrift des Inhabers – Rufname, Familienname)

Größe in Zentimetern 1,58 | Augenfarbe
Körperbauform | Haarfarbe
Besondere Kennzeichen (z. B. Brillenträger)

Blutgruppe

I. Angaben zur Person

1	Familienname	
2	Vornamen (Rufnamen unterstreichen)	
3	Geburtstag, -monat, -jahr	1928
4	Geburtsort, Verwaltungsbezirk (z. B. Kreis, Reg. Bezirk)	Köslin
5	Staatsangehörigkeit (auch frühere)	
6	Religiöses Bekenntnis	kath.
7	Familienstand	led.
8	Beruf (nach Berufsverzeichnis)	erlernter; zuletzt ausgeübter
9	Eltern	Vater (Rufname, Familienname); Beruf (nach Berufsverzeichnis); + 1940 (wenn verstorben: † und Sterbejahr) (wenn gefallen: gef. und Jahr); Mutter (Rufname, Familienname); geb. (Geburtsname) (wenn verstorben: † und Sterbejahr)

Zahl der leb. Kinder

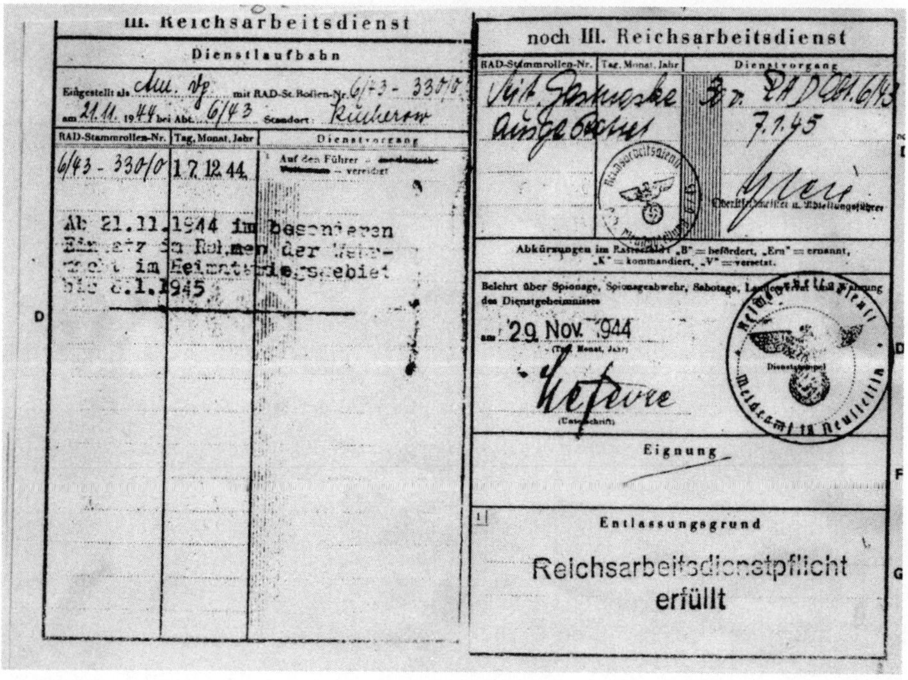

III. Reichsarbeitsdienst

Dienstlaufbahn

Eingestellt als Arb. Mn. mit RAD-St. Rollen-Nr. 6/43 - 330/0 am 21.11. 1944 bei Abt. 6/43 Standort:

RAD-Stammrollen-Nr.	Tag, Monat, Jahr	Dienstvorgang
6/43 - 330/0	17.12.44	Auf den Führer – vereidigt

Ab 21.11.1944 im besonderen Einsatz im Rahmen der Wehrmacht im Heimatkriegsgebiet bis 6.1.1945

noch III. Reichsarbeitsdienst

RAD-Stammrollen-Nr.	Tag, Monat, Jahr	Dienstvorgang
		RAD Abt. 6/43 7.1.45

Oberstfeldmeister u. Abteilungsführer

Abkürzungen im Rahmen „B" = befördert, „Ern" = ernannt, „K" = kommandiert, „V" = versetzt.

Belehrt über Spionage, Spionageabwehr, Sabotage, Landesverrat und Wahrung des Dienstgeheimnisses

am 29 Nov. 1944 (Tag, Monat, Jahr)

(Unterschrift)

Dienststempel

Meldeamt in Neustettin

Eignung

Entlassungsgrund

Reichsarbeitsdienstpflicht erfüllt

Figures 5.2 and 5.3. Stanisław Szroeder's military passbook. Stanisław Szroeder's archive

"It's interesting, how could Adolf Hitler picture me on the front? A Mauser, the Wehrmacht rifle, was one meter, ten centimeters long. Unloaded, it weighed four kilograms. How far, according to Hitler, could a boy walk in a uniform too large, and shoes too loose, carrying a rifle, ammunition, and a rucksack? Hitler probably didn't picture anything. By the end of 1944 the Third Reich's situation was plainly hopeless. Hitler had to fight on two fronts, eastern and western, at the same time. The army's strength was declining. In the fall of 1944 the *Volkssturm* was created. It recruited old men and children who were able to run at least two hundred meters toward the enemy. And then die. The Wehrmacht draft also affected *knôps* like me. But, as it happened, I was not going to die."

"The telegram came at the beginning of the year. It stated that on January 8 I was supposed to appear at the station in Bütow, which is now Bytów, and take the designated train to my unit in Rummelsburg, that is to say, Miastko. But I decided not to go. I didn't say anything to anyone. My mom and my siblings wouldn't understand. Everyone knew that any private could shoot me for desertion. Even talking about Hitler's imminent defeat was considered treason. The penalty was hanging.

"My family would also be worried about themselves, that the Gestapo would come to ask why I didn't show up at the front. Perhaps only my *òjc*, which means father in Kashubian, could understand me? But he wasn't there anymore.

"So I was silent. It was my decision. I have no idea where my strength was coming from.

"That day I got up in the morning. I put a loaf of bread from my mother into my rucksack, large and fresh. And a piece of pork fat. I slung a pack with a gas mask across one shoulder. My brother Zygmunt went to get a horse and sleigh. He was supposed to take me to the station. We set out. I was afraid of what was awaiting me."

"My mother, Franciszka, was standing in front of the house, waving her hand. Was she crying? I imagine that every mother cries when she sends her son to war. She had borne twelve children. The first died. I was the seventh. When she couldn't see the sleigh anymore, she went back to the house. She had already given two older sons to the Wehrmacht. Both of them survived the war. She had been a widow for two years."

"We arrived in Bytów. My brother said he would wait for my train to leave. So I would feel safer. Holy Mary and Joseph! How should I get rid of him, so he wouldn't realize I was getting away?

"'You know, Zygmunt,' I said. 'It's cold, the horse is hungry, and my *Bahn* [train] is coming. So, go! And safe journey.'

"He left, and I was exuberant.

"My train to Rummelsburg was on the platform. But I jumped onto the other one, heading in the opposite direction, to Lauenburg, that is to say, Lębork. My plan was to get off at the station in Wutzkow, which is now Oskowo, and from there to reach Aunt Justyna's house. She was my father's sister. She lived in Łyśniewo, that was on the Polish side before the war.

"So I was sitting in the train car, but in terrible fear and confusion. Then I looked through the window and saw two soldiers with rifles leaving the station building, and getting onto my train! I knew they would be checking the documents of all passengers. They got in, we set off, and there I was, already a deserter—still in my civilian clothes, to be sure, but with a draft notice that served as a ticket—in the opposite direction.

"What now, Stach, what now? I knew they would be checking the train starting from the rear, and I was sitting up front. At the station of Gross Pomeiske, now Pomysk, I jumped onto the platform and ran back to the end, passing the train car where they now were, got on, and rode two stations more, to Oskowo.

"Perhaps at that moment I thought, 'What would my father say?' I don't remember."

"I loved my father and obeyed him. When he forbade me to raise my arm when the national anthem was played, I didn't.

"'You are a Pole. You may stand at attention and take off your hat, but you don't have to raise your arm like the Germans,' my father used to say.

"My teacher whacked me with a short wand, but it was a long time before I groaned.

"My father, Antoni Schröder, considered himself a Polish Kashub who was jinxed by the Treaty of Versailles. After World War I, when the borders of the new Europe were delineated, Kashubia was cut into three pieces like a birthday cake. The largest part fell to the Second Polish Republic and a smaller one to the Free City of Danzig. A tiny piece stayed in Germany, including Bytów-Lębork Land where our native village Kłáczëno (Kłączno in Polish, Klonschen in German) sat in the middle of a forest, a few kilometers

Figure 5.4. Antoni Schröder. Stanisław Szroeder's archive

from Poland. So my father, a citizen of the Reich, happened to live at the borderland, but according to him, on the wrong side. He was not going to give up. He organized meetings aimed at reconnecting Bytów Land with Poland. He spoke Polish, but at home with us he spoke only Kashubian. He read and wrote in Polish. He subscribed to *The Voice of the Borderlands and Kashubia* and *The Catholic Guide*. He tried to open a Polish school in the village. Yet he never received permission to do so, and what is more, the building burned down in unexplained circumstances.

"Dad was active in the Union of Poles in Germany. In 1933 he began to work with the intelligence unit of the Polish Border Guard. We only found out about this dozens of years later. You are asking why he cared so much about a Poland that he didn't know well, having spent all his life under German rule, about a Poland that never repaid his love? I don't know. That's the way it was.

"Most Poles didn't care about Kashubs. They treated us as outcasts and misfits, and thought our language was Germanic, though it's Slavic. But Germans were even more hostile to Kashubs. For them, we were second-class citizens. You wanted to get promoted? You had to be Germanized. What's more, Germans are mainly Protestants, and Kashubs are Catholics. My father could have chosen a third way—the most popular among Kashubs who were disenchanted with both Poles and Germans. They were just the People-from-Here, Ourselves. Their motherland didn't extend farther than three more villages and they didn't know any other language, just Kashubian. But my father didn't want to do this.

"After I was whacked by my teacher, my *òjc* sent me to Kwidzyn, where I could attend one of the Reich's only two Polish high schools. The other was in Bytom. I completed first grade there. I spent my summer vacation in 1939 at home and in September I went back to Kwidzyn. This time my dad couldn't take me there. The authorities had called him to Berlin.

"When the war broke out, our school was surrounded by German soldiers. We were transported in trucks to Tapiau in East Prussia. For a month we lived in an abandoned psychiatric hospital. Then we were sent home."

"I got off the train. There were sixteen kilometers on foot ahead of me. The road to Aunt Justyna's place ran through the fields and woods. I ran without knowing what was awaiting me one or two kilometers ahead. There was a thaw and the snow was melting. I didn't know whether I was soaked because of fear or exertion. Maybe because of snow? Every hundred or two hundred meters I would throw myself to the ground and dip my head in the snowdrifts. I wasn't carrying much gear but it was weighing me down anyway. Yet I couldn't abandon it. What if someone found my gas mask and followed my footprints? You have no idea how much I prayed there. 'Holy Mary and Joseph! Stach, keep going, because either you survive or you will be buried somewhere here.' So I kept going and suddenly I saw my aunt's backyard. Two hundred, three hundred meters more and I was there! I came closer to the window and saw some strangers at the table, talking to my uncle and my aunt.

"All of a sudden I was surrounded by yapping dogs. Boleś, my cousin, a bit older than I, stepped out of the house.

"'Who's there?' he shouted.

"I was quiet.

"'Who's there?' he repeated.

"'Stach is here,' I finally responded."

"For betraying the Third Reich my father was sentenced to death. The Germans found his name in documents from Polish intelligence that fell into their hands in September 1939. In his last letter he wrote to us, 'My beloved wife! My beloved children! Today I was informed that I will have to die. I send you hugs and greetings. When this letter reaches you, I will not be alive.'

"On April 1, 1943, an executioner employed by the Plötzensee prison in Berlin cut off his head. Harald Pelchau, a prison chaplain who was present at executions, set down his memoirs. I will read a fragment to you: 'The loss of blood was enormous. Each time the legs of the convict trembled so much that his clogs flew into the air.'

"The Reich announced that our farm was to be confiscated by the state. We were supposed to be taken to Mecklenburg for our final Germanization. You know, after the war I changed my name. In my father's document the name was Schröder; I turned it into Polish."

"I was seated at my aunt's table. Someone praised me for deserting.

"'The Krauts won't last long,' I heard.

"I learned that the strangers I had seen through the window earlier were four Russians who had fled German captivity. They were hiding in Łyśniewo, waiting for the imminent arrival of their own.

"My mother didn't know where I was. Since I didn't write to her, she probably thought that her little boy had died at the front. But she didn't have any problems resulting from my desertion. The Gestapo didn't pester her. They had more important issues to deal with. The war was about to end. They were getting ready for their evacuation. In Łyśniewo I was helping my uncle and my aunt on the farm. And like everyone else I was waiting for the Russkis. My God, how eagerly was I waiting for them! Like for salvation. The Red Army was about to bring me freedom from the army, from the front, and from death. We waited four or five weeks. One morning I woke up and there was silence all over."

Silence. Perhaps not as silent as the grave, because the rooster was crowing, the chickens were clucking, and there were noises coming from the cowshed. Nevertheless, on March 8, 1945, the farm was immersed in silence. Fog was hanging low over the fields. No shots were heard. No orders given in German. No engines of military trucks. No grinding of tank treads. Stach would sleep a bit longer but Boleś shook his arm.

"The German army is gone! There is not even a single soldier digging trenches! They must have gone to Gdańsk," he shouted.

Stach got up and stepped out onto the porch. He was listening to the silence, nervously touching his pocket. He could feel his folded Wehrmacht draft card. Aunt Justyna, Uncle Piotr, cousins Ksenia and Wanda, cousin Boleś, and the four Soviet soldiers stood by him on the porch in silence.

Nobody knows who saw the soldiers first. They were running from the village of Pusdrowo, or Puzdrowo. They were moving with their backs bent, and with rifles in their hands. Germans or Russkis? Too far, you can't see.

"A tank is coming!" Someone on the porch broke the silence.

"With a star! They are Russkis! Hurrah! Holy Mother of God! Hurrah!"

In the village of Łyśniewo ten people, squeezed together on Aunt Justyna's porch, were shouting and waving their hands.

"Like in the most wonderful movie," Stanisław Szroeder, the son of Antoni Schröder, told me sixty-nine years later.

JUNE 1945

Today, Sunday, June 3, the County Committee of Social Welfare in Lublin is organizing a street fundraiser for poor children in the care of the Committee. The Committee expects that, following tradition, society will not fail to show its generosity.

—*Gazeta Lubelska*, June 3, 1945

Maria Curie-Skłodowska University will buy fish tanks. Information at the Supply Office, 21 Racławickie Avenue.

—*Gazeta Lubelska*, June 3, 1945

The Food Rationing and Commerce Department in Radom has received 6,000 kilograms of meat. This meat is earmarked principally for industrial workers. First and foremost, meat rations will be offered to the employees of the metal and chemical industries, power plants, railways, police and security service.

—*Dziennik Powszechny*,
Radom-Kielce, June 3, 1945

On November 20, 1944, our newspaper published an article, "A Gallery of Traitors." The article stated, "Mieczysław Kołakowski, residing at 15 Krzywińska Street, is accused of collaboration with the Gestapo." A proper investigation conducted by the Prosecutor's Office at the Special Criminal Court of the Polish Republic proved the groundlessness of this accusation, a result of a personal dispute.

Detainee Mieczysław Kołakowski has been released from custody.

—*Życie Warszawy*, June 3, 1945

Maksymilian Cybulski recants his verbal abuse toward citizen Stanisław Grabowski, office worker.

—*Dziennik Bałtycki*, June 7, 1945

Russian-language course. The Society for Polish-Soviet Friendship is organizing basic courses for the population at large. A variety of musical events are planned for closer rapprochement and cultural exchange so both nations can be better informed about achievements in this field.

—*Życie Warszawy*, June 7, 1945

Chocolate bars labeled "E. Wedel" are still on the market, although the Wedel factory is not producing chocolate bars at all. According to our sources, this chocolate is counterfeit and bears stolen labels.

—*Życie Warszawy*, June 11, 1945

Today, Tuesday, at 4 p.m., in its series From the History of German Barbarity in Poland, Polish Radio will broadcast "People in Auschwitz," an account by the prominent writer Zofia Nałkowska.

—*Życie Warszawy*, June 12, 1945

Due to the intensified efforts in debris re-moval, the health authorities have started to exhume bodies buried beneath side-walks and green spaces during the Upris-ing. Exhumations requested by individu-als are carried out by the City Sanitation Department. The charge for exhuming a body and transferring it to the cemetery is 800 zlotys.

—*Życie Warszawy*, June 16, 1945

• • • • • • • • • • • • • • • • • •

The Maritime Department of the Minis-try of Industry has issued a warning that anyone impersonating an employee of the Maritime Department in order to acquire an apartment or confiscate furniture in the Coastal Area, will be pursued to the full extent of the law.

—*Dziennik Bałtycki*, June 17, 1945

• • • • • • • • • • • • • • • • • •

Citizens of Gdynia, shame on you! Out of 70,000 people only 2,000 showed up for volunteer work before Sea Day.

—*Dziennik Bałtycki*, June 19, 1945

• • • • • • • • • • • • • • • • • •

I will take in as my own an orphaned girl, age 10–14, from a fine family and preferably from Warsaw. Information: Krakow, 3 Na Ustroniu Street.

—*Dziennik Polski*, Krakow, June 20, 1945

• • • • • • • • • • • • • • • • • •

Please, does anyone have any information about Leszek Buczyński, age seventeen, who during the Uprising was in the People's Army in Żoliborz. Parents, 27–17 Puławska Street.

—*Życie Warszawy*, June 22, 1945

• • • • • • • • • • • • • • • • • •

Lost goat, black with white spots, no horns. Last time seen near Morska Street. Gener-ous reward. Gdynia, 29 Kapitańska Street.

—*Dziennik Bałtycki*, June 23, 1945

• • • • • • • • • • • • • • • • • •

I inform my Honorable Clients and Retail Merchants that I have come back from the concentration camps and I continue to manage "Canada," the Warehouse of Hab-erdashery and Cosmetics. I recommend my diverse merchandise. Low prices! Manu-facturers' prices! Józef Cepura, Krakow, 37 Main Square.

—*Dziennik Polski*, Krakow, June 24, 1945

• • • • • • • • • • • • • • • • • •

The only thing I have left is my brown sheepdog with a collar. She got lost between Polna and Mokotowska Streets. I sincerely implore the finder to return her. Reward. 57 Mokotowska Street.

—*Życie Warszawy*, June 27, 1945

• • • • • • • • • • • • • • • • • •

I tell fortunes from rare cards, water, hands, photographs, and writing. Clairvoyance. Counseling. Daily, between 11 a.m. and 5 p.m. Excluding holidays. 1–7 Mała Street.

—*Życie Warszawy*, June 27, 1945

6

First, Reviving Warsaw

RUINS

The writer Janina Broniewska wrote: "I am driving alongside completely incinerated houses. Piękna Street. Wilcza Street. At the end of the rail spurs there are piles of rubble, a few meters high. A bit farther on, a view of ruins, ruins, ruins. A pile of rubble in the middle of the road. We are going past it.

"Friends, Varsovians! Try to understand! There is nothing here. There is nothing here. Your mother is not here, not a single janitor is here. This is a cemetery. Death is here. These are not Marszałkowska, Wspólna, or Nowogrodzka Streets. This is the worst nightmare."

Józef Sigalin, a prominent architect, recalled: "Wind. Frightening. The corner of Jerozolimskie Avenue and Nowy Świat. A huge hole in the road. Like a crater a dozen meters wide. A collapsed ceiling over a tunnel on a cross-city streetcar line. The gorge of Nowy Świat. A horrifying view. There is nothing here. An ominous ravine. . . . It is more empty here. Castle Square. . . . Silence all around. A desert. I grabbed the driver's hand: 'Watch out! A dead body on the road!' We almost ran over it. I jumped out and started to brush off the snow. King Zygmunt. He was lying on his back, looking up at the sky. I cried."

Figure 6.1. Warsaw, March 1945. Castle Square and the ruins of the Old Town. In the foreground: the statue and column of King Zygmunt III, destroyed during the Warsaw Uprising by a German projectile on the night of September 1, 1944. PAP

Lilka Frindt, in 1945 an eighteen-year-old student, reminisced: "Two pictures. The Old Town with the King Zygmunt III monument lying on the ground and the former ghetto. The Old Town was in ruins but fragments of buildings were sticking out. Although from the basements you could see the sky, there were traces of the former construction. The ghetto, however, was a stone desert. The ground was a bit rutted but nothing attracted attention, nothing protruded. I couldn't believe that houses had once been standing here, that it had been an ordinary Warsaw neighborhood with rows of apartment buildings and people."

The prominent writer Jerzy Putrament recorded: "I am driving haphazardly. The ghetto was too large. Without asking anyone, I found a tall, red wall. A few hundred meters more and here it is, a gate. In the past, geography textbooks used to mention Poland's largest sandy Sahara, the Błędów Desert, with a certain pride. Today, a stone, concrete, and brick desert sits in the middle of Warsaw. Who knows? Maybe it is even larger than the other one. . . . The piles of rubble stretch out in regular coils like dunes. And only this makes it possible to grasp where the former houses used to be."

MIN NYET

Mines, unexploded ordnance, projectiles, and aerial bombs were everywhere. The Germans didn't manage to blow up everything they were preparing to destroy. They didn't manage to take away all their weapons and ammunition. If you left the beaten path and made one careless step into the ruins, you were blown up. *Życie Warszawy* was soon to be filled with obituaries about tragic deaths.

In January 1945 Eugeniusz Ajewski, an insurgent of the 1944 Uprising and architect, had to spend a night in the ruins of 103 Puławska Street together with his cousin.

He remembered: "In the morning, at dawn, we retraced our footsteps left in the snow the night before. We were petrified when we noticed two powerful antitank mines at our feet. Five centimeters farther and one of us would have stepped on them."

The Polish Army Command set up the Central Staff for De-Mining the Capital City of Warsaw. A Russian colonel, Piotr Puzerewski, commander of the Second Combat Engineer Brigade, was appointed its chief. As early as January 18, 1945, he dispatched the Second, Fourth, and Fifth Autonomous Combat Engineer Brigades, the Third Pontoon Bridge Brigade, and some Soviet units to clear the city. The capital was being de-mined by over four thousand soldiers.

But they couldn't manage on their own. In mid-April 1945, the headquarters of the Army Corps of Engineers appealed to all Poles for help: "Society should on its own enclose all mines and places filled with ammunition, and mark them with signposts." What served as signposts were two-meter poles with a bundle of straw on the top. In addition, after completing special courses in their municipalities and counties, citizens were supposed to carry out simple de-mining jobs on their own. Were such courses held in Warsaw? Nobody today knows, not even historians.

Looking at sappers working, people were astonished. They recalled articles from prewar illustrated magazines about mine detectors, mine-protected vehicles, and magnetic dollies pushed before tanks. In the meantime, soldiers were "armed in a strange way. Long poles topped with steel rods. Their uniforms, gray and shabby," noted Jerzy Hryniewiecki, an architect.

Figure 6.2. Sappers working in the ruins of Warsaw. Collection of the Karta Center

Hryniewiecki talked to the sappers. They spoke with the accent of Vilna and they moved at a leisurely pace as in a slow-motion movie. Was this a result of their character or a work habit?

Soldiers marked dangerous places with the inscription "MINES!" Places free of peril were labeled "NO MINES" or "This place was de-mined on . . ." Russians wrote "MIN NYET" in Cyrillic. Sometimes they added their signatures. Monika Żeromska, the famous writer's daughter, was touched. "Here and there you can see 'Min nyet' with the signature 'Kuś' below. Good morning, Mr. Kuś."

Hryniewiecki noted, "This struggle is taking place amid ordinary life, among stalls with moonshine, piles of breakfast rolls, and used clothing."

By the beginning of March, the sappers had completed their most important assignment toward their de-mining of Warsaw. They had managed to remove and destroy 15,000 mines and 75,000 projectiles of other kinds. In doing this, 33 soldiers died and 28 were wounded.

ARCHAEOLOGY

Andrzej's grandmother was despairing. She picked up a piece of rubble and tossed it aside. She kicked a wooden slab and cried. What was left of her house at 17 Chopin Street, where she had been living many years, was a pile of bricks, ripped curtains, broken furniture, and a mass of flying papers.

"I have buried everything in the basement," his grandmother sobbed. "Dollars, gold. If we could reach it, I'd take some," she lamented over the heap of debris.

"But how are you going to get there? How?" Andrzej's mother asked her helplessly.

This was the end of January 1945. Andrzej Pstrokoński, who later became a basketball player and an Olympian, was nine years old. Just half a year ago he had lived here with his parents and his younger brother. But when the Warsaw Uprising failed, the Pstrokońskis locked the door to their apartment and on October 5, 1944, joined the multitude herded by the Germans toward the Pruszków Camp. The Nazis allowed everyone to take a small piece of luggage and expelled more than a half million people from Warsaw. Almost all its living residents.

A few months earlier Andrzej's grandmother had gone down to the basement. How did she pack her dollars and gold? Did she wrap them in a scarf? Did she lock them in a box? Did she put them in a jar? Nobody knows. Where did she hide them? Did she manage to dig a hole in the dirt floor? Or perhaps the basement floor was made of brick, so she hid the bundle among the pickle jars, or covered it with coal. Nobody remembers anymore.

But everybody knows that tens of thousands of Warsaw residents had been doing the same for weeks. They were hiding their paintings behind closets, their crystal in the attics, and their silverware under mattresses. They were filling their safes with valuables and locking their books in their bookcases.

Monika Żeromska stashed four cases of her father's manuscripts, six volumes of press clippings, and personal belongings in the basement of her house at Old Market Square.

Friends of Eugeniusz Ajewski, future architect, stowed away his photographs, books, and a wicker suitcase with his clothing in the basement at 14 Pańska Street.

Everyone was sure they would soon come back to their city and recover their treasure from its hiding place.

It had been Adolf Hitler's wish that after his victorious war Warsaw should become an insignificant, provincial city. But at the beginning of August 1944 the Führer demanded that the city be wiped off the face of the Earth. During the city's doomed Uprising by the Polish resistance in August and September, over 150,000 people were killed and 25 percent of the buildings were destroyed, including the entire Old Town.

On October 3, 1944, the specialized German brigades, the Vernichtungskommando and the Verbrennungskommando, that is, Annihilation and Incineration Units, entered Warsaw. First, the Germans robbed house after house. They pulled paintings from behind closets, and fur coats from the closets. They took away bookcases, ripped safes from walls, rolled up carpets, found valuables, and loaded everything onto trucks. They took machines away from factories, pulled telephone cables off poles, and ripped tracks from railroad ties.

Did they walk down to the basements? Did they forage in the garbage left by those hiding during the Uprising? Did they move the bodies of insurgents and civilians to look for treasure hoards? Did they tap on the walls or inspect the jars against the light? Probably not.

Taken altogether, they drove away from Warsaw with 45,000 freight cars and several thousand trucks loaded with Polish property.

They incinerated what was left with flamethrowers. Burned houses, palaces, museums, and places of worship were mined and blown up. By January 1945 they managed to destroy 30 percent more of the left bank of Warsaw.

Due to the war the city lost 84 percent of what had been there in 1939.

The Russians entered Warsaw on January 17, 1945. Right behind them, in the first group of Warsaw residents, walked Eugeniusz Ajewski. He recalled, "Everyone wanted to get to his or her house to see what survived. . . . Perhaps at least a basement remained." But first Ajewski went to the courtyard at 5 Belgijska Street where, right before he surrendered to the Germans after the Uprising, he had hidden his pistol, his documents, and his Home Army ID in a wrecked car. Everything was there the way he had left them.

The renowned writer Maria Dąbrowska arrived in Warsaw soon after.

Figure 6.3. Warsaw, 1945. Aerial view of Napoleon Square (previously Warecki Square, now Warsaw Insurgents Square). The Prudential skyscraper and Świętokrzyska Street. Karol Szczeiński / East News

She was lucky. The apartment building at 40 Polna Street, where she had lived since 1917, survived. Dąbrowska noted in her diary, "I was robbed of all the 'easy' things, but the furniture, and what's more important, my library and archives have survived." The floor was covered with damp, trampled piles of photographs, books, letters, and manuscripts. There were no glass windows in the apartment, snowdrifts sat in the bathroom and the kitchen, the ceilings leaked, and the plundered furniture had been knocked over.

By contrast, Eugeniusz Ajewski's house was turned into a pile of rubble. "Suddenly, I realized there might be some undamaged basement rooms under this eight- or ten-meter-high burial mound, with my stuff in them," he wrote in his memoirs. He decided to begin "archaeological work" and to dig out everything that was left. Shovelful after shovelful, he removed the debris. He carefully examined every piece of trash, damp and dirty with plaster. He put aside books and photographs, wet and devastated by limestone. He quenched his thirst with champagne because he had found an unopened bottle. In the evening he reached the basement. The crater he had created was twelve meters deep but too narrow at the bottom. Through a crevice Ajewski could see his wicker suitcase, but he couldn't pull it out. It was already too dark to work further. He decided to come back the next day. However, in the morning he discovered that he had been beaten by a looter who cut a hole in the suitcase and stole his clothing.

Eugeniusz Ajewski dipped his hand into the suitcase and pulled out only a single necktie, missed by the thief.

Monika Żeromska started her "archaeological work" in April. Although some basements under the Old Town had survived, after several attempts she was still not able to reach the chamber with her father's manuscripts. She then formed a brigade of forty-nine women, "all of them sturdy Warsaw females," hired three skilled workers and a foreman, borrowed money to pay their wages, and began to clear away debris. The women collected rubble from the ground where the apartment building at 11 Old Town Square used to stand, and the men buttressed the walls. They attracted the attention of the tour groups coming to Warsaw to see the reconstruction. At night, looters attempted to dig in this place on their own. After a month the treasure was found.

From the rubble Monika Żeromska recovered her father's letters from famous Poles, including Henryk Sienkiewicz and Marie Skłodowska-Curie. She found her grandmother's sugar bowl, her mother's coat with the seal-fur lining, her own reindeer-fur coat, a pillow, and a woolen blanket. Every day she discovered something new. An untouched basket of chinaware, wrapped in old panties and shirts, gladdened her more than the surviving porcelain cups and creamers. Finally, she had the manuscripts. The covers of the novels *Ashes*, *Elegy for a Commander*, and *Wind From the Sea*, which had been locked in a chest, were slightly damaged but the paper was dry and the ink was clearly visible.

Żeromska's brigade was admired by a man who used to live at the corner of Market Square where Zapiecek and Świętojańska Streets met. He was wealthy. During the German occupation he had put his dollars into glass jars and his precious carpets into metal tubes. Then these had all been sealed and buried in the basement, under the coal. Now, he made an offer to the writer's daughter. He would point out the basement with his hidden treasure, and she would dig it out with her team. They would split the money fifty-fifty. But Monika Żeromska refused.

Eugeniusz Ajewski worked in the Warsaw Reconstruction Office and was in charge of apartment buildings. He remembered a worker knocking a hole in the wall to emplace a ceiling beam in some burned-out house. This worker had come across a wall a quarter as thick as a brick. "Suddenly, a treasure hoard started to spill out from the hole. Silver items and other valuables kept falling along with the dust and debris. The worker, standing on a wobbling ladder, wanted to grab everything, but he caught nothing. Small precious items mixed with rubble were falling to the floors below through the cracks in the wooden scaffold, as far down as the basement. Shouting, havoc, and people snatching the treasure," wrote Ajewski.

Every day Andrzej Pstrokoński's grandmother would go to the heaps of rubble at 17 Chopin Street. She had neither the means nor the strength to take a spade to the debris. She found a few family mementos among the bricks and trash. She never found her dollars or her gold.

STINK

Warsaw stank. People stank. Water was hardly available, and could only be used for drinking. There was no soap; there was a shortage of towels, bathtubs, washtubs, and showers. "Life means giving up the elementary requirements of culture and hygiene," noted Maria Dąbrowska, the writer. For the first two weeks she slept on the floor at her neighbor's, next to fully dressed strangers lying down on mattresses. In her apartment there was no glass in the windows and the door lock was missing. She couldn't sleep there.

Trash stank, too. There was no waste removal service, at least not at the beginning. Garbage was tossed away right outside the door. Bomb craters served as temporary trash chutes. The sewage system didn't work and there were no public toilets, so people relieved themselves in the rubble.

Życie Warszawy blamed janitors for the filth, claiming that they couldn't keep their territory clean. The newspaper also asked who had allowed a temporary garbage dump at Starynkiewicz Square. It reported that the carters paid by the city council didn't come to pick up the waste. In May the reporters were worried that epidemics of typhus and dysentery might break out in that city of 400,000 people. The authorities ordered mandatory typhus vaccinations.

That spring the stink accelerated and that summer it became unbearable. Readers of *Życie Warszawy* complained that in front of the Polonia Hotel on Jerozolimskie Avenue all kinds of rotting waste and garbage were thrown through an opening in the ceiling of the train tunnel below the street. There was a dead horse in the tunnel, completely decomposed, poisoning the air in the neighborhood. "Millions of flies hover over the garbage dump."

But the worst foulness came from the decaying corpses. "We were followed by the constant and relentless stench of decomposing carrion somewhere nearby. At that time Warsaw stank from all kinds of rotting," wrote Jan Tereszczenko, an architect who was twelve in 1945.

"The odor of decaying bodies was killing," recalled Andrzej Pstrokoński. "At the end of April they started to open the insurgents' graves. They were everywhere. I couldn't stand it. When I was coming back from school and I saw people with shovels, standing over a ditch with cadaverous slime, I held my nose and ran quickly to avoid it."

EXHUMATIONS

The body of a blond kid, an insurgent whose back had been hit by shrapnel, was still lying in the shop at 5 Belgijska Street. He died there when they were dressing his wounds and there was no time to bury him. "His body was preserved by the freezing temperatures, so the blond boy looked like he had died the day before," Eugeniusz Ajewski, his companion from the Uprising, recalled later. "His young, handsome face was disfigured by a rat that had bitten off the tip of his nose."

In the City Center the writer Kazimierz Brandys tripped over the body of a young boy with a rifle. He noticed that some merciful person had covered the boy's face with a helmet, a resourceful person had pulled off his shoes, and a third person, a believer, had placed a little cross between his fingers.

Janina Broniewska leaned over the frozen body of an elderly woman who lay next to the trampled path near the Vistula. She made a note, "Her dark coat and her leg with one shoe has been covered with snow. Her face resembles a piece of wood, desiccated, without any features. Through her gray hair the wind blows."

A dead body hanging head down, with its legs caught in a little window, barred the way to the basement in which Monika Żeromska looked for her father's manuscripts. She pushed the body out of the way with a long stick and forced her way through.

At the end of June 1945 reporters from *Życie Warszawy* visited the Old Town. They met a bricklayer, whose son, playing in the rubble near the Baryczkas' house a day earlier, had found a man's shoe protruding from under a sheet of steel. "Following this clue, they found three dead bodies, or rather three skeletons covered with skin—a man, a woman, and a child. There are many more such corpses here."

In January 1945 the left bank of Warsaw was one gigantic cemetery.

If you wanted to live there, you had to get used to the sight of dead bodies. You had to be unmoved. "Everyone . . . lived near or walked past unburied bodies just as indifferently as today we pass by a street lamp or newsstand. For a long time, the corpses were lying on the sidewalks. . . . During the first weeks we didn't have time to take care of them. We had to find some shelter in the rubble for ourselves," noted Ajewski.

Dead bodies lay on the streets and in entry ways. Tens of thousands of cadavers filled sewers, occupied basements, and waited under debris for someone to get to them. Other bodies occupied the ground under Warsaw. There were no longer any flagstones in the sidewalks; during the Uprising they had been used to build barricades. Where the sidewalks used to be, there were now graves. There also were no squares, parks, urban gardens, courtyards, and playgrounds. They had turned into cemeteries.

The essayist Jerzy Waldorff noticed the graves in front of the former café at Warecki Square. "During the most prosperous times there weren't as many living clients in the cafés as now there are dead ones," he wrote.

In August 1944 Adolf Hitler demanded that all residents of Warsaw should be killed. Erich von dem Bach-Zelewski, SS-Obergruppenführer, commander of the military forces assigned to suppress the Uprising, ordered the killing of every civilian and every insurgent. Taking prisoners was forbidden. Heinrich Himmler commanded his subordinates to "kill tens of thousands."

When the Uprising broke out the Nazis began the slaughter. They dragged people from homes, threw grenades into basements, torched houses, and shot individuals escaping fire. They murdered the residents of entire neighborhoods, herded people from the streets into one spot and executed them, and used civilians as human shields. In the Russian Orthodox orphanage at 149 Wolska Street they used their rifle butts to smash in the heads of dozens of children. They executed captured insurgents. They finished off the wounded. They abandoned the bodies or piled them up and burned them.

On August 5 Bach-Zelewski eased up on Hitler's order and forbade killing women and children. They were to be sent to the Pruszków Camp. A week later he forbade killing male civilians. He had decided it would be a pity to waste a good workforce.

Altogether, according to various estimates, during the Warsaw Uprising 150,000–180,000 civilians and about 16,000 insurgents were killed.

In February 1945, according to the City Council's Exhumation Department the number of temporary graves and unburied bodies was estimated as 200,000. They had to hurry while it was still cold. Heat would accelerate body decay, making identifications more difficult. There was also the risk of an epidemic.

Working on exhumations was very difficult and therefore very well paid. Red Cross volunteers, nurses, and medics applied, mostly women. They were provided with gray and green overalls, masks, gloves, and pliers. But it also happened from time to time that they worked with the dead bodies with their bare hands, wearing their own clothes.

In mid-April 1945 reporters from *Życie Warszawy* interviewed a medical student working on exhumations. He complained, "We haven't gotten any protective gloves or aprons. Even worse, we can't wash our hands after we finish our work because nobody thought about the soap ration. . . . And it's unacceptable that there is no chlorine powder."

Janina Rożecka, nom de guerre "Dora," a medic, worked at Czerniakowska Street. Ten workers dug out a pit and in it placed the bodies found in houses, ruins, and temporary graves. After many years she recalled, "It was a disgusting job. Once, someone came to me and told me that there were people in a septic tank. So I said, 'How come?' . . . It was Sadyba, a well-off neighborhood. In front of the church there were septic tanks. The Germans threw live people into them. The workers lifted the covers and picked up the bodies with pike poles, or whatever they are called. The corpses were, well,

Figure 6.4. Exhumations in the streets of Warsaw. March 1945. PAP

it's terrible what I'm saying, as finely preserved as if they had been placed there just a moment earlier. The manholes were just clogged and some of the gases from the septic tanks slowed down the decay."

Red Cross volunteers examined each exhumed body very carefully. They identified the cause of death. A hole in the skull—executed. Bits of bandage or plaster cast—died from wounds. There were also those who had been buried under debris and those who had died from projectiles and bombs. All details mattered. If there were any documents in a pocket, the case was simple. People buried in makeshift graves often held sealed bottles under their arms. Inside, on a piece of paper, someone had written who had died, when, and where. But, most often, the dead had nothing on them. In that case the next step was that one had to make a note of their hair color, the condition of their teeth, and the clothes they had on. Sometimes it was very hard to determine the sex of the decomposing bodies. One of the foreign correspondents noted how nauseated he felt when he observed an exhumation and watched women working.

Życie Warszawy informed its readers that unidentified bodies were marked with the letters NN (*non notus*, or "no name). All items found on them were carefully preserved by the Polish Red Cross. They planned to organize some kind of exhibition soon that would make it easier to find many of those who had disappeared without a trace. "Photographs, wallets, prayer books, medallions, purses, etc., will be collected together. Personal documents, sorted and ready to be picked up by the families of those killed, will be placed in envelopes."

The fence near the Red Cross station at Pius XI Street, now Piękna Street, was covered with notices about the identified dead.

Exhumations were performed where there were renovations or new construction. But the cemeteries were full and there were no wagons or trucks to carry the bodies. Someone had the idea to burn the bodies after a detailed description had been recorded. The idea caused outrage. These methods had been employed by the Germans during the war! So for the time being, exhumed bodies that had not been identified and claimed by families, were buried in mass graves. One of them was installed in Dreszer Park.

In May 1945 *Życie Warszawy* informed its readers that the grave had been opened again. "For a few days, residents of Mokotów have been witnessing the disturbing procedure of opening the mass grave in Dreszer Park, just to satisfy some tardy citizen looking for a dead relative."

The newspapers reported the exhumations of the remains in detail. In June readers learned about the demolition of the indoor market at Kazimierz Wielki Street. During the Uprising several hundred fallen fighters had died here and were now under the rubble. The Municipal Department of Health and Welfare's Exhumation Section began to bury the exhumed bodies. "The victims' families are called on to appear at the site in order to identify their loved ones." Relatives of the victims of the Uprising, who had been temporarily buried between Savior Square and Żurawia Street and between Union of Lublin Square and Teatralny Square, were also summoned.

By the end of May, 27,000 bodies had been exhumed in Warsaw.

About some of the exhumations no one was informed, especially at the beginning. Home Army soldiers dug out the bodies of their brothers-in-arms from the graves they had marked during the Uprising, and moved them to the cemeteries. They wanted to get to them ahead of the authorities who were trying to erase any traces of the Polish Home Army resistance fighters by burying their unclaimed bodies in the gravesites for the soldiers of the communist People's Army.

For epidemiological reasons, Red Cross volunteers working on exhumations were forbidden to release the bodies to private individuals without permission from the public health authorities. Janina Rożecka remembered that despite the senior doctor's orders she sometimes would yield to the pleas of relatives.

She recalled, "A young man has shown up, hunched and limping, and he says, 'Miss, I would like you very much to let me take my mother, my wife, and my child from this mass grave. . . . ' What shall I tell him? 'No?' He has come with some coffins. I told the workers, 'Listen, if you expose me, I will never talk to you again.' They have seen everything. How could I not do it? There were more situations like this."

Monika Żeromska was also not going to wait for an official exhumation. In April 1945 she informed the Polish Red Cross that in the Old Town she would like to exhume the body of Roman Padlewski, nom de guerre "Crusty," a composer, musicologist, and her friend, who had died in her arms during the Uprising. She knew where he had been buried, she had attended his funeral. Żeromska got a permit to dig out the body. The Red Cross health inspectors appeared at the designated spot near the old walls at Nowowiejska Street. Roman's mother, Nadzieja Padlewska, the pianist, attended the exhumation. She wanted to take her son's body to the Wilanów Cemetery where her husband was buried. Together with the inspectors, Żeromska removed the rubble. The grave, with its marked cross, was found where she expected. They dug out the coffin, opened it, and from behind the corpse's head they pulled out a bottle with documents. Monika noted in her diary: "The health inspectors are giving us a permit to exhume the body and take the coffin away." She had to arrange transportation of the body to the cemetery. She wrote later: "Mrs. Padlewska looks as if she is going to faint and I seat her on a broken wall, a bit farther from the open grave, and I beg her not to move. I promise to come back soon." After a long search she stopped a man with a wagon. He agreed to take the coffin to Wilanów where the priest was already waiting.

The planned exhumations would continue until 1948. At the beginning of the 1960s Józef Sigalin noted in his diary: "Even now, at many Warsaw construction sites, workers carrying out earthmoving tasks find human bones. . . . No, there is no end to this citywide exhumation."

THE SOUGHT

How to find anyone if there were no personal ads in the newspapers? Well, you had to take a piece of paper, a pencil, and write down where you were staying. Then you rolled up the paper and squeezed it between the bricks of the house you used to live in. Or you wrote with chalk directly on a wall. In mid-1945 these were the most reliable sources of information in Warsaw.

Pola Gojawiczyńska, the writer, noted: "At the end of the street, on the wall, you can read 'Kwiatkowska, Maria now lives at Bednarska Street.'"

"There were notices on the devastated entranceways. 'Zosia! Kasia! I am in Podkowa Leśna, in Pruszków, in Praga, at 12 Targowa Street,' and so on," Eugeniusz Ajewski recalled.

"Thanks to some people I met by accident I left a message on a fire-damaged doorframe saying I was going to Praga to look for my friends. Later on, that notice made it possible to find my entire family," reminisced Janusz Orszt, who was thirteen in 1945.

Andrzej Pstrokoński remembered: "When it turned out our house at Chopin Street had been destroyed, my mom, my grandma, my younger brother, and I spent the night in the entranceway. Of the entire house only this part survived. In the morning we spotted inserted notices all over. It was neighbors looking for one another. My mom and my grandma burst into tears. How will we find my dad in this ruined city? We walked around, read all the notices, pulled pieces of paper from walls or from under stones. And nothing, there was no letter from my father.

My grandma and my mom decided that we had to cross the frozen Vistula to get to Praga. We had family there. My heartbroken grandma kept walking around in thick snow till the last moment and suddenly she spotted a piece of paper. 'I live at 85 Jerozolimskie Avenue. If you've gotten here, come. Edek.' A letter from my father! Later, my mother would recall through her entire life how, letter in hand, she was racing to my father so fast that even Zatopek wouldn't have caught her."

Figure 6.5. A notice board at Three Crosses Square in Warsaw. Among the scribbled names and addresses, one notice reads: "Jadzia, I am at Three Crosses Square, the pastry shop, Felix." Spring / summer 1945. Karol Szczeciński / East News

DEBRIS

The city was covered with twenty million cubic meters of debris. Piles of crumbled bricks and concrete, broken furniture, and trash had been temporarily moved to the sides of the streets. They were several meters high. It was not possible to take them away. There was no transportation, no wagons, horses, trucks, or gasoline. And after all, where should the junk be taken? But things couldn't be left like this, either. Although in May *Życie Warszawy* informed its readers that debris from Puławska Street was taken away by one hundred wagons every single day, it looked more like play than real work. The piles of rubble in the city were enormous. If necessary, debris might be shoveled into the basements, but one had to be careful not to cover drains and gutters. In July a trolley started operating in Żoliborz to speed the rubble removal. A second line was supposed to cross the Old Town and the Center. But it was nevertheless not enough.

Ruins that were still standing could collapse at any time. Special teams were in charge of their demolition. Everything had to be done by hand since at the beginning there were also no cranes or excavators in Warsaw.

Jan Tereszczenko reminisced: "First, a work brigade sent one man who, risking his life, would climb a pile of debris and would install a steel cable there. Then, the cable was pulled to the other side of the street. Other workers hung on the cable and, swinging rhythmically in the clouds of dust, would knock down the unstable walls."

Each demolition attracted many spectators.

In May the Rubble Commission was formed at the Warsaw Reconstruction Office (WRO). There were proposals to move the debris to the bottom of the Vistula embankment in Powiśle, but someone claimed that covering the wetlands with rubble would destroy seeds and vegetation, and make the soil infertile. Somebody proposed to cover the pond at Puławska Street or to use the debris to build a dike between the reservoirs of the River Pumping Station at Czerniakowska Street. But this was unacceptable because of possible bacterial infection. There was also a suggestion to heap up a mound, but there was no machinery. Finally, the commission decided to cover depressions and ponds, as well as barren lands, on the right bank of the Vistula, if transporting debris was worth the trouble. The commission also considered making the left bank of the Vistula more regular in designated areas. Selling the debris for building Polish roads was also contemplated.

People started moving into the burned-out, ruined, and unstable houses. In July violent thunderstorms with strong winds passed over Warsaw. Some ruins collapsed, burying the residents alive. Many people died or were injured. A six-story house at 29 Wilcza Street fell down. Dozens of people perished under the rubble. The building had been already hit in 1939 and then seriously damaged during the Uprising.

In August the newspapers informed their readers that the WRO had announced a contest for the best plan for the debris. Dozens of innovators applied. *Życie Warszawy* wrote: "First of all, the WRO received several projects for how to produce porous crushed-brick concrete. The concrete blocks can be used for building walls that are light, warm, and strong."

In September the same newspaper reported that the debris problem had not been solved yet. There was a plan to use half of it as crushed stone for the construction of reinforced concrete frames.

TRADE

JANUARY 1945

Wheat flour, 1 kilo—106 zlotys

Sauerkraut, 1 kilo—68 zlotys

Potatoes, 1 kilo—13 zlotys

Milk, 1 liter, costs almost 44 zlotys

Butter, 1 kilogram, costs 483 zlotys

Pork, 1 kilo—285 zlotys, lard—483 zlotys

Distilled spirits, 1 liter—1,100 zlotys

Box of matches—25 zlotys

Pair of men's socks—350 zlotys

Nylon stockings—800 zlotys

An official would hand out 500 zlotys and cut off the corner of the *Kennkarte*, the German-issued ID, as evidence that the money had been collected. In February 1945 Maria Dąbrowska collected 500 new zlotys at the designated post near the National Museum. She still had *młynarki* in her wallet, that is, the currency used during the occupation, but these notes had just become invalid. The authorities replaced them with zlotys issued by the Lublin government. Every person who returned to Warsaw and appeared at the correct agency would receive an identical amount as a onetime allowance. The money helped people survive for the first few days. There would also be Food Coupons, divided into five categories, according to type of employment.

Already in January, Warsaw, mainly on its less-damaged right bank, had 232 grocery stores and 130 soap shops. Each month their number would grow. In December 1945, there were 1,246 registered shops in the entire city, including 74 shops with coal and wood products, 230 soap shops, and 213 potato stores.

In May, a journalist from *Życie Warszawy* using the pen name Joker wrote mockingly, "Despite the variety of names, these shops don't specialize in anything. You can enter a secondhand shop and ask for a cookie or milk. They will find it. And in a creamery you can quite often purchase a hat, an umbrella, or a coat."

Residents of Warsaw registered kiosks with carbonated water and newspapers, cigarette stalls, refreshment pushcarts, flower stands, personal scales, cameras, shoeshine stands, and counters where fashion accessories were sold. The intersection of Jerozolimskie Avenue and Marszałkowska Street became the city's commercial center. A few apartment buildings had survived there and among the ruins some were only partially collapsed. Each niche was suitable for a shop, sometimes quite elegant. Zofia Nałkowska was looking at the shop window of the luxurious florist's "planted at the foot of the ruins." At Marszałkowska Street the reporter Ksawery Pruszyński caught sight of "some shop with every possible item, but with a slight majority of dusty cameras." In the city center, Eugeniusz Ajewski's friend ran a small business buying silver.

But the real commerce of Warsaw was wild and unregistered. It was run from baskets and suitcases, so you could quickly pack your goods and escape the police. It took place in bazaars and shabby markets, on both sides of the Vistula. It was temporary. Makeshift stalls were built overnight. Building materials—bricks and wooden planks—lay directly on the ground, but nobody cared about building permits. According to reporters, the Citizens' Police were not able to solve the problem. The officers chased away the vendors and their baskets but they were helpless against the shabby stands defacing the city. Fines for unlicensed stalls were just calculated as part of the cost of doing business, so after a few months the vendors were making a slight profit despite them.

You could buy and sell everything. Maria Dąbrowska wrote in her diary: "Commotion, crowds, marketplace. Stores are displaying hams and sausages and the stands are full of . . . our looted items. Tons of cigarettes, and . . . tangerines, 50 zlotys each. A lot of white bread, pastries, and jelly doughnuts."

Whenever she had free time, Jan Tereszczenko's mother would go to the market at Poznańska Street. She was a painter and she could tell the difference between true art and rubbish. Her son reminisced: "My mom, with her expert's eye, would buy Persian carpets for the price of a doormat, or Saxon porcelain for the price of some trashy pottery."

Figure 6.6. Street vendors selling bread in ruined Warsaw, 1945. PAP

In the magazine *Przekrój*, Wiech (Stefan Wiechecki) also described the bazaar at Poznańska Street: "Private businesses enjoy an incredible success. They boil, surge, and spill onto the sidewalks and out into the middle of the street."

Hucksters dealing in gold and foreign currency operated near the Central Station. One of them pestered Ksawery Pruszyński. "Despicable type whispering softly, 'dollars, dollars, hard and soft.'"

In May the newspapers were warning their readers against counterfeits. The American "York" cigarettes—in a pink pack—turned out to be fake. The cigarette label "Navy Cut" was printed as "Novy Cut," and a further giveaway was that the inserted cardboard stiffening in the boxes came from local Ekonomiczne cigarettes. You also had to be cautious about food products purchased in the bazaars. Meat was sometimes putrid.

Soups, dumplings, and cakes were made at home and then brought to the street for sale in pots bundled up in newspaper. Temporary bars opened in the streetcars that had served as barricades during the Uprising. In September 1945 Wiech wrote: "Right away, on da second day, as soon as dose goddamm Krauts had left, da first stalls toined up at Jerozolimskie Avenue. You could order a modest but hearty snack that paired well with a shot of rotgut infused with carbide, known as *karbidówka*."

In February 1945 Leon Czarzyński came back to Warsaw for a while. He remembered: "You could buy hot tea, pierogi, and cabbage. The street trade was everywhere."

There was a coffeehouse on every corner. Jan Wedel resumed production of chocolate in a Praga factory and opened an outlet at Szpitalna Street. Jelly doughnuts, already famous before the war, were served in Gajewski's patisserie at the intersection of Marszałkowska and Wspólna. The singer Mieczysław Fogg opened Café Fogg, where you could have a cup of tea and listen to his prewar hits.

Prices were arbitrary. Sometimes they depended on the merchant's mood, usually on the patron's appearance, and often on the neighborhood. A cup of coffee cost 25 zlotys in a little café at Zgoda Street, but for the same cup, though of lesser quality, you would pay 70 zlotys in the newly opened place at Three Crosses Square. A pastry at Puławska Street—18 zlotys, a pastry of inferior quality at Central Station—35 zlotys. The price of a glass of bouillon varied between 2 and 20 zlotys and of water or coffee between 5 and 15 zlotys. The same happened with prices of books, bread, and cold cuts. The courts imposed a fine for usury from 12,000 to 25,000 zlotys.

If you were caught selling vodka illegally, you paid a fine of 1,000 to 2,000 zlotys. But still the city was drunk. A *Przekrój* journalist, Roman Burzyński, remarked that the number of bars was what grew most rapidly. He counted thirty in a row at Jerozolimskie Avenue between the corner of Marszałkowska and the former Central Station. "Every wooden stall is a cheap clandestine bar. And it doesn't matter if this is a fruit stall, a carbonated water stall, or a potato stall. In front, carrots and kvass, in back, homemade booze," he noted. When stalls were not available, the bar was thrown together on the spot. Two chairs and an old flower stand pulled from the ruins were enough. "Instead of a flower pot, you place a bottle on the stand, with two glasses and a snack, and the bar is ready." A *Życie Warszawy* reporter observed that alcohol was available in every location. You could ask about booze in the soap shop or in the depot for bicycle parts. "The hard stuff can be found everywhere."

APRIL 1945

Wheat flour, 1 kilo—95 zlotys

Sauerkraut, 1 kilo—24 zlotys

Potatoes, 1 kilo—6 zlotys

Milk, 1 liter, costs almost 36 zlotys

Butter, 1 kilo, costs 441 zlotys

Pork, 1 kilo—196 zlotys, lard—411 zlotys

Distilled spirits, 1 liter—1,140 zlotys

Box of matches—8 zlotys

Pair of men's socks—173 zlotys

Nylon stockings—512 zlotys

QUARTERING, OR SHARING YOUR APARTMENT IS OBLIGATORY

"Crowded streets and deserted houses. Where do you people live?" some foreigner asked a reporter from *Życie Warszawy* in June. "In the ruins," answered the reporter. "In buildings that look like they are about to collapse. In sheds. And in basements from which the only thing protruding above street level are pipes from cast-iron stoves." And he presented the official data: there were 11,063 inhabited buildings in Warsaw, including 5,794 buildings on the left bank. It was 50 percent less than in 1939.

But not everyone had to live in the ruins. The lucky ones, whose houses had survived flamethrowers and mines, came back to their plundered apartments; but there was already someone else living there.

Jan Tereszczenko's mother had always carried her apartment keys with her. Her apartment building near the train station had survived! When she came back to Warsaw, she noticed someone else's nameplate on her door. She turned the key and entered. Later on, her son would write in his memoirs, "A woman came out of my room by the kitchen and introduced herself, 'I am Warwasińska.' 'And I am the owner of this apartment,' my mom introduced herself. 'Nice to meet you. We took this room.' Mrs. Warwasińska pointed to *mine*. 'We've received a quartering order for it.'"

"My father was an engineer and from January 1945 had been working at City Hall. He was lucky, because it was his friends who decided who got apartments, so for us he arranged a room with a kitchen, first floor, at 85 Jerozolimskie Avenue. That building miraculously survived," recalled

Figure 6.7. A family meal in a destroyed building. Warsaw, September 1945. PAP

Andrzej Pstrokoński. "Of course, it was not *our* apartment. The owner soon showed up and we moved to a bigger place at 50 Słoneczna, in front of the Russian Embassy. At first, half our family lived there with us."

Eugeniusz Ajewski didn't want to take someone else's apartment. He moved into a vacant building on the corner of Puławska and Szuster, whose construction had been halted even before the war. It had never been occupied. Right away, he appeared at the neighborhood Quartering Office to legalize his stay. The local official, picking his teeth with a pocketknife, wrote a quartering certificate on an excise stamp removed from a carton of Mewa cigarettes.

Maria Dąbrowska was surprised that she had to get a quartering order for the apartment she had lived in since 1917. But as a well-known author she was warmly welcomed. First, Władysław Czerny, Warsaw's deputy mayor, whose office in January 1945 was temporarily located in the school on Otwocka Street, accepted her application for the apartment at 40 Polna Street. He wrote a note in the margin "with some embarrassingly flattering words about my oeuvre, and ordered the Quartering Office in my neighborhood to take care of my request, promptly and favorably," Dąbrowska recalled. Next day, a young official, while eating some soup, handed Dąbrowska a quartering order. It had to be affixed to the door as a proof of residence. If it was torn off, a duplicate would be issued. Maria Dąbrowska's apartment would be plundered a few times more, but nobody ever squatted there, and she didn't have to share it with anyone.

Very few Varsovians were so lucky. Officials visited the surviving Warsaw apartments and measured the space. The phrase "quartering order" was terrifying. It meant that nobody could have an individual apartment. Statistically, in Warsaw there was one room for 2.2 people. *Życie Warszawy* consoled its readers, observing that before the war these figures had not been any better, and that in working-class neighborhoods 2.1 people had lived in one room. But it also added that during the coming winter, the density would be higher, because people now camping outdoors would have to be placed somewhere.

Wiech told the story of his friend, Alojzy Skubliński, who had come back to his apartment on Marszałkowska. The friend had three bedrooms and a kitchen, but one room was missing a wall, two rooms had no ceiling, and the bathroom floor had collapsed. "So he felt a bit uncomftable when one day tree guys wit briefcases showed up and said dey were da commission. . . . Because dere were tree rooms dere, dey claimed, nine people should live in dis apartment, and da friend wit his wife and no children were only a couple."

Finally, Skubliński's apartment got assigned one tenant, who was supposed to live in the kitchen.

FINNISH HOUSES

Marian Marzyński lay down on the grass, closed his eyes, and pretended he was sleeping. It was 2014, summer, in the center of Warsaw. But for a moment the man on the ground is eight years old again and lying under the covers. In his dream the year is 1945, and his bed stands in a little house, new and of wood, among ninety identical houses, in Górny Ujazdów.

At first, nobody knew if Warsaw would be the capital at all. The government in Lublin was considering moving the capital to Łódź, and leaving Warsaw in ruins, so that future generations would remember it as a symbol of Nazi barbarity. But Stalin needed the provisional government in Warsaw, and Poland with its old capital.

So at the beginning of January 1945, the State National Council made the decision to rebuild Warsaw and proclaimed it the capital of independent Poland. Later that month, the Warsaw mayor Marian Spychalski, an architect, created the Warsaw Reconstruction Organizational Office that, in February, turned into the Warsaw Reconstruction Office. The WRO was led by Roman Piotrowski, and his deputies were Józef Sigalin and Witold Plapis. They were devoted communists, and known as "the modernizers." The other group within the WRO, led by Jan Zachwatowicz and Piotr Biegański, loyal to the London government-in-exile, was called "the traditionalists." These two groups would have opposing visions of the city's reconstruction.

The WRO's job was to inventory war losses, modernize the city's infrastructure, and devise plans for the reconstruction of historic landmarks. By July the office would already be employing 1,500 people, including architects, urbanists, all kinds of engineers, economists, and lawyers.

The war had not yet ended when Joseph Stalin presented Warsaw with five hundred ready-to-assemble houses. The Polish capital was in ruins, people lived in the rubble, so the wooden dachas were gifts not to be underestimated. They were made by Finns in a factory in Kemi. In this way Finland was paying off a portion of its war reparations to the Soviet Union in the amount of $300 million. (One of the Finnish workers in this factory was Franz Vilena, the grandfather of Jari Vilena, a future ambassador to Poland.)

In April 1945 freight cars filled with gigantic stacks of pine planks arrived at the Gdański Station. Protected with sawdust, they waited to be picked up, while getting soaked in the rain and blocking the station. What should be done with them? Where should they be put? Who should receive them? Who was going to take care of all of this?! Nobody other than the Warsaw Reconstruction Office.

So where should they put these five hundred little houses? Józef Sigalin would remember that the deliberations were heated. This housing development was to be temporary, ready for demolition in five years when there wouldn't be any housing shortage in Warsaw. And it should be close to the city center, the largest construction site, because house keys would be given to those working for the capital's reconstruction. However, it turned out that Warsaw had no single site vast enough for five hundred houses. A

Figure 6.8. Construction site for Finnish houses. April 1945. PAP

decision was made. Ninety houses were sent to Górny Ujazdów, and the others to Dolny Ujazdów or Wawelska Street (the future Mokotowskie Field).

And here engineer Daniel Marzyński came onto the stage. He was a Jew, a Polish Army officer, and a former prisoner of war in Woldenberg who had lost his wife and child in Auschwitz. At the end of the war he met Bronisła-wa Kuszner, the widow of an engineer he used to know. This woman and her son, Marian, had escaped from the Warsaw ghetto. The boy was cared for by some Poles and in 1944 she found him in the orphanage in Łaźniewo.

Daniel fell in love with Bronisława, married her, and her son got his last name. But Marian, Bronisława's son, protested. Why should they live with a stranger, why was mom sleeping with him in one bed? But with the passing of time he would love this man like his own father.

The engineer Marzyński got a job in the Warsaw Reconstruction Office. His first task was to oversee the construction of the Finnish houses in Górny Ujazdów.

In 2014 Marian Marzyński, now a prominent film director, got up from the ground to show me where his little bed used to stand in the Finnish house. He told me, "My mom, my stepfather, and I were here first. We moved into one of the pavilions that survived the destruction of the Ujazdowski Hospital. I remember the Soviet trucks entering the construction site, bringing wooden planks. Our house was one of the earliest."

The housing development in Górny Ujazdów was put up first. Construction work began on March 20, 1945. *Życie Warszawy* had been excited about the project for a few months. Workers leveled the ground, demolished the hospital ruins, and cleared away the rubble. The wooden components were on the way; there was an ongoing selection of doors, walls, windows, and floors. The cement and limestone for the shallow foundations were stockpiled. The Fire Safety Commission sent some instructions to the WRO about protecting those houses from fire. Small reservoirs and barrels with water would be installed in the housing development.

Bronisława Marzyńska appraised the women who excavated and scraped the bricks. At night, using an indelible pencil and five sheets of carbon paper, she prepared the lists of workers' wages. She ran a bread depository and made sure that soup and baked goods were distributed fairly among the people.

In May, journalists visited the house of one of the construction managers (probably the Marzyńskis' house). "We climb the cement stairs under the graceful columns of the arcades and enter the hallway. On the right, there is a living room, then a bedroom, and a dine-in kitchen. . . . There are three closets in the bedroom—for underwear, clothing, and outer apparel."

The houses were placed in long rows and grouped into smaller colonies, a dozen buildings in each. The workers were in a hurry. On May 1, Labor Day, twenty-four houses were ready—but not to be inhabited. Even after a year it would turn out that some roofs leaked, the keys didn't open the locks, the toilets didn't flush, the windows didn't close, water spurted over the ceilings, and smoke flowed inside the house instead of being exhausted through the chimney. Fifteen-centimeter-thick walls, insulated with cardboard, didn't protect from cold. People would also complain that the houses were so close to one another, that without curtains their neighbor's lingerie was clearly visible.

In June the newspaper announced that at the end of July the lights would be turned on in the Finnish houses in Górny Ujazdów. But it happened much faster. In mid-July tenants moved into the first thirty houses. *Życie Warszawy* reported that work was still in progress. Workers built a cobblestone road and brick sidewalks that had a chevron pattern. Two shoe repair shops and a nursery were already operating in the neighborhood.

The ceremonial opening of this urban development took place on the first anniversary of the Warsaw Uprising. Ninety Finnish houses were ready to be inhabited: sixty-four three-room houses and twenty-six four-room houses. Warsaw's mayor, Stanisław Tołwiński, who in March replaced Spychalski, received the symbolic keys to the development. As a reward for their efficient labor, the twenty most devoted workers got a two-week vacation. Portraits of eight of them hung above the podium. Representatives of the Śląsko-Dąbrowski Committee for Warsaw Reconstruction brought a gift from the Silesian labor teams and factories: a freight car of soap and twenty-seven freight cars of cement.

The engineer and WRO director, Piotrowski declared that 75 percent of the houses would be taken by workers, and the rest by project designers and technicians. According to *Życie Warszawy*, General Sergyey Shatilov, the Soviet head of mission, "spoke in heartfelt words about the friendship between the two brotherly Slavic nations, Poland and the USSR."

Wanda Hoppe's husband got the keys to house number 5a/3. He was a technician and a construction supervisor. The house had fifty-three square meters. The Hoppes had two children.

"It smelled of wood and resin," reminisced Wanda Hoppe. "Planks smooth as a breadboard, white, spick-and-span. A wooden ceiling, a brick oven, and a charcoal burner. There was no bathroom, just a toilet. My mother-in-law lived on Złota Street. I remember leaving our beautiful neighborhood and walking on horrible debris just to get there. Nevertheless, people would sometimes say that we lived in higher quality shacks."

"It was a paradise," said Marian Marzyński. "In Warsaw people were fighting for every square meter, but we lived like royalty, in a park."

"Electricity, water, and a sewage system. In 1945, here was the biggest luxury in Warsaw," said Stefan Szczerbiński, the son of Barbara, a war widow and an accountant in the WRO. They and four members of their immediate family moved into their house. "I remember that on the first day the main door was boarded up, probably as a sign that it was a fresh house. We had to pull the planks down and then we could move in."

The neighborhood got its first bathhouse, built in the pavilion of the former hospital's morgue. The bath attendants made sure everything was spotlessly clean. You could take a shower for a few zlotys. A hot bath in a tub was a bit more expensive. The house next to the Hoppes' was occupied by the family of Tadeusz and Jadwiga Gorczyński, botanists. The WRO hired them to inventory green spaces in Warsaw. They lived in a fifty-four-square-meter house with ten children and a maid. Ewa Długosz, the Gorczyńskis' daughter recalled: "Once a week, with towels and soap, we walked in single file to the local bathhouse."

It was not possible to remove all the debris from the area; therefore, the houses stood on leveled rubble, and they were not fenced. Nobody had been officially allocated a backyard. So people demarcated areas around their residences at their own discretion. In order to plant anything, they had to remove crushed bricks and stones.

"My parents removed the debris and brought soil. Otherwise, nothing would grow. Then, they started to import fruit trees for the entire area, and finally, they designed a whole infrastructure of greenery here," said Ewa Długosz.

The temporary housing development in Górny Ujazdów, later called Jazdów, would survive seventy years. Dolny Jazdów and the Wawelska housing development vanished earlier. Some houses were demolished, and others were purchased, disassembled, and shipped to summer resorts.

Marian Marzyński got married and moved to a different house in the neighborhood. After 1968, with his parents, wife, and son, like many other Jews, he emigrated from Poland. His house was handed over to someone else. His parents' house would end up a dacha on the Zegrze Reservoir.

When the city authorities decided to demolish the remaining buildings during the second decade of the twenty-first century the residents fought to stay in these Finnish houses presented by Joseph Stalin to Warsaw in 1945.

WHAT SHALL WE PLAY?

In May 1945 Warsaw had almost 64,000 children below the age of sixteen. Andrzej Pstrokoński had been attending school since February. For the moment, classes took place in a private apartment at Three Crosses Square.

There were three rows of school desks in one room and each grade occupied one row. After their classes, they played. Warsaw boys mainly played war.

Marian Marzyński said, "We kids found one another. We had our own unit. We rolled dry leaves, twisted them, and used them as cigarettes because we couldn't afford real ones. And since we were soldiers, we had to find weapons."

Andrzej Pstrokoński recalled, "It wasn't difficult. Sometimes a gun was lying right on the street. You just had to pick it up. Later, we discovered some Home Army cache full of weapons. Where should we hide them? I snatched the key to our basement."

Marzyński added, "Franio Mleczko from the neighboring quarter was a colonel's son and had access to his father's gun. Loaded! He showed us how to shoot at trees. Then, at the head of our unit, he was storming the ruins of Ujazdów Castle. The castle had housed a hospital until the end of the war. Shooting was wonderful. In the debris we found containers with aborted fetuses. We gunned them all down."

Pstrokoński said, "Two boys from our school wanted to duel. Both of them died. We were throwing grenades into the Czerniakowskie Lake to catch fish. One boy lost his arm because he was juggling grenades for fun."

In the ruined houses children found mines and projectiles missed by the sappers. The newspapers were filled with obituaries of youngsters who had died tragic deaths. In February 1945 Jerzy Putrament noted: "The Old Town Square . . . There are three or five unexploded bombs in the square. Rusty, bulky, and large. They are just waiting for some enterprising twelve-year-old to fiddle with them, and thereby choose this rapid means of transportation to the other world."

A reader who was disturbed by teens playing with unexploded ordnance sent a letter to *Życie Warszawy* signed "Dr. M. S." "The fearful passersby avoid these kids because an explosion can happen anytime, and the shattering shards . . . can easily cause serious bodily harm." This reader believed that these children were war orphans, deprived of any care. The only way to help them was to send them to houses of correction, where "they would be taken care of, and they could study." Those fit to work could be directed to rubble removal.

Playing war was not the only thing that occupied the boys of Warsaw. Andrzej Pstrokoński and his friends occasionally ran to Old Town Square where the famous pigeon lady lived. "This old woman, she lived somewhere

Figure 6.9. The Pigeon Lady of Warsaw. The poster behind her says: "I kindly ask for a gracious offering for the traditional pigeons of the Old Town." PAP

in the basement, and when she went out, the birds would fly to her. We were waiting, because the sight was incredible."

In the castle ruins Marian Marzyński's group spied on some couples in love. "With such a shortage of apartments and vacant rooms it was the ideal place for people eager for sex. We would go there every day to watch them. We waited until the gentleman finished and pulled up his pants, and then we began to spook them, we let them know we had seen them. Our best achievement was to roll a sewage pipe along in which some couple were weaving their nest. I don't remember how it ended."

"WARSAW LOOKS INTO THE FUTURE"

Przekrój (June 1945): "One should not expect that Hoża Street will be rebuilt in June, Wilcza in July, and Grzybowski Square in August. It will happen neither this year, nor in two years. In the first year of reconstruction practically nothing will happen. That means, nothing spectacular, visible from the outside. . . . After a year the work will be going full swing. In ten years Warsaw will become the most modern 'urban agglomeration,' a capital of two million people envied by the entire world. . . . The old Center will be replaced by a new 'directorial' neighborhood. Government buildings, embassies, diplomatic missions, banks, commercial centers, and administrative headquarters. Where the Wola neighborhood used to be, 'The Western Provisioning District' will stand. Around it will be three residential quarters—Żoliborz, Saska Kępa, and Mokotów. In these five parts of the city only 700,000 people will be living. The other 1,300,000 will find accommodations in more distant residential districts, from Góra Kalwaria to Modlin. These neighborhoods will be connected by excellent transportation routes. . . . Each house and each bloc of residential buildings will be surrounded by green space. The whole city will be one extensive garden city with utterly 'dispersed' development. . . . The entire city will be electrified, 100 percent. What is more, even living spaces and kitchens will have electric heating. . . . These projects are very modern, but because of tradition, the decision was made to faithfully rebuild some historic landmarks of old Warsaw. . . . This conception, despite opposing viewpoints, may no longer be questioned.

"That is how Warsaw will look."

JULY 1945

Have you been to "Telimena" for the best ice-cream, torte, and coffee? Krakow, 39 Dietl Street. This establishment is operated by former Ravensbrück prisoners.

—*Dziennik Polski*, Krakow, July 1, 1945

• • • • • • • • • • • • • •

I apologize to Mrs. Maria Białkowska, office worker at the Gdynia Municipal Administration, for hurting her feelings unintentionally by talking about her in a derogatory way and questioning her Polish nationality. M. Błażejczyk, Gdynia, 3 Indyjska Street.

—*Dziennik Bałtycki*, July 4, 1945

• • • • • • • • • • • • • •

Because women have been raped, the Minister of Justice has authorized the Polish Red Cross [PRC] to perform medical procedures. Victims may come forward to the PRC. It has the authority to allow a procedure, if appropriate requirements are met.

—*Dziennik Bałtycki*, July 6, 1945

• • • • • • • • • • • • • •

LOT Polish Airlines is seeking young women (no older than 28), with at least 6 years of gymnasium education, fluent in at least one foreign language (excluding German), and familiar with hotel services. Graduates of the Hotel School in Krakow highly preferred.

—*Życie Warszawy*, July 10, 1945

• • • • • • • • • • • • • •

Warning. Fake products packed in jars stolen from us have appeared on the market. We declare that the original products bear our signatures on the labels. Those guilty of counterfeiting will be prosecuted. Cosmetic Laboratory of Dr. Zofia Restkowska and Dr. Feliks Restkowski.

—*Życie Warszawy*, July 11, 1945

• • • • • • • • • • • • • •

Custom-made clogs manufactured speedily by "Vogue," Krakow, 24 Poselska Street.

—*Dziennik Polski*, Krakow, 12 July 1945

• • • • • • • • • • • • • •

Typist needed urgently. Polish and Russian a must. Apply at Governing Board for Military Construction, WP Ursus, 1 Piłsudski Street.

—*Życie Warszawy*, July 14, 1945

• • • • • • • • • • • • • •

We will sell for almost nothing, for only 10% of their prewar value, 4 summer houses next to the Electric Commuter Railway. Also a few villas, several houses, and some lots in Warsaw and in summer resorts. Pacek—Central Office, 2 Żurawia Street.

—*Życie Warszawy*, July 18, 1945

• • • • • • • • • • • • • •

I will buy prominent artists' paintings that were damaged by wartime events. Stanisław Dybowski, 21 Marszałkowska Street, the shop.

—*Życie Warszawy*, July 18, 1945

• • • • • • • • • • • • • •

Little Hell, a romantic establishment. Best drinks, most delicious appetizers, and something else. Where, what, and how? Soon!

—*Życie Warszawy*, July 18, 1945

• • • • • • • • • • • • • •

A Warsaw woman, expelled and completely robbed, whose house burned down, pleads for clothing assistance: dresses, underwear, stockings, and shoes. Otherwise, she cannot get a job. Please donate these items at the Piasek Company, Krakow, 8 Gołębia Street.
—*Dziennik Polski*, Krakow, July 19, 1945

• • • • • • • • • • • • • • • • •

I will give an infant girl to a good family. Information: Krakow, 9 Szlak Street, midwife.
—*Dziennik Polski*, Krakow, July 19, 1945

• • • • • • • • • • • • • • • • •

Two Russian medals "For Military Service" have been lost. If found, please send to Major Gubarev, Piastów near Warsaw, 28 Bohaterów Wolności Street. 1,000 zlotys reward.
—*Dziennik Bałtycki*, July 22, 1945

• • • • • • • • • • • • • • • • •

Mr. Thief is kindly requested to return the following documents: 2 ID cards and a Cashier's ID for Wł. Grzybowska and Władysław Grzybowski, husband and son's photos, letter of authorization, and Proof of Fire Loss. Keep the money. Discretion guaranteed. Return this to the narrow-gauge railway station, Paderewski Square.
—*Dziennik Bałtycki*, July 22, 1945

• • • • • • • • • • • • • • • • •

To the prisoners of Pawiak and those coming back from camps in Germany. If you know anything about Witold Ludkiewicz, student at the Rey Gymnasium, born July 2, 1926, residing in Warsaw, 6 Mazowiecka Street, and about his friends, arrested on February 2, 1944, after the assassination of Kutschera, please contact Władysław Ludkiewicz, Kielce, 47 Sienkiewicz Street.
—*Życie Warszawy*, July 24, 1945

• • • • • • • • • • • • • • • • •

Muslim General Meeting will take place on July 29, 1945, in the community's building at 50 Mokotowska Street. Agenda: (1) Introduction; (2) Selection of Presidium; (3) Selection of Imam and his deputy; (4) Selection of Community Board; (5) Suggestions. All Muslims are obliged to appear.
—*Życie Warszawy*, July 26, 1945

• • • • • • • • • • • • • • • • •

At the last session of the Municipal National Council in Sopot it was decided to turn one of the villas into a resort hotel for the members of the Polish Committee of National Liberation. In addition, the Sopot Communal Savings Bank was created, and 3 streets were named after President Bierut, Prime Minister Osóbka-Morawski, and Marshal Żymierski.
—*Dziennik Bałtycki*, July 27, 1945

• • • • • • • • • • • • • • • • •

Tęcza Movie Theater, Żoliborz, 4 Suzin Street. Premiere! Opening! Superb Soviet musical comedy *Anton Ivanovich Is Angry*.
—*Życie Warszawy*, July 27, 1945

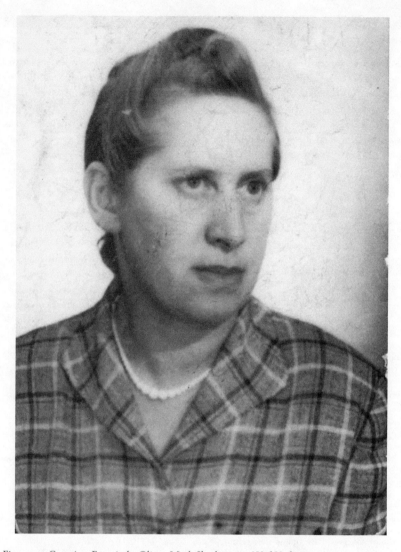

Figure 7.1. Caregiver Franciszka Oliwa. Mark Shreberman / Yad Vashem

I'm Not a Shiksa, I'm a Jew

Never ever did they use the word *orphanage*. It was home.

FRANCISZKA

A strange group. Ten children in rags and a Soviet soldier. He holds their hands. They wander in the streets of Otwock, bewildered.

A woman walks on Prus Street. She is thirty-one and her face isn't unattractive, but she looks as if she were drawn with a thick crayon by a three-year-old. Her forehead is too high, her nose and ears too large, her lips too full. She limps a bit in her left leg, a polio souvenir. And she has lost the use of her left hand. But you can't see this because she has put her gloveless hands into the pockets of her shabby coat. Her name is Franciszka Oliwa. The soldier approaches her, pointing at his group.

"These are Jewish children, homeless," he says. "They've been hanging around the soldiers stationed in Otwock, without purpose. They're a nuisance to us. Now you take care of them."

Franciszka protests, "But I don't have any home, either."

The soldier points at random at a villa, number 11. "You'll live here." And he walks away.

During the first night Franciszka and the children sleep on the floor. This building, the prewar guesthouse Zachęta, has survived, but in poor condition. There is no glass in the windows, no water in the faucets, and patches of plaster flake off the walls. It is cold and everyone is hungry. In the house the children look for hideouts and conceal themselves in the nooks. In the morning residents of neighboring houses bring them bread and hot tea.

"I've realized that these children have no place to go, and that they will stay with me. That I am the only person who must protect them, help them, and take care of them," Franciszka Oliwa will write after many years.

It is the end of January 1945.

What a pity that everything I have written above is not true.

Except for three details: the woman, the children, and the guesthouse Zachęta in Otwock. They are real.

Everything else was made up by Franciszka Oliwa, a caregiver for the intermediate age group at the House of the Jewish Child in Otwock.

I know almost nothing about her. The children from her group called her "Miss Oliwa." Never "Mom," like the younger children there called their caregivers. She was not too warmhearted, not too tender, although many years later she would be writing about the cuddles and kisses with which she used to wake up her children on Sunday mornings. They wouldn't be able to recall this. But they would remember that she was kind and devoted to them. She loved them very much. She would write about this in her memoirs.

She never had children on her own. She was a communist, Jewish, anti-Zionist, and had lived in Otwock before the war. Was she educated? I don't know this, either. During the liquidation of the Otwock ghetto in August 1944, she escaped to the Aryan side and worked as a maid at 53 Wilcza Street in Warsaw. After the failure of the Warsaw Uprising she escaped from the transport heading to the labor camp. Until the end of the war she was hidden in Kielce by Joanna and Rudolf Nowak. They treated her like a member of their own family. They never accepted any money for helping her. In 1991 they were awarded the medal for the Righteous Among the Nations.

In January 1945 she left Kielce and returned to Warsaw. "The basement in which I had buried my modest possessions was plundered." She crossed

Figure 7.2. Franciszka Oliwa (second row, in the middle) with her co-workers and children. Yad Vashem

the pontoon bridge over the frozen Vistula and made her way to Otwock. She didn't find any relatives.

I am not supposed to believe that in Otwock she met a group of children who were with a Soviet soldier. The former residents of the Otwock children's home I spoke to, Aviva, Janusz, Irka, Linka, Włodek, Judyta, Israel, and Ludwik told me not to. Franciszka was not its founder, nor was she its first director, as she claimed after many years had gone by.

However, nobody knows exactly how and when the children moved into the villa Zachęta. Not even the former residents themselves, or the Jewish Historical Institute (JHI), or Yad Vashem. Who assigned this guesthouse, the former property of Rywka Flunt-Zylberbaum, to them? It is known that the first director of this children's home was Michał Kokoszko, a pediatrician from Otwock, who had been hiding during the occupation under the name Kosowski. He probably had known Franciszka before. Maybe it was he who offered her a job? Franciszka worked in the home from the very beginning. But later she erased Doctor Kokoszko from her memory.

When she left the home in 1948, she took with her some documents, photographs, and the Memory Book, in which the children had written about their war experience. Later, she made a gift of everything to the Jewish Historical Institute.

"It is to her credit that she took these materials, because nobody else would have done this," Luba Bielicka-Blum, former director of the Otwock children's home and Kokoszko's successor, would write after years had passed.

To the souvenirs from the home Miss Oliwa added her own recollections that she would write down later. Not everything in them was untrue.

IRKA

Irka was sure that everything had begun earlier, in the fall of 1944. She was twelve then and weighed at most 30 kilos. Later, in the children's home, at the table for starvelings, she would be receiving an extra portion of cream and a hard-boiled egg.

She remembered very well opening some door halfway and hearing two men speaking in Yiddish. One of them noticed the girl and told the other, "Go and see what this shiksa wants here." Irka understood some Yiddish, so she burst into tears and said in Polish, "I'm not a shiksa, I'm a Jew." This man invited her inside. His name was Olek Awol and he was from Warsaw. He had two daughters and a second wife. Before the war he had been a diamond merchant.

After the war he was active in the Central Committee of Polish Jews (CCPJ), directly supervised by Edward Osóbka-Morawski, chairman of the Polish Committee of National Liberation. The CCPJ was founded in November 1944. It had been providing assistance to all Jews who survived the Holocaust and had a branch office in Otwock.

"My name is Irka Młotek. I have two brothers, Janek and Danek," said the little girl and continued her story. Before the war they had lived in Otwock at 16 Racławicka Street. In August 1942, when the Germans started to liquidate the Otwock ghetto, they, their mother, Lea, and Grandma Borucka hid under the roof of their veranda, in a special hideout prepared earlier by their father, Shulim.

Through the cracks in the wooden planks they were watching Poles plundering the deserted ghetto and carrying away porcelain figurines, silver utensils, and a wall clock from their house. Their mother was crying, but their father was consoling her. If they survived, they would buy new ones. If they didn't, they wouldn't need these things.

After a few days they ran toward a village where all the farmers knew their father and liked him. Before the war, he used to buy fruit from them. He would sit with them at the table and paid them fairly. They called him "Our Shulimek."

Later, many a farmer would shed a tear when they heard that in the fall of 1943 he had been killed by Poles. They dragged him from the house of a woman he knew and told him, "You will go to the woods with us to fight the Germans." Later they shot him.

One day, grandmother walked toward her native village and nobody ever saw her again.

Nobody had heard from their mother since September 1942, when she crossed over to the ghetto in the village of Sobienie-Jeziory near Otwock in order to say good-bye to her family there. The milkman, paid by her husband, waited for her outside, but precisely on that day the Germans were liquidating the ghetto.

Only Irka and her brothers survived the war. They were hidden, separately, by farmers from the villages of Piotrowice, Kosumce, and Kępa Nadbrzeska. They worked as farmhands and concealed themselves from strangers. When in July 1944 Otwock was liberated, they stayed with the farm owners. Because where could they go?

On that day Irka and the farmer's wife came to the Otwock market. Just as they were displaying potatoes and carrots for sale, the Germans started shelling from the other side of the Vistula, which they still held. People scattered, but Irka ran to see if her family house was still standing. It was. With someone else's name on the mailbox. She was afraid to knock. She asked a passerby whose house it was now. "Did you live here?" he asked. She nodded her head. He understood immediately. "I can't help you, but I know that on Warszawska Street, near the turn to Kościelna, there is a Jewish Committee. Those who have survived are looking for one another there."

She raced there. She opened some door halfway. She heard two men speaking in Yiddish.

"There will be a children's home in Otwock, soon," said Olek Awol to Irka Młotek.

"Sir, I am strong and able to work on a farm for the rest of my life. Both my brothers are weak and the older is always sick. I visit them sometimes, take off their shirts, and pick off the lice. I cook carrots and potatoes for them in a pot I got from a farmer's wife. But they won't last much longer. I'd very much like them to come to this home. If there are any limits, I will give up my place," responded twelve-year-old Irka.

"When the home is founded, Jewish children without parents will have priority," said Awol. "Listen, I have two daughters. Dana is your age. Soon, I will take her from the Poles, from the hideout. I live in Otwock. Stay with me and wait for Dana. Her mother was killed in the ghetto. It will be easier for her with you. We plan to go to America. We will take you with us."

"I can't do it now, sir. Until the children's home is set up, I will stay in the countryside, close to my brothers. I am staying with good people. But on the day you place Janek and Danek in that home, I will come live with you. And I'll stay until you leave for America. I promise," said Irka.

The Młotek brothers moved into the Otwock children's home in March 1945. Other children were already there.

Soon, Irka Młotek and the Awol family would move to Katowice. She would go to school. When in late fall 1945 Olek Awol and his family left for Germany, and then to America, Irka went back to Otwock and became a resident of the home.

Olek would be sending her pictures from overseas.

SRULEK

He didn't want to be Srulek. After a few weeks he wanted to be called Israel.

Franciszka Oliwa wrote about him: "The war experience turned him into a tough grownup. He was of medium height. His face was concentrated, serious, resolute, and concerned. It was difficult to understand his psyche. His heart was filled with sorrow and pain."

Franciszka really loved only him. That was how the other children would remember it. She called him "sonny." When he grew up, she kept sending preserves to him in Israel. She wrote a newspaper article about him and she devoted eleven pages of her memoir to him, more than to any of the other children.

Israel Nojmarek's sister, Bronka, told Franciszka about his life during the occupation.

In October 1942 they and their mother escaped from the ghetto in Legionowo during its liquidation. In pursuit, the Germans shot their mother. Bronka hid in the forest and Israel in a doghouse on one of the farms. He slept with the dog and shared a bowl with him. The farmer knew about the Jewish boy and always left more food by the doghouse. Israel also begged in the villages. Occasionally, he would meet his sister in the woods. She was hiding in deserted houses, wells, and in garbage dumps. Sometimes people offered her food. Israel didn't have shoes, so he got frostbite on his feet. They were affected by gangrene and he lost most of his toes. He couldn't walk. Until the end of the war he had to crawl.

As soon as the Germans withdrew, people from the CCPJ moved into the areas occupied by the Soviet army and they looked for Jewish children who were in hiding or were wandering around, who had been taken in or adopted. From the Council to Aid Jews (Żegota), they received addresses of Poles who had been hiding Jewish children. People from the committee visited convents, knocked at doors, and looked around towns and villages. They searched basements, attics, and tombs. They pulled children from closets, sheds, and coal containers.

Three million Jews had lived in Poland before the war. According to various estimates, 30,000–150,000 survived the war, including some 5,000 children and teenagers. Sooner or later all the children came under the committee's care, and 1,600 of them ended up in one of the nine Jewish children's homes in the country.

Thanks to the CCPJ, at the beginning of March 1945 Israel and Bronka arrived in Otwock. Israel was nine years old.

WŁODEK

Before the war Helena Kazimiera Sztykgold had a husband, servants, and an apartment building in Warsaw. In February 1945 she had a nine-year-old son, Włodek, a daughter, Wanda, and torn shoes. At the end of the war, she was surviving by hiding in Otwock with her daughter. There, at the end of February 1945 and thanks to her friendship with Felicja Winawerowa, she was hired at the Jewish home. She became a hygienist. She had no credentials whatsoever.

Winawerowa had been the prewar proprietor of one of the guesthouses in Otwock. She was a real beauty and a lady. Artist Henryk Kuna, in love, had sculpted a bust of her. In the children's home she was "a supervisor for health and administration."

Helena Sztykgold's son was somewhere in Żyrardów, in a house in the suburbs. His mother didn't know that for the last half year he had been hidden in a shed by Poles. His only companion had been a billy goat. When she traveled to him by handcar and they saw each other, Włodek was swollen and his body covered with sores. His protectors coated them with onion, using the only one they had. His mother appreciated their gesture since they could simply have eaten it. But she went back to Otwock without her son. The Poles demanded money for returning Włodek but she didn't have it. At the beginning of March, she received cash from a Jewish activist she knew. Soon after, hygienist Sztykgold introduced her son to the Otwock children's home.

It was evening. Fearful Włodek could see dark figures in blankets.

JUDYTA

At the beginning of March 1945 Judyta Finkiel was enrolled in the home by her mother. Many Jewish mothers wanted to send their daughters and sons there.

For a bit.

While they were poor and had no place to live.

While they couldn't afford anything.

They would return for the children as soon as they were not afraid to love them anymore.

In 1943 Judyta and her mother walked out of the Warsaw ghetto to the Aryan side. They survived the war with Polish papers. In 1945 the girl was eight years old and she didn't know who she was.

Not so long ago she had been told she was Polish. She had learned how to cross herself. Touch your forehead, chest, left shoulder, right shoulder, with your right hand. She knew her prayers and she knew Mary. She knew that Jews killed Jesus.

All of a sudden Judyta was told that she was Jewish after all.

LINKA

Eda Szternes met Andzia Sztarkman in Targówek. It was the end of February 1945, at the latest the beginning of March. The women knew each other from the ghetto. In the building where the Sztarkmans used to live,

Eda was running a secret center for a few children. She was teaching them about things that, according to the Germans, were no longer useful for Jews. About Eskimos, for example, or about Japan. One of her pupils was Linka, born in 1933, Andzia's daughter. In the future Linka would marry her friend from the children's home, Władek Kornblum.

We can imagine a conversation between Eda and Andzia.

"You're alive?" asked Eda.

"Yes, we are. But the rest of my family is dead."

"What are you up to, Andzia Sztarkman?"

"I have no education, so I stand in lines and buy pepper. I divide it into portions and sell it in smaller packages."

"Andzia, why don't you send your daughter to the Jewish home? One has just been set up in Otwock. I'm on the staff there. Please, come to the Jewish Committee at Targowa Street and enroll her."

On March 5 or 8, Linka Sztarkman climbed on a truck's cargo bed. Her mother waved good-bye to her. She promised to visit her in Otwock every Sunday.

Linka was a great-granddaughter, in the seventh generation, of Dawid, zaddik of Lelov. In September 1939, during the bombing of Warsaw, all pious Jews from the neighborhood wanted to stay with her and her mother in the same basement at Grzybowska Street. They believed the holy zaddik would save his relatives.

Besides Linka there were sixteen other children on the truck, and Eda. The truck set off. The guardian began a song. In Yiddish and loud. Linka's Polish was impeccable. She hadn't known Yiddish but she picked up some in the ghetto. After escaping from the ghetto she and her mother hid in various apartments. In the last months before the liberation they were living in a basement in the Warsaw suburbs with thirteen other Jews. Linka was the only one with "the right looks." She was the only one who could go out without arousing suspicion to get food, pour out the waste, or bring a doctor to a woman suffering from dysentery. The lives of all of them depended on the flawless accent and self-confidence of an eleven-year-old.

And now, she was traveling toward Otwock at twilight, singing Jewish songs aloud.

They arrived. The building at 11 Prus Street, its white walls, modernist

Figure 7.3. The entrance of the Jewish Children's Home in Otwock. Mark Shreberman / Yad Vashem

plateglass windows, balcony supported by simple columns, and large surrounding garden were not visible anymore. It was dark, almost night. They were welcomed by several children. Among the adults there were Doctor Kokoszko, Franciszka Oliwa, the cook Katarzyna Raguzowa, called by others Odesowa, and the hygienist Helena Sztykgold.

The children gave up their clothing. It would be burned out of fear of contagious diseases. It was the hygienist's idea. The Jewish Committee had not yet delivered any change of clothes. So all the children got military blankets and wrapped themselves in them. Their heads were shaved, without any inspection of whether they had lice, so nobody would stand out.

Linka had lice and although she felt sorry about her short braids, she didn't protest.

For dinner they got bread dipped in fat. In the children's home, they called it stearine. It was a gift from the army. The cook melted the stearine on the pan and dipped bread in it. The solidified fat looked like wax. Onions, if available, could be fried in the stearine. What a treat!

Figure 7.4. A meal. Otwock, 1947. Aviva Blum/Yad Vashem

HOME

Soon, in a few months, the floors there would shine from morning to evening. The walls would be painted.

Dinner would consist of three dishes and dessert. Meat would be served twice a week, including lungs, loved by so many.

There would be plenty of bread and cheese.

Flowers would bloom in the garden and a beehive would be constructed.

Felicja Winawerowa would get hold of covers for the children's beds.

The girls would be wearing ribbons in their hair.

Each child would eventually receive a new American briefcase of checkered canvas.

But not yet. It was April 1945 and the children's home in Otwock was visited by health and education inspectors sent by the Jewish Committee.

The war was still going on, and getting underwear for children or potatoes for dinner bordered on the miraculous. But Doctor M. Simchowiczowa and her companion K. Fuswerk, who didn't provide their first names in the report, turned up their noses as if they were expecting a hundred-year-old finishing school for rich girls.

Well, the truth is the children's health was not the best. Nine children had flu, one suffered from bone tuberculosis, two had pleural effusion, and seven were isolated because they had been in contact with typhus. Fortunately, all the other children were relatively healthy and cheerful. As soon as a Roentgen apparatus was available, all of them would be x-rayed.

On the other hand, the hygienic conditions of the children and the space were not satisfactory. There was a shortage of bedsheets, underwear, diapers— there were five diapers for four babies—handkerchiefs, and towels. Children going to school wore their friends' clothes. Thirty-six children didn't have proper footwear. There was not enough furniture, so during meals some residents had to kneel. There were no toys, writing accessories, or gym shoes.

The furniture was covered with dust, the toilets stank, and the bedrooms were messy. Despite washing every day and baths twice a week, some children still had lice.

The room for nine children, none older than three, was deplorable. They lay in large beds without any side support, covered with blankets. They were under the care of a single person who fed them, washed them, changed their diapers, cooked for them, washed their clothes, played with them, and watched them at night. The beds were too close to one another, "which is absolutely impermissible because it may lead to contagion or sexual deviation, etc.," noted the inspectors. The lack of spittoons and chamber pots was clearly visible.

Older children slept, sometimes in twos, on military cots made of canvas stretched on wooden frames. Paper bags filled with hay served as their mattresses.

The kitchen was approved by the inspectors. It was very clean, and the meals were tasty, regular, and nutritious.

The primary conclusion of the report recommended the immediate hiring of a genuine director for the children's home. Perhaps Doctor Kokoszko was a fine pediatrician, but as it turned out, he was not the best administrator.

THE MEMORY BOOK

Every night one of the girls woke up, screaming, "Don't kill my mom! Don't kill my dad!" Others cried in their sleep. Many wet their beds. They sucked their fingers. Bit their nails. They looked for hideouts under the beds. They stored bread under the pillows.

Later on Franciszka Oliwa would write: "As soon as a child arrived, the staff tried to write up his or her wartime experience." The CCPJ also recommended recording the children's accounts. In the future they would be used as evidence against the Nazis.

But some things were never written down. Stories of molested girls, raped by their guardians or by random men, stayed inside the head.

"The matron had to repeatedly ask one girl who had been hiding in the countryside, not to tell anyone what the peasants had done to her in an attic. Because young, well-mannered ladies don't talk about such things in society," Marek Edelman, a friend of the director Luba Bielicka-Blum, would recall in the future.

All the girls underwent gynecological checkups, so none of them was stigmatized. Venereal diseases were not uncommon.

Little children's memories were written down by the staff, but the notebooks would be lost. Older children wrote entries in the Memory Book on their own. Those who couldn't write dictated to their friends or confided to their caregivers.

"The Memory Book written by the older residents is the original document." Franciszka Oliwa passed this information to the Jewish Historical Institute.

This was not fully true. Of the twenty-five children's recollections, Franciszka would rewrite a few, in her characteristic flowery style.

She would make up others. Which?

Each child, who came to Otwock, got a number. Zula Goldminc had number 1. She was brought to the home by her older, nineteen-year-old brother. Zulejka was seven years old. She had red hair and freckles. According to her brother, her father hid Zula and her mother in some basement in the ghetto. He left them food and water, and walled up the entrance. He went to fight in the Ghetto Uprising and was killed. Zula's brother knew where she was hiding with her mother. He told his friends. When they broke through the wall, they found the girl sitting by her long-dead mother.

In the home, initially fearful Zula was elected president of the intermediate group. She was well-liked, especially by the younger children. She took care of them, and at the same time she kept order among the intermediates.

Out of longing she wrote: "A child without a mother is very unhappy. So, all of you who have mothers, respect them and love them!"

Found by a female relative, she left the Otwock children's home and died of meningitis on a ship to Palestine.

The former residents remembered pleasant, red-haired Zula.

But they recommended not believing the story about the mother and daughter walled in the basement.

Bobi should have been in the group for toddlers. He was only five years old. But he was in the intermediate group because he didn't like little children. He often cried. His mother, who brought him to Otwock, said that during the liquidation of the Warsaw ghetto she had escaped with her husband and one-year-old son to the Aryan side. A female friend took the boy under her care. But her neighbors became suspicious that she was hiding a Jew. So she left Bobi at the door of an apartment where a sect was performing some secret prayers. Its members believed "in a prophecy that a child will appear and save them," noted Franciszka. From that moment until the end of the occupation, Bobi, dressed in liturgical robes, was treated as this deity.

Well-fed, groomed, fussy, and opinionated, he didn't want to live with his mother after the liberation. He didn't like the home, either. The only person he was fond of was Srul.

I wrote to Israel Nojmarek, formerly Srul: "Is it possible that during the occupation Bobi could have been a deity in a sect?"

He replied, "The answer is no."

How did it happen that a seven-year-old German child called Gertruda ended up in a Jewish children's home? She was sent by the CCPJ. Her mother was a maid in a Polish household that had no place for her daughter.

"It was a careless and insensitive decision that put me in an uncomfortable situation. I knew how Jewish children, whose fate had been to suffer so much cruelty from Germans, would react," Franciszka Oliwa would recall in the future.

Nobody liked Gertruda. Nobody talked to her. Her name was not mentioned. She didn't know Polish, so she didn't understand the question, "How many Jews were killed by your father?" The staff's explanations that children were not responsible for the acts of their parents were useless.

"One day a puppet troupe called Baj came to the home. The lead part was played by a puppet resembling Gertruda. She had a long face and a prominent pointy nose. Her name was Petronela. . . . After the show the children surrounded Gertruda and told her that from now on she would be called Petronela. And they started playing with her," Franciszka wrote. "Animosity toward the girl was gone."

Soon after Gertruda-Petronela and her mother left for Germany.

None of my interlocutors remembered her. A German girl in the Jewish children's home? That was a whopper, Miss Oliwa.

During the war Karol Bal and his parents escaped from Zamość, where he was born in 1934, to Warsaw, and then to the Soviet Union. His father joined the army, his mother died in the Minsk ghetto, and Karol joined the partisans, some of whom were his parents' friends. In the Memory Book he wrote: "I spent a year and seven months with the partisans. I was a liaison, I took care of the farm, I cleaned weapons, sometimes I tended cows. . . . Occasionally, there were skirmishes with the Germans."

There were a thousand people in Karol's unit, including five hundred children. All the partisans were Jewish. After the war the boy was taken to a Soviet orphanage, where he was found by his father. They went back to Poland and Karol ended up in Otwock.

I didn't have to verify if Franciszka Oliwa invented this little partisan. In April 1947, Karol Bal, age thirteen, was decorated with the Partisan's Cross, the Medal for Freedom and Victory, and the Grunwald Badge for "his guard duty and passing important material to the intelligence service."

This information was published in the Bulletin of the Jewish Press Agency.

WIESIA

She longed for the company of other children so much, that she left her mother, Luba Bielicka-Blum, the new director of the Jewish children's home in Otwock, even though they had good living conditions.

Wiesia Blum was thirteen years old and she preferred to live in a four-person room in the Otwock home. She liked the discipline, getting up early, exercises, breakfasts in a common room, clothes with embroidered numbers, and baths in one of the two tubs that used to be a luxurious symbol of the Zachęta guesthouse. On the very first day Wiesia made friends for life.

Before the war her mother had been deputy director of the Nursing

School at the Jewish Hospital in Warsaw. Thanks to her efforts, the school was moved to the Warsaw ghetto and was the only educational institution allowed by the Germans. Wiesia's father, Abrasza Blum, was one of the leaders of the Bund, a member of the command of the Jewish Fighting Organization, and a participant in the Ghetto Uprising. He escaped through the sewers. The caretaker of the house in which he was hiding denounced him to the Gestapo. Blum escaped through the window, but a rope made of bedsheets untied itself while he was at the third-floor level. He fell and broke both legs. He was murdered at Gestapo headquarters on Szuch Avenue.

Wiesia, her mother, and brother Aleksander, younger by four years, escaped from the ghetto. They obtained false papers. Wiesia's brother was taken by the Borkowski family in Warsaw. She and her mother went into the Holy Cross Mountains, to the village of Grzegorzewice. Until the end of the war her mother took care of two handicapped children at the manor of the Rauszer family.

Only for a little while did Wiesia's brother want to live with his mother in a small house she rented. Soon, he, too, would move to the children's home.

It was June 1945.

LUBA

For the little ones, called *deborzątka* after their caregiver Debora Adler, a former prisoner in Auschwitz, she was Mama Luba. Among the older children she evoked respect. And love, too.

"The affection I have for you fills me with inexpressible sweetness. It is love combined with enormous and deep appreciation." In the archives of the Jewish Historical Institute I found an anonymous letter to the director written in a child's hand.

Surely, she loved them like her own children. Otherwise, why would she use her Wiesia's date of birth for those who didn't know when they were born? All of them were treated equally. They were not insulted or belittled. Her daughter was not favored. Luba kept her distance.

The prominent journalist Hanna Krall, a former resident of the Otwock home, would remember her, "Down to earth. Very energetic. In flat shoes. Straight hair. Only washed, never styled by hairdresser. No makeup. Always in white blouse. Short nails. Like a veteran Girl Scout or nurse, although in the children's home she wasn't that old."

In June 1945 Luba Bielicka-Blum was only forty.

Figure 7.5. Director Luba Bielicka-Blum with her husband Abrasza Blum on their wedding day.
Aviva Blum Wachs/Yad Vashem

Thanks to Dawid Guzik, the prewar director of the Polish Section of the Jewish Joint Distribution Committee, parcels and money from American Jews were coming for Polish Jews. They were distributed by the CCPJ. Luba Bielicka-Blum often went to Warsaw, to the committee. For her children she was able to get cash, American dresses, 100 men's outfits, shoes, 83 kilograms of chocolate, blankets from the United Nations Relief and Rehabilitation Administration, athletic equipment, a piano, blank canvases, notebooks, vegetables for winter, 27 tables, 28 wardrobes, 6 office desks, 15 school desks, 203 chairs, 21 stools, 5 multishelf stands for small objects, 200 iron beds, 5 deck chairs, 40 shelves, and 1 ping-pong table.

The director hired someone to take charge of supplies, also an accountant, cleaning ladies, seamstresses, washerwomen, kitchen aids, nurses, and hygienists.

In total, about 200 people would be living in the former guesthouse Zachęta, including 130–150 students. The number of children kept changing. Some of the staff were their parents or relatives.

Calm and competent under any conditions. Luba Bielicka-Blum never fell apart. She wanted to pass this faculty to her pupils. She believed that order, principles, and impeccable manners might save anyone at some critical moment.

"In the ghetto she made sure that all nurses had sparkling clean and starched caps. In the children's home she reminded the children that they should respond politely and in full sentences," Marek Edelman remembered after many years.

His wife, Alina Margolis-Edelman, a former student at the Nursing School, said, "She simply never accepted that the School was in the Ghetto. . . . We had notebooks, we wrote out the lectures, and we got grades."

At breakfast in the dining room, the guardians, hygienist Sztykgold, and Felicja Winawerowa, used to sit at the head of the table.

"We don't smack our lips and we don't slouch," they intoned. "We hold the knife with the right hand and the fork with the left hand," they repeated.

Some children were seeing cutlery for the first time.

Felicja Winawerowa inspected the students before they went to school. She adjusted ribbons, pulled down cuffs, and pulled up socks. If she didn't like the appearance of some of the girls, she changed their clothes until they looked right.

Figure 7.6 Bee-keeping workshop run by Berta Górecka. Mark Shreberman / Yad Vashem

Everything in the Otwock home had to be top quality.

Homework was done after the classes. And then there were extracurricular activities. The choir was led by a well-known musicologist. Irena Prusicka, the prewar owner of a famous dance school, came from Warsaw to give dance classes. She noticed that Irka Młotek was exceptionally talented. Izabella Szereszewska, a singer and theater director, offered voice-training classes. There were painting classes and foreign-language classes in English, Russian, and Yiddish. The student journalists' club, including Wiesia Blum, regularly published the school magazine. Berta Górecka would come from Warsaw with bunches of cut flowers. She donated wall hangings—kilims and macramés. She planted roses in the garden and put up beehives. She trained the children in beekeeping. There was a short-lived Scout troop. Professor Henryk Ehrich taught Jewish history and culture. He explained how to celebrate Jewish holidays.

Once a month the children cleaned the place themselves.

All the orphans learned to sew on buttons. Each girl from the intermediate and senior groups was assigned a boy. She had to supervise his appearance and, if need be, darn his socks.

During summer vacation children with weak hearts would go to the seaside and those with ailing lungs were sent to the mountains. There was a trip to France, where Polish Jewish children met French Jewish children.

Włodzimierz Sztykgold told me, "Other children's homes bred cows, we grew roses. You should also know that some of our orphans were children of the prewar intelligentsia, the Jewish aristocracy, with money and connections, so they were able to hide on the Aryan side. Besides, Jewish children from Warsaw and neighboring areas, even if they didn't come from wealthy families, attended Polish schools and spoke fluent Polish. They had no Jewish accent that would give them away. But in 1946 other Jewish children, who had been taken away to the East during the occupation, started coming to Poland from Russia. Some of them ended up in Otwock. We had nothing in common."

For a while Luba Bielicka-Blum, following instructions from the CCPJ, was breeding a few pigs on the premises. But this undertaking that was supposed to save money would in fact cost a lot and would eventually fail.

On the other hand, the flowers grew frantically.

On days off the children went to Warsaw, to the theater or the movies. They were frequently visited by activists of various organizations, artists, writers, and poets. Pianists played Beethoven for them and dancers presented traditional Jewish dances. They were visited by Jewish miners from Wałbrzych wearing shakos with feather plumes, who brought them coal for the winter, and by soldiers from the Jewish Brigade created in 1944 in the British Army. They reminisced about the war and talked about wonderful Palestine.

Journalists and filmmakers showed up a few times. Jurek Glass, the only one who spoke English, was the child on call for interviews with foreign reporters. Also a favorite with the journalists was Tomek Buergenthal, the only one of the orphans who had survived Auschwitz. The celebrated poet Julian Tuwim was a frequent visitor in Zachęta, so was the writer Zofia Nałkowska. She noted in her diary: "I was grabbed up and taken to Otwock. . . . It is about a visit to the Jewish Orphans' Home. I give a cordial speech but not too skillfully. . . . At the very moment when I entered among the children I thought there was a mistake. All of them have Aryan looks, almost no black eyes or curly hair. What does this mean? Well, that's

Figure 7.7. Playing ball. 1946. Aviva Blum / Yad Vashem

why they are here! That's why they survived the camps, the burrows, the basements, and the ruins where they had been hiding. This is a very specific selection."

The children didn't like those visits very much. They had to answer questions asked by increasing numbers of ladies and gentlemen, politely. They had to tell them where they had been hidden and how they survived. They had to move these people by telling them about Jakubek, who had been dressed as a girl during the war, but who only in the children's home found out that his name was not Zosia. They had to ask Stefa, who had lived on garbage dumps, to dance in front of the guests. (After moving to Israel she would become a prima ballerina.) Or they had to encourage Lilka to recall her life in a tomb.

The best stories were rewarded by the guests with tears, halvah, or a ballpoint pen.

But after the children had spoken, came the most difficult thing for them—listening to what the visitors had to say. "Every Sunday at lunchtime another guest would appear. Leaning against the doorframe in the dining room, visitors would talk about the disasters of war and the brotherhood of men and would assert something or account for something," Hanna Krall wrote in her book *The Subtenant*.

CHILDREN

The former residents of the children's home warned me that I shouldn't think I would be able to understand everything.

No present-day criteria should be applied!

"Don't be fooled by us" they advised. "By our innocent faces, braids, and short pants. We only pretended to be children."

Hanna Krall wrote about Julian Tuwim in *The Subtenant*: "He wasn't duped by these cynical characters with the appearance of seven- and ten-year-old children. He glanced at them, asked something, and apparently got scared, because he walked away in a hurry without even turning his head. Later, when he was coming every Sunday, they tried to get his attention. They would play hopscotch or run in a circle holding hands and laughing, carefree, like all other children, but it didn't help. Tuwim went past them quickly, without looking, ran to the infants, and read them his poems for hours."

"I can't understand you," I told them.

"Don't try to understand!" responded Włodek Sztykgold.

"During the war we were not allowed to cry, so nobody would hear. There was nothing to laugh at," said Judyta Finkiel. "I forgot both things. This was not unusual. At first, nobody would laugh spontaneously."

"We were not normal. Neither the children nor the staff. It was a mad-house," added Włodek Sztykgold

"We were all a bit loony," said Linka Sztarkman. "It was difficult not to be. I tried hard to be a child. But I have always remained a person nobody had ever played with. You know, I have a small plastic tree at home. Before my guests come, I can decorate it with cherry tomatoes for hours, just to surprise them."

"It was my birthday and I received a cake. I was unsettled," explained Irka Młotek.

Janusz Karcz said that some of them had gone too far over on the adult side and were not able to return. He remembered fifteen-year-old Janek who confided to him after many years, "Listen, in the ghetto I found my father's body. He had starved to death. I took him downstairs and put him on a cart. I could hardly get used to this artificial childhood." People like Janek were gone.

"But don't forget that, for most of us, the children's home in Otwock was a return to life. I was like a crocus starting to sprout through the snow after the winter," said Linka.

"I had been a piece of garbage," said Irka. "Suddenly, I realized I had dignity."

"Later in life, I was never as happy as there," admitted Ludwik Eisenbach.

LUDWIK

A little master was brought by some lady in a horse-drawn carriage. She said his name was Ludwik. Born in Łódź. A Jewish orphan. She didn't provide his last name and date of birth. Perhaps she didn't know. She left.

The boy looked like a six-year-old, so in the register they wrote down 1939 as his year of birth. He would be called Rabinowicz. In the future his adoptive father would give him his name, Eisenbach. Naming there was arbitrary. Someone would be called Zachęta to honor the guesthouse, another child named Gwiazda, or Star, because he arrived at Otwock on a very starry night.

Ludwik didn't talk very much. He only cried vehemently after some "Miss." The staff suspected that the boy had been under the care of wealthy people and "Miss" was his nanny. But why did they give him away? Nobody knew. Ludwik joined the *deborzątka* with the younger children. But to alleviate his despair, they placed him under the care of Tamara Buchman, the leader of the senior group. This girl was a guardian's right hand and the other children looked up to her. Temporarily, she had to replace his "Miss."

It happened sometimes that provisional Polish mothers gave away their Jewish children, and then came back for them. Franciszka Oliwa remembered a Polish woman who had brought a five-year-old girl. She took the money she was owed for her care. She unfastened the fingers of the girl, who was trying to catch her skirt. She left, hearing the child cry, "Mommy, don't leave me here." She returned the next day. "Here's your money, give me my child back."

But, Ludwik was not so lucky. The lady from the carriage visited him a few times, then didn't appear anymore. He would never know who she was.

Of 130 Jewish children from Otwock registered for the American Jewish Joint Distribution Committee, probably in the summer of 1945—there is no date on the list—58 were full orphans, 71 were half-orphans, and only 1, Samuel Gruszka, born in 1930, had both parents.

Everybody was looking for everybody. Mothers and fathers left their hiding places, returned from the camps, and sent letters to the home. They asked if Rywka was there or if, perhaps, Dawid lived there. They came in person. They looked around. Aunts, uncles, cousins, and sisters showed up, too. Miracles happened. Families were reunited. The lucky ones disappeared instantly. Sometimes without saying good-bye.

In the evening Linka lay down next to her friend, Lucynka. In the morning Lucynka was gone. Had she been found by her relatives? Had she been adopted? The staff didn't explain anything.

Not all departures were happy. Ewa, who joined her uncle and aunt in Uruguay, became a maid for her own family. She escaped to Israel. Larysa, too, became a domestic servant at her relatives' in Paris.

Irka Młotek hated Sundays, visiting days. Her parents wouldn't come. She couldn't stand looking at those hugs and kisses. She couldn't stand this breaking up of the group and taking of individual children to corners. Tereska Pinczower's mother brought grated carrot—a lot of vitamins!—and fed her daughter with a spoon, surreptitiously, so nobody could see her. Irka couldn't enter her shared room because it was locked from the inside. Probably one of her friends was being forced to gobble up chocolate. Without witnesses, without sharing it with anyone.

Linka was visited by her mother every week. She got one pastry.

"You're not eating?" asked her mother.

"Later. I'll share it with those who haven't been visited by anybody," replied the daughter.

The staff tried to suppress the children's dreams about their families. It was better not to be waiting. Not to be looking back. One should be looking ahead. That was easier.

In the home, those who knew they had no parents played tough guys. Tomek Buergenthal was sure that his mother and father were dead. So he was a tough cookie. He would write in his memoirs: "In some perverse way, our attitude towards children who were not full orphans resembled the way repeat criminals, speaking their prison jargon, proud of their prison status, and known as hard men, treat 'punks.'"

Tomek tried hard not to think about his parents and looked for oblivion in sports. Until the day he received a letter from his mother. "In the blink of an eye, the 'tough guy' mask, so carefully nurtured by me, fell off. . . . I had a mother, and that meant I could be a child again."

And there were adoptions.

A letter from the Jewish Historical Institute archives: "After having read about the orphanage in Otwock . . . I would like to bring an orphan who has no relatives to my home and adopt her . . . I mean a girl no older than six. I am a woman of decent means and I would like to help an orphan. Sincerely, B. Lew."

But Irka Młotek wouldn't allow herself to be adopted, not for the world. She had an aunt in Otwock, but she preferred to live in Zachęta with her brothers. Her uncle from America had found her after he heard her sing a Jewish song on the radio. He would like to bring her, Janek, and Danek to America, but Irka refused him politely. The only place she would go, if she were to leave Poland, was Palestine.

Tomek Buergenthal explained, "For us older children it was a matter of honor to say no to adoption."

Israel was rejecting candy offered by a woman who wanted to adopt a child. Franciszka Oliwa remembered that he was shouting: "I am not a beggar. I begged enough during the occupation."

But adoptions sometimes took place. The most wonderful one happened to Mendel Gwiazda. The story of the sick and handicapped three-year-old who had been hidden in a basket by a peasant woman, who didn't talk or walk, and whose weight and height were those of a one-year-old, was told in Canada by a representative of the Jewish Committee. This story reached a millionaire whose name, by chance, was also Gwiazda. He came to Poland after the war looking for his family, but didn't find anyone.

"It's a sign from heaven! He will be my son!" he said and sent a nurse to bring the boy who came to the home on a starry night.

However, it was usually less romantic. Franciszka Oliwa would write that potential adoptive parents were evaluated by the CCPJ and the director of the children's home, without consulting the staff and the children: "There was no problem with the little children but the older ones were not told they were being adopted by strangers. They were informed that, happily, their parents, whom they didn't remember, had been found. Or their relatives, mostly aunts or uncles."

The children were lied to? What for? It seems improbable. I can't confirm Franciszka's information with other sources. In the JHI archives I have only found the "Register of Children in the Children's Home in Otwock" signed by the director Bernhautowa, who replaced Luba Bielicka-Blum in 1948. There are only seven names on the list. Six girls (the oldest born in 1937) and one boy (born in 1939).

Younger children, at least some of them, wanted to be adopted. Ludwik remembered a rumor spread among the residents, that the children's home would soon be transferred into Polish hands, and the children would have to wear striped clothing, like in the concentration camps. Adoption seemed a better option.

JANUSZ

I would know him the least. During our interview he was sitting turned a bit away from me. I asked questions to win him over but he would answer reluctantly and with sarcasm. Later on, Irka Młotek sang me a song written about him in Otwock: "He looks like a little flea, but he stings like a little bee, tra la tra la la la lee!"

He lost his father during the occupation. The liberation found him and his mother in the Warsaw neighborhood of Praga.

"You have to leave," said the man who had been hiding them. "You are free. If you hang around here, people will find out I was hiding Jews. I can't afford this."

So for ten months they moved to Siedlce, his mother's native city. Janusz went to school at the end of the second semester. He attended the first year of the gymnasium for two weeks and right away passed the exam to get into the second year, but he had to retake biology since he didn't know what algae were.

In July 1945 he turned up in Otwock where his aunt Czesława Czarnobroda worked as a nurse. Among the residents he met Wiesia Blum, his friend who was two weeks older, and who had lived in the same apartment building at 9 Mylna Street before the war.

In his luggage he kept the report card certifying that he had completed the first year of gymnasium. In Zachęta this was a very unusual document. He was unable to finish the second year.

In the ghetto some children had attended underground classes, but those were individual cases. The lucky ones, hiding with close relatives, learned how to read and write. But most children were not studying anything throughout the entire war. There were children who had never held a pencil.

But they would rather not have had to attend school. They didn't want to walk in the town streets among Poles. They didn't want to share school desks with Polish children. They argued that they could study in Zachęta.

"You have to understand that between us and Polish children there was a natural difference, distrust, and antagonism. Polish boys and girls grew up during the war, at a time when a Jew was filth and something repugnant. And we were filled with fear and distrust," Janusz told me.

The staff at the home argued, however, that attending school was a must. And right away, before June 1945 was over, even for a few weeks. Otherwise, the former guesthouse Zachęta, full of Jewish children, would turn into another ghetto.

But which schools were they supposed to go to? Which grade should an illiterate teenager, who had spent the entire war in the woods, attend? And what about Ludwik Rabinowicz? He said he'd like to go into the second year. Let him. Wiesia Blum would be enrolled in the first year of gymnasium on a faster track. Janusz Karcz and his friends would go into the second year. After all he had a report card. The idea of school was explained to Włodek Sztykgold by his friend who had attended some classes after the war. He told Włodek to go into the gymnasium's third year, skipping previous years. Włodek, who knew nothing about school, wanted to know if this was all right. Very all right, confirmed his friend. So the son of the hygienist became a third-year student.

During summer vacation the children filled the gaps in their knowledge and studied. On September 1 they left Zachęta in pairs.

Right behind the children's home, if you followed Prus Street toward the center, there was a Polish orphanage. It was run by nuns, austere women without makeup.

Here came the Jewish children. First elementary school, followed by gymnasium. Polish children ran along the fence and shouted, "Yids! Moishes! Itzeks!" Their words were followed by stones. The nuns could see this but didn't intervene.

A walk to school took half an hour. Polish children from Otwock, mostly schoolmates, waited in a woodlot. They had insults and stones at hand. Almost every day. The cavalcade from Zachęta would close ranks, and little children, and girls, were pushed into the middle.

The little town had something to tell them, too.

"Look, people, Hitler couldn't handle all of them, after all," said adults not far from the school.

Did they defend themselves? Did they sometimes throw the stones back? Maybe they should have used some insults, shouted something about Polish swine?

"We probably didn't understand that we could throw stones at someone as well," reflected Linka. "We were the ones who were beaten. That's how things were."

But Janusz Karcz remembered that when they were verbally abused, occasionally they would fight with their Polish peers.

For a while the children were escorted to school by their guardians. It didn't help much.

In September 1945 the Jewish Committee ordered director Bielicka-Blum to put a "No Trespassing" sign on the gate.

Sometimes Polish and Jewish children sat together at the school desks. Usually when the teachers seated them according to their height. But they didn't talk to one another during recess, nor did they visit one another after classes. They were not curious about one another.

While the Polish children prayed every morning, the Jewish children stood. In some grades they stayed for the religion class. In some they left at the nun's command, "Children's home, leave the class." The Jewish children irritated the religion instructor because they knew the answers to all her questions. And they prayed better. Not so long ago "Our Father" had been their pass to life.

Sometimes the teachers did their best.

"These beloved little Jewlets! They are such great students!" Helena Dybowska, the second-grade teacher, praised her eight-year-olds.

And she didn't understand why Franciszka corrected her, "Miss Dybowska, please, these are Jews."

It was true that Jewish children read better and more, wrote dictations without spelling errors, and solved math problems quickly. They wanted to be better than the Polish students.

"These Jewish girls, they always know more," sighed Wiesia Blum's teachers, giving her a high grade.

And they admitted that Jewish children treated learning very seriously.

Other teachers didn't care. Janusz Karcz remembered Father Jan Raczkowski, a religion instructor and Scoutmaster. At a Scout meeting, he condemned two students from their school who had fled abroad.

"Listen, boys!" he told the Scouts. "We won't abandon Poland. We won't leave our country in the hands of communists and Jews."

During the occupation the same priest had helped hiding Jews, supported them financially, and provided fake baptism certificates. Janusz would learn about this many years later.

However, there were exceptions. Someone would remember that in Primary School No. 4 Jewish and Polish children talked to one another, and that Helenka Brenner from the children's home was Teacher Czyżowa's favorite.

In 1946 people with rifles lay down on Zachęta's flat roof. It was right after the Kielce pogrom that July. Poles—citizens, police, and soldiers—murdered about thirty-seven Jews and wounded thirty-five. All because of a rumor that in the house at 7 Planty Street, where the Jewish Committee had its office, Jews were holding eight-year-old Henryk Błaszczyk in order to carry out a ritual murder. Later on it would turn out that the boy had run away from home for a few days. To avoid punishment, he made up a story of abduction.

But in Otwock nobody knew that the boy, Henio Błaszczyk, was a little liar. Instead, people said things like: "Who knows? Won't Jews kidnap a Polish child here as well?"

The CCPJ ordered extreme vigilance. Five guards were dispatched and a sixth was to be hired. They had six light machine guns and one automatic rifle to defend the children.

Fortunately, nothing happened.

EDA

I don't know the date of her birth or the date of her death. I have a few photographs showing a gentle-looking young woman with black eyebrows. I know that in the ghetto she was active in the Central Association for the Care of Orphans. She made a living teaching in the "secret corners." Linka was one of her pupils. Eda was an ardent Zionist. Most likely educated, she must have known Doctor Korczak's methods.

Figure 7.8. Caregiver Eda Szternes. 1945. Aviva Blum / Yad Vashem

When in March 1945 she arrived in Otwock with a transport of children, she was not even thirty.

Franciszka Oliwa couldn't stand her. She was jealous.

Jealous about the residents' self-government, modeled on Korczak's ideas, introduced by Eda in the oldest group. From now on, children were supposed to have a say, to some extent, about what happened in the home. They chose theater plays and movies they wanted to see in Warsaw. Director

Bielicka-Blum should consult them about vacation. The children's court could on its own determine punishments for misdemeanors. For plunging the tip of Tamara Buchman's braid into the inkwell, Tomek Buergenthal was sentenced to two weeks' carrying her schoolbag.

Soon, such a self-government would be constructed in the middle group tended by Franciszka. She was jealous of Eda's manual skills. That she taught children paper art, and that she knew how to cut letters out of glossy paper. Soon after her arrival she cut out the slogan "For the memory, glory, and honor of those who perished, we will study and work," and she placed it in the arched passageway separating the dining room from the auditorium. The children would love this inscription. For example, it helped Linka Sztarkman understand that although she shouldn't forget the past, studying and working were her primary goals.

Franciszka couldn't read as nicely as Eda. Every Sunday Szternes took the children to the little wood beyond the tracks and read to them about animals or cities. Sometimes it was Bambi, sometimes Kraszewski. She did this splendidly and the listeners asked her not to stop.

Franciszka would write about Eda: "She was a very energetic person, a superb organizer, strict, and occasionally uncompromising. She introduced sharp discipline and order in the group. She managed to control the less orderly children."

It was Eda who defined the rhythm, shape, and character of the Otwock children's home. Franciszka couldn't bear it.

Quite often Eda was cross with the children. She tormented them. Ill-tempered, she slapped Teresa when she made a mistake reciting a poem of Broniewski. She never parted with the whistle hanging around her neck. She was unkind to her own younger, beautiful sister Krysia, who sometimes visited her from Warsaw.

"When are you going to get lost?" she asked her in the children's presence.

Linka swore that for the first two weeks in Zachęta, Szternes had been a poised and energetic caregiver. Only later did something happen to her. But nobody else believed this. They didn't like her. Neither did Linka Sztarkman. "I remember you from the ghetto," Eda said to her. But her tone was as if she remembered Linka from a house of ill repute, and not from the "secret corner" of the ghetto.

In the summer of 1945 Szternes picked the students who would be able to skip sixth grade and go directly to gymnasium. Linka was an outstanding student, but she heard Szternes say, "You are too young. You will go to elementary school." It was unfair. Less talented children her age were getting permission. Linka remembered a similar situation from the ghetto. The children were to memorize a poem selected by Eda. When Linka finished her declamation, Eda told her, "Your friend recites better than you." Władek Kornblum, Linka's future husband, hated Eda. It was mutual. She didn't allow him to go to dance parties, although she knew how much he loved to dance. "You are too little," she told him.

Irka Młotek was also not permitted to participate in the evening parties. But all the children asked for her since she knew all the songs and dances. "Too fresh from the cradle," decided Eda and sent her to bed. Irka was scared of this guardian and found her repulsive. When Szternes stroked her casually, the girl wiped herself surreptitiously.

I don't know if Tomek Buergenthal was one of Eda's favorites, but he would remember her in the best possible way. "All of us, including me, adored her."

Franciszka Oliwa wrote: "It seemed as though our little community was doing well, but that guardian cared mostly for its older residents."

Eda Szternes sent the self-government's leader to supervise the girls taking a bath. But she herself supervised the boys personally. The oldest were invited to her room. After a while, at the director's order, she would have to share her room with two resident children.

Luba Bielicka-Blum was a Bund activist. She believed that the future of Polish Jews was in Poland. To her, Zionists, who wanted to go to Palestine and build Israel, were dreamers.

In the CCPJ, the Bundists argued with the Zionists. Otwock supported the Bund; Zionists were not welcome. In Bielicka-Blum's opinion, the children should study, finish gymnasium, graduate from the university, and stay in Poland.

The children's home in Biały Kamień near Wałbrzych was under Zionist influence. There, children and teenagers belonged to HaShomer HaTzair, an organization that could be compared to the Polish Scouts. They wore neckerchiefs and uniforms, and they were being prepared for future life on a kibbutz.

Eda Szternes was a Zionist. She helped people from HaShomer HaTzair penetrate Zachęta. She knew that every few weeks children from the oldest group sneaked out to the meadow in the woods. There, they met with Aron, who was not very tall and had lovely curls. The girls called him Arończyk. Linka and the others were captivated by his words about a new life in Palestine.

"Do you want them to throw stones at you all the time?" asked Arończyk. They didn't.

"Do you want to finally have your own country?"

They did.

"So get ready for departure."

Only Wiesia Blum knew nothing about HaShomer HaTzair. She was their friend, but also the director's daughter. They were afraid she might betray them.

One night, at the beginning of 1947, twenty residents from the oldest group would disappear from the home. They went to Biały Kamień near Wałbrzych, and from there through France, to Palestine.

One of them would be Israel Nojmark.

Irka Młotek, picked up by her aunt, would leave Zachęta a day earlier and would join her friends on the train to Wałbrzych.

Wiesia Blum joined HaShomer after their departure. She went to Israel after gymnasium.

Irka Młotek and Judyta joined her a few years later.

Ludwik Eisenbach and Włodek Sztykgold left in 1957, when they graduated from the university.

Janusz Karcz, son of a prewar Zionist, was already there.

Eda Szternes had disappeared from the children's home before the escape of her wards. Franciszka Oliwa would write in her memoirs that this guardian of the oldest group was crazy about the uniformed guards protecting Zachęta. But nobody could confirm this. She might have gone to Biały Kamień to see her pupils. But they didn't want to see her. Someone told me that she had moved to Switzerland, where she graduated from nursing school, and had died there years later. But nobody knew for sure.

Franciszka Oliwa left the home in October 1948. "I had to go due to personal matters," she wrote in her memoirs.

She was hired at the Ministry of Industry and Commerce. There were rumors that she was the eyes and ears of Minister Hilary Minc. Later on, she got a job in the Jewish Historical Institute. She married a Polish Army officer named Cynamon.

In April 1949 the last of the children who had parents or relatives left the Jewish children's home. The Jewish Committee had less and less money to provide for these institutions. They only had places for full orphans.

In mid-1949 Luba Bielicka-Blum left Otwock to become the director of the revived Nursing School. She visited Wiesia in Israel a few times but she never wanted to move for good to the "powder keg," as she called that country.

Her post was taken for several months by Alfreda Bernhautowa. By the end of 1949 the last fifty-two children had left the home in Otwock. The younger were sent to the Jewish children's home in Śródborów and the older to the boardinghouse at Jagiellońska Street in Warsaw.

In 1950 the Central Committee of Polish Jews ceased to exist.

FRANCISZKA

On the internet I come across a photograph from a Purim party. Twenty-three children.

I recall that Franciszka Oliwa described this party in her memoirs. The residents were supposed to disguise themselves as the people they wanted to become in the future.

The little German Gertruda—Petronela—whom nobody would remember, wanted to be a maid. She was given a white apron, a cap, and a feather duster.

If this is true, Petronela should be somewhere in this picture, I presume. There is a miner, a clown, and a painter, a Gypsy girl, a woman from the Tatra Mountains, and a Chinese girl. But no maid.

"Franciszka Oliwa, you lied after all."

But after a moment I notice that the party photo has been scanned front and back. I read the inscription on the reverse side: "Children's home in Otwock. Petronela, girl in white cap, first row. Miss Oliwa."

I look at the picture once again. How could I have missed her? A cheerful girl is sitting cross-legged between a gardener with a basket on her head and a dancer with a flower coronet. She is propping her chin on the duster.

Figure 7.9. Purim carnival in the Jewish Children's Home. Petronela (first row) in a white cap. 1948. Mark Shreberman / Yad Vashem

Franciszka Oliwa is standing a bit to the side, behind the children. She is smiling faintly, with her eyes closed.

Postscriptum. I receive a letter from Wiesia Blum. Olek, her brother, has written from the United States that he remembers Petronela.

AUGUST 1945

For sale: painting worth as much as a Rubens, cheap. Rulski, 2 Żurawia Street.
—*Życie Warszawy*, Aug. 1, 1945

Bolesław Hozakowski, born March 21, 1925, in Toruń, arrested in a roundup in Warsaw on January 1943, was at Pawiak Prison. Together with others he was summoned by name out of his cell and then disappeared without a trace. I am looking for anybody who was with him at Pawiak, witnessed that summons, or knows anything about his fate. Bronisław Hozakowski, Toruń, 8 Mostowa Street.
—*Życie Warszawy*, Aug. 1, 1945

I am looking for Irena Gryl, age 4, who on September 1, 1944, was placed with a foster family in Płudy. Leave message at Youth Detention Center, Płudy.
—*Życie Warszawy*, Aug. 1, 1945

Generous reward for anyone who returns a little dog, a fox terrier with a black spot on his back, or who provides any information about him. In September he was seized by a German from a woman in the Pruszków Camp. Michalski, 51 Mokotowska Street.
—*Życie Warszawy*, Aug. 2, 1945

I take back my slur against Citizen Musiał, a member of the PSP [Polish Socialist Party]. Regina Centlewska.
—*Dziennik Bałtycki*, Aug. 3, 1945

A childless couple will take as their own an orphan, age 1–4, from a good Catholic family.
—*Dziennik Bałtycki*, Aug. 4, 1945

Bass and baritone needed for prewar barbershop choral group. Czerniaków, 10 Cecylia Śniegocka Street.
—*Życie Warszawy*, Aug. 10, 1945

I will take a 3-year-old girl to bring up as my own, preferably an orphan. Piotrowska, 19 Śniadeccy Street.
—*Życie Warszawy*, Aug. 10, 1945

Dąbrowska, a midwife, offers her services. Discounts for unwealthy ladies. 21 Wileńska Street.
—*Życie Warszawy*, Aug. 10, 1945

Szelązek Janina is looking for her husband E. W. Szelązek, owner of a Warsaw bookstore, who was recently in Oranienburg, and for her daughter Maria Krystyna Szelązek, age 18, recently in Ravensbrück. Please leave message at: Krakow, 9 Żuławski Street, Orphanage.
—*Dziennik Bałtycki*, Aug. 15, 1945

5-year-old Wojtuś Malarski is looking for his parents. Since the Uprising he has been staying with Dobrzyński Stefan in Babice Stare.
—*Życie Warszawy*, Aug. 16, 1945

For room and board, an aged teacher will prepare children for school and improve their performance. French language. 10 Dynasy Street.

—*Życie Warszawy*, Aug. 20, 1945

• • • • • • • • • • • • • • • • • •

If Mr. Miodek, owner of the home appliance store at 46 Solec Street, doesn't return by September 1, his establishment will be managed by the Administration.

—*Życie Warszawy*, Aug. 20, 1945

• • • • • • • • • • • • • • • • • •

Since false news has been spread that blemishes my reputation in the public eye, I proclaim that I have nothing to do with my namesake Czesław Krause from Puck, who at one point was expelled from the Polish Republic, or with other individuals bearing the same name who are social parasites. I am not related to the above-mentioned Czesław Krause in any way. Augustyn Krause, former mayor of Gdynia.

—*Dziennik Bałtycki*, Aug. 21, 1945

• • • • • • • • • • • • • • • • • •

The Gablenz and Son Factory of vinegar, mustard, and canned food, Krakow, 33 Królowa Jadwiga Street, alerts the public that falsified vinegar with our labels has appeared on the market. We inform the public that from August 1, 1945, we have been sealing our bottles with wax, and only sealed and stamped bottles are authentic.

—*Dziennik Polski*, Krakow, Aug. 22, 1945

• • • • • • • • • • • • • • • • • •

Once again Convent Sacre Coeur has opened a boarding school for children ages 7–16. Healthy location, forest, lake. Good nourishment. Considerate, individualized upbringing. Languages, sports. Send applications to: Mother Superior, Polska Wieś Center, Pobiedziska train station and post office, County Poznań.

—*Życie Warszawy*, Aug. 22, 1945

• • • • • • • • • • • • • • • • • •

I will give a baby away into good hands. Girl, 4 months. Not baptized. Distraught mother. Mokotów, 14 Lewicka Street.

—*Życie Warszawy*, Aug. 24, 1945

• • • • • • • • • • • • • • • • • •

Before you see Wanda Wasilewska's movie *Tęcza*, read her book under the same title first! Book price 16 zlotys. Available in the bookstore of Czytelnik Publishing Cooperative, Gdynia, 9 Mściwoj Street.

—*Dziennik Bałtycki*, Aug. 25, 1945

• • • • • • • • • • • • • • • • • •

Wanted immediately. Experienced sommelier to manage the fruit wine factory. Apply to "Wino," Czytelnik.

—*Życie Warszawy*, Aug. 28, 1945

• • • • • • • • • • • • • • • • • •

I will hire a boy or a girl to tend a cow. Gdynia, 21 Peowiacy Street.

—*Dziennik Bałtycki*, Aug. 28, 1945

The Thirty-Six Days of
Bolesław the First

The piece of paper, torn out from a pocket notebook, is really tiny. The man who holds it pushes through the crowd at Market Square in Krakow. He looks for Doctor Bolesław Drobner, a short man, but with such a handlebar moustache that Joseph Stalin himself would be jealous. Besides, Drobner has met Stalin on a few occasions. The national demonstration against fascism continues. Drobner adores rallies, marches, and protests. He should be here somewhere. Perhaps he will give a speech. Here he is! He stands under the Cloth Hall arcades surrounded by workers he knows. The man hands him the piece of paper with the short note. Its contents won't survive, but it could have said, "Bolek, you've become mayor of Wrocław. Contact Ochab as soon as possible."

It is March 24, 1945. The war hasn't ended yet. Fortress Breslau is still resisting.

1913, NO LATER THAN 1914

Atelier Adela was very close to the Drobners' house. You would leave the residential building at 3 Szczepański Square in Krakow, take a few steps, and here it was. The photo studio. Ignacy Pretzel, owner of the Modern Photography Studio, was a well-known artist, both in this city and in the world. His works were appreciated at exhibits in Paris, London, and even in nearby provincial Karlsbad.

Therefore, for the meeting with Pretzel the Drobners put on their carefully selected outfits. Bolesław, a Cracovian for generations, put on a frock coat. Underneath, he put on a vest and fastened a tie around the stiff collar in the Austro-Hungarian emperor's style. He slicked back his thick dark hair and twisted his moustache. He was thirty-one, but this outfit made him look at least ten years older.

He was a son of Abraham Roman Drobner, who was an assimilated Jew, an insurgent of the January Uprising of 1863, and a city councillor. On the ground floor of the number 3 building, Roman had run a wholesale depot with paints, toiletries, and toys. On the other side, facing Planty Park, he had built a coffee shop called Drobneiron.

Drobner couldn't know that in twenty-two years, wearing a dark tunic known in the East as a *gymnastyorka*, he would come back from Moscow, from his daughter's funeral. He never took it off. In the 1950s an informer with the cover name "Four-Eyes" wrote about him in his report for the UB, the Secret Police: "He would wear this quasi-worker's outfit all the time. He approached every worker with a smile and asked about health, home, and family. Simple workers were captivated."

Luba Tauba Hirszowicz, Bolesław's wife, a year younger, had the beauty of a Greek statue. She parted her hair and tied it in a loose bun. She put on a black velvet dress and under her neck she pinned a lace ruffle with a silver brooch. She had been born in Moscow. She was a granddaughter of Leib Hirsz, a jeweler and an authorized engraver for the Russian nobility. Her father, Józef Hirszowicz, established a printing shop at Jerozolimskie Avenue in Warsaw, one of the largest in Poland.

Bolesław Drobner seated his daughter, Irenka, on his lap. The four-year-old girl, dressed in a sailor's outfit, had the sad look of her mother. She would later die of tuberculosis in a luxurious clinic outside Moscow. Ida, one of Luba's sisters, also posed for the picture, but nothing is known about her. When the Drobners were ready, positioned on chairs with their backs against a little table, they became motionless in front of a painted backdrop depicting a bourgeois interior. Pretzel asked them for a moment of attention and took a photo. The Drobners hadn't brought their little son, Mieczysław. In the future he would become a prominent musician and his simple compositions for piano would be played by children even after

Figure 8.1. Bolesław Drobner's family about 1914. From left: his daughter Irena, Bolesław Drobner, his wife Luba, and his sister-in-law Ida Hirszowicz. YIVO Institute for Jewish Research

a hundred years, but at that moment, the youngest Drobner was only two and he stayed at home.

LATE AUTUMN 1914

Bolesław Drobner, soldier in the Austrian army, posed for a photograph in full gear. His right hand leaned on a rifle barrel and the left one he dropped along his body. He had his haversack thrown across a shoulder. He wore a peaked cap. An entrenching spade was attached to the rucksack on his back. Drobner didn't look into the camera and his face seemed apprehensive.

Being a soldier, a subordinate following orders, didn't suit him. He wanted to rule, authorize, instruct, lead into battle, put others on the spot, advise others himself without listening to anybody, deliver pompous speeches, and credit himself with achievements larger than life.

If he had been born in some other time, he might have been a theater director. His father's apartment building shared its facade with the Old

Figure 8.2. Bolesław Drobner in Austrian army uniform. 1914. Historical Museum of Krakow

Theater. Bolesław had worked there as an extra since he was five. He played a page who carried the actresses' long trains on the stage, or a blacksmith's boy in Władysław Anczyc's play *Kościuszko at Racławice*. He was friends with the theater staff and acquainted with Ludwik Solski. Drobner would never stop loving the theater, remaining devoted to cultural matters his entire life. When after World War II he became a Krakow councilor, he insisted that the Under the Rams Palace, occupied earlier by the Soviet Military Authority, be turned into a cultural community center. He would help to bring into being a literary nightclub, The Cellar under the Rams, located in its basement.

Bolesław Drobner, the child of a wealthy bourgeois family, student of the Sobieski classical gymnasium, taking lessons in music and foreign languages, loved socialism more than theater. Reportedly, from early childhood, he had been appalled by the destitution of beggars and had cared about the fate of workers. Reportedly, his parents regarded themselves as democrats. Reportedly, they approved of the meetings of young socialists from Krakow organized in their apartment by their oldest son, Józef. At the age of fifteen, Bolesław Drobner joined the Polish Social Democratic Party of Galicia and Cieszyn Silesia, one of several similarly named parties of the day.

He studied chemistry in Berlin, where they arrested him for participating in a protest against the beating of Polish children in Września. He was expelled from the capital of the German Empire and was banned from entering it for ten years. He therefore completed his studies in Zurich. Over there he ran a course, "Chemistry in Everyday Life," teaching young socialists how to construct homemade bombs. In 1907 in Freiburg he defended his doctorate in chemistry. He went to work for a gas company in Switzerland, then for a biochemical laboratory in Vienna, and in 1909 in Krakow, using his father's money, he founded his own analytical laboratory. His father's company went into the hands of outsiders after his death in 1913. Bolesław found a job as director of technical sciences at the Society for the Hygiene of the Chemical and Pharmaceutical Industry. What exactly did this society do? Nobody knows. Luba, Drobner's wife, was also a chemist and worked in the same place. Like her husband, she was active in the Polish Socialist Party (PSP).

Most of all, Drobner was politically active. He attended workers' rallies in all the partitioned pieces of Poland. He made friends with Ignacy Daszyński, a chemist and prominent Polish socialist. He became a member of the PSP. Within this organization they considered him a leftist. In 1914 he joined Józef Piłsudski's Riflemen's Association for a short while, but soon after that he was drafted into the Austrian army. They dressed him in a uniform, took his photo, and sent him into the war. He came back in 1918. Where had he been and what had he done for a such a long time? Nobody knows.

1925, 1932, AND LATER

Luckily, he had this bushy moustache, making it easy to recognize him even in the blurry photographs taken with portable cameras during socialist congresses and meetings.

They adored him. They hated him. State authorities and socialists didn't exhibit any moderate sentiments toward Bolesław Drobner.

He was everywhere. He was on the Board of the Workers' University Society, in the Trade Union of Office Workers, and in the Socialist International executive. He was one of the best-known PSP activists in Poland. City councillor, speaker at rallies, prone to brawling during May First parades and during skirmishes with members of the right-wing National Democracy—known from its initials, ND, as the Endeks—and police. His favorite song was "The Red Flag," the socialists' anthem. In 1968 it would be played over his coffin for the last time.

During the interwar period he was detained repeatedly. Tried and sentenced to prison many times, he served six years in all. They called him a man with clean hands. He was famous for his honesty and uncompromising stance. At the same time, Drobner was able to antagonize people, find fault, and nitpick as no one else could.

Years later "Four-Eyes" would note: "In his work and his activity, he doesn't contribute anything constructive or productive. He somehow breaks everything. And he doesn't demolish something at once and from the outside, rather he enters the core and shatters it, cracks it from the inside. He has no friends and knows nothing about people."

Dissatisfied with the PSP, in 1922 Drobner founded his own Independent Socialist Labor Party, but he soon became critical of its activity, rejoined the PSP, and was appointed to its Supreme Council.

Irena, his daughter, fell into socialism up to her eyes. She attended the kindergarten and school run by people from the PSP. She studied ethics

Figure 8.3. Active members of the Independent Socialist Labor Party. Bolesław Drobner seated, center. December 1925. Historical Museum of Krakow

there instead of religion. When she was sixteen, she joined the Young Communist League. She worked as a photo retoucher and married a communist, Salomon Stramer, who later changed his name to Roman Kornecki. There was a rumor in town that during a brawl she bit one of the rightists in the hand. In 1928 for the first time Irena ended up in St. Michael's prison in Krakow where she contracted tuberculosis. Five years later she was very sick. Her mother's sister, Manya, invited her to Moscow for treatment. Manya was married to Boris Stomonyakov, a Bulgarian. Boris was a member of the council of the Soviet People's Commissariat's Section on Foreign Relations. He arranged a trip to Crimea for his wife's niece, and then he found her a place in the Kremlin's hospital. Irena died at the end of 1935. Her parents were at her bedside.

After returning from Moscow Bolesław embarked on a series of lectures: "What I Have Seen in Soviet Russia." He delivered them all over Poland. Dziunka, or Comrade Wanda Wasilewska, a friend from the PSP, sent him a special invitation to Warsaw. The party authorities thought that Drobner had become a communist, and in 1936 expelled him. However, they had no time to announce that decision because at the same time a court sentenced Drobner to four years' imprisonment for communist activity, as his lectures on Soviet Russia were characterized.

1939, UNTIL THE SPRING OF 1944

In September 1939 Bolesław Drobner and his family reached Lvov, which was now Soviet Lviv. He had gotten leave from Polish prison during the summer and never went back. A few months later he was arrested by the NKVD and accused of attempted departure for Germany. He suspected he had been denounced by a friend from Lvov, but the thing was that Drobner was not planning to travel anywhere.

Drobner ended up in Siberia, in Asino. He was one of four thousand camp prisoners. He worked as a postman. When there was a prisoners' strike demanding better living conditions, Drobner tried to convince them that their protest was senseless, but the NKVD accused him of counterrevolution anyway. After a nine-month investigation in Novosibirsk, the court sent him to Beregayev on the Arctic Ocean. He worked as a woodcutter, an accountant, a canteen inspector, and a swineherd.

The almost-sixty-year-old Drobner could hardly bear camp conditions. He was weak and suffered from malaria. Fortunately, in September 1941 he got a permit to go to Cheboksary in the Chuvash Republic, where his wife, son, and daughter-in-law were waiting for him. He got a job as a chemist in a brewery and in a cooperative of disabled workers, where he launched the production of aspirin made from willow bark, and also made ether, school chalk, ink, metal-cleaning polish, and matches.

The Drobners wanted to leave Cheboksary at any cost. They even thought of leaving on foot, but were deterred by fear of wolves. One day, by chance, Bolesław Drobner came across the newspaper *Polska*, published by the Polish embassy in the temporary Soviet wartime capital of Kuybyshev. He read about the Polish army that was being formed in the Near East. In his memoirs he would write: "I learned from one of the deportees that this new Polish army is commanded by a Colonel, or General, Anders. I had never heard of him before." When at the end of summer 1942 the magazine *New Horizons*, also published in Kuybyshev by Wanda Wasilewska, reached Cheboksary, Drobner wrote her a letter. Dziunka replied with cordial greetings, and in October she invited him to Moscow. Drobner's life had just gained momentum.

There are no photos from his Soviet imprisonment. Who would take a camera to Siberia? Perhaps later there were some photos in Moscow, with Wanda Wasilewska, or even with Stalin. Unfortunately, they have not survived.

In Moscow he talked for hours with Wasilewska and her third husband, the Ukrainian writer Olexandr Korniychuk. They went to the theater. He frequented the library and met the Polish communists Hilary Minc, Zygmunt Modzelewski, and Edward Ochab. He was introduced to Colonel Zygmunt Berling.

After three weeks he returned to his wife. For the trip Dziunka offered him Moscow sausage, real tea, and chocolate. She informed him that he and his family would have to move to Moscow for good. The Union of Polish Patriots (UPP) was about to be formed and people like Drobner would be needed. Wanda Wasilewska created the UPP in consultation with Stalin. After the war this union could be the center of power in Poland. However, Joseph Vissarionovich played both sides. He knew very well that the new Polish government should be created in Poland. Initially, he didn't even rule out an agreement with the government-in-exile in London.

In March 1943 Wasilewska wrote to Drobner: "I invite you to the meeting of the Union of Polish Patriots. Come to Moscow as soon as possible." Three months later, at the First Congress of the UPP, Drobner was elected to the General Board. After the congress, Stalin sent him a congratulatory letter and expressed his wish for "strengthening Polish-Russian friendship and collaborating on the resurrection of a strong and independent Poland by all necessary means."

Drobner now found himself in the communist milieu that he hadn't known well before. The communists treated him, a socialist, with caution. Yet he was aware that he was indispensable to them. He would write in his memoirs: "Besides Wanda Wasilewska's name, for many participants in the congress, mine was the only one they knew."

They didn't trust him. He was not charged with any significant tasks. Bolesław Drobner performed ceremonial functions. He attended parades, meetings, and gatherings. He met Stalin a few times and considered him a kind man who could speak about any subject. But within the UPP Drobner would like to talk about the future of Poland. He had ideas and projects, yet nobody treated his opinions seriously. To cheer him up, they nominated

him to be head of the Social Services Commission at the UPP, whose job
was to protect Poles living in the Soviet Union. Drobner thought that job
below his ambitions.

His old spirit awakened in him again. He criticized the leadership of the
UPP, accused them of violating their own governing rules, carried a grudge
against Wasilewska, and complained in writing that he was a member only
of the General Board of the Union, but not of its Presidium.

Many years later Dziunka would write of him: "He was an amazingly
wonderful person, but he failed as an organizer and as an ideologist." For his
peace of mind, they elected him to the Presidium of the General Board of
the UPP. According to Wasilewska, "this gesture must have nicely stroked
Bolesław Drobner's political ambitions."

In the meantime, in 1943 on New Year's Eve in Warsaw at 22 Twarda Street,
Władysław Gomułka, member of the Polish Workers' Party (PWP), con-
spiratorially formed the State National Council (SNC) without any consultation with Moscow. The SNC, a sort of parliament, was supposed to
represent the Polish nation. Bolesław Bierut, Michał Rola-Żymierski, and
Edward Osóbka-Morawski, among others, were a part of its Presidium. In
May 1944 a delegation of the SNC arrived in Moscow. Drobner talked to
Osóbka-Morawski for hours. He was also involved in creating the program
of the Polish Committee of National Liberation (PCNL) that was being
established. The committee was supposed to be a provisional executive
power for the Polish Republic, dominated by communists and fully controlled by Stalin.

The communists wanted to create the illusion of a multiparty government that was above all divisions. They needed representatives of other
political factions. Andrzej Witos represented the Peasants' Party that had
been cofounded by his brother Wincenty; Wincenty Rzymowski represented the Democratic Party; and Drobner, the only representative of the Polish
Socialist Party, became head of the Department of Labor, Social Services,
and Health. Edward Osóbka-Morawski of the Polish Workers' Party was
named committee chairman and Wanda Wasilewska became his deputy.

On July 22 Radio Moscow broadcast the PCNL Manifesto, lying, however, that it had been signed that same day in Chełm, a town taken over
by the Red Army. In reality, Bolesław Drobner and other members of the
PCNL only reached Chełm at the end of the month.

APRIL 13, 1945, AND A BIT EARLIER

Bolesław Drobner is not in this photograph from near Breslau a month before the war ended. Instead, there are six uniformed men—three Polish policemen and three Soviet soldiers. They don't pay any attention to the photographer, and bask in the sun. Only one of them, under the Polish emblem and the white and red flag, rifle on shoulder, stands guard in front of the small residential building.

Paul Majunke, a plumber, used to have a workshop in this building. The inscription in German lettering, right above the storefront, informed potential clients of his services, but it was a long time ago, perhaps a few months ago, in a different world, when this house stood in the town of Kanth near Breslau. Now the house belonged to the Soviet army. It was temporarily hosting Bolesław Drobner's operational group that was on its way to Wrocław. Nobody cared what had become of Majunke the plumber. Soon, as part of the repolonization of the Piast Lands, the front wall would be painted over and Kanth would change its name to Kąty Wrocławskie. It might happen that in several dozen years a decorative "M" from Majunke would resurface. Prewar paint was of truly top quality.

Comrades from the PCNL, who had been on duty in Lublin since August 1, 1944, might have known how to tame Bolesław Drobner. He had to be given an assignment. Even better, he had to be sent into the field. So Drobner, accompanied by other members of the committee and escorted by soldiers, visited the sites occupied by the Red Army. He took control and created self-governing bodies. He was in Rzeszów, Łańcut, Stalowa Wola, and Warsaw's Praga district.

On January 18, 1945, the Soviets entered Krakow. A day later, Bolesław Drobner and his wife arrived in a specially assigned Dodge automobile driven by a Russian, Niko Kartoshkin. By then the Polish Committee of National Liberation no longer existed. On December 31, 1944, it had been replaced by the Provisional Government of the Republic of Poland, created by the State National Council. Osóbka-Morawski was prime minister and Edward Ochab was minister of public administration. In April Ochab would be appointed plenipotentiary general for the Recovered Territories. Drobner had not been invited into the government, but he was still a member of the State National Council and deputy chairman of the Polish Socialist Party.

Figure 8.4. Headquarters of Drobner's Operational Group in Kąty Wrocławskie. April 13, 1945. Reproduced from *Trudne dni. Wrocław 1945. We wspomnieniach pionierów*. Zakład Narodowy im. Ossolińskich, Wrocław 1960

The citizens of Krakow welcomed him enthusiastically. His old party comrades were at his disposal. He said he had the full authority of the government behind him and that he would be in charge there. He was lying. He didn't have any authority, but nobody from Krakow would scrutinize someone like him. The government didn't disavow him, but it did give orders to follow Drobner and report on his movements.

Drobner began to look for a worthy office for his party. Main Square would be the best location. Unfortunately, the Under the Rams Palace was occupied by the Russians, and the Polish Workers' Party had taken the next building, at the corner of Main Square and Wiślna Street. It didn't matter. Two days later Drobner started to govern in the ceremonial Szołajski Palace at Szczepański Square, not far from his family home. At that moment, the Drobners lived at 25 Staszewski Street. The Palace became PSP headquarters.

Some people noticed that Drobner looked tired. He had gotten older in Siberia. His hair had become gray, his hands trembled, and his memory was weaker, but he didn't pay any attention to this. He was in his element. Drobner renewed his old connections and filled administrative positions in the city with socialist friends. He attempted to form a PSP police force, and openly claimed that no one other than he could be the best mayor or voivode of Krakow. He attended rallies and gave speeches during demonstrations. His support among Krakow workers was growing. He made clear that socialists and communists should never unite. He didn't want to march with communists in the same May Day Parade and he even ordered separate May Day pins.

And this could be disturbing to higher authorities. Once again, Drobner was out of control. In those days it was the communists from the Polish Workers' Party that were supposed to predominate. Although the first mayor of Krakow appointed by Warsaw, Aleksander Żaruk-Michalski, belonged to the PSP, he was in charge for only a month. Then he was replaced by Alfred Fiederkiewicz, a committed prewar communist.

Was Edward Osóbka-Morawski bothered by Bolesław Drobner on the rise? Maybe he thought hard about how to get the Krakow socialist out of the city? Was this why on March 24, 1945, he nominated that man, not generally known as the best organizer, to be mayor of Wrocław?

The message about his nomination, scribbled on a piece of paper torn from a notebook, was delivered to Drobner by Stanisław Szwalbe, a socialist and deputy chairman of the State National Council. On the same day in the evening the news about Drobner's appointment was announced by BBC Radio.

Bolesław Drobner had never been to Wrocław, but he didn't hesitate even for a second. "It was true that nobody talked to me about this nomination, but at that time Poland was showered with appointments, decisions, resolutions, and directives. Clearly, in the case of Wrocław the Provisional Government had to act swiftly. . . . Refuse? I couldn't!" he wrote in his memoirs.

So he went to Warsaw to talk to Ochab. Wrocław was still besieged by the Soviet army, but the Poles were already counting their unhatched chickens. They drew up a plan that when the city became Polish, it would be autonomous, like Warsaw and Łódź and its mayor would, de facto, perform the function of voivode. Minister Ochab rushed him, "But first and foremost, Comrade Drobner, get to work as soon as possible." Drobner had a free hand in everything but, most important, he had to collaborate with the Soviet Military Authority.

That day Drobner was not able to talk to Osóbka-Morawski in person. The prime minister was busy, so he delegated his representative to meet the new mayor of Wrocław to tell him: "Do what you want in whatever way you want to do it."

At the beginning of April Drobner announced in the press and among PSP members that he was hiring a team to govern Wrocław after the expected German defeat. Engineers, specialists, and scientists who would know how to secure, and later restart, factories, power plants, gas plants, streetcars, universities, and theaters, were asked to appear in the office at 55 Floriańska Street, and later at Kleparski Square. Assembling the operational group took longer than expected. There weren't so many volunteers. Nobody knew what to expect in Wrocław. Were there any buildings standing? Wasn't that too risky?

In the meantime, on April 7, the chief of the Department of Military Authorities of the First Ukrainian Front, Lieutenant Colonel Repin, arrived in Krakow. He had a document for Bolesław Drobner allowing him to go to Wrocław and ordering the city commandants to assist his team. Soon, Ochab sent money to Krakow and pushed for a reconnaissance trip to Wrocław. Its purpose was to symbolically mark the presence of Poland in still-German Breslau, even before the fortress was defeated.

On Friday, April 13, 1945, Drobner rode toward the city whose mayor he was. A dozen people went with him in three cars, including journalists and photographers. He was fully aware of the propaganda power of this expedition. The convoy was guarded by fifteen armed policemen, but Drobner didn't trust them very much. They took with them Polish flags, a few metal plates with the white eagle, and armbands with the inscription "City Council of Wrocław," but they didn't have maps. They asked randomly encountered people for directions. They made stops in Katowice and Opole, where district offices were already functioning. At the nearest bridge on the Oder they nailed on the first plate with the eagle and posed for a group photograph. They planned to spend a night in the small town of Kanth near Wrocław.

On the way there they ran over a black cat.

Figure 8.5. Wrocław City Hall. 1945. East News

JANUARY UNTIL MAY 1945

How to choose one photograph that will tell the story of the city turned to rubble in seventy-six days? A photo of the Wrocław City Hall barely standing, an aerial photo of the burned ruins, or perhaps a photo of the cathedral lacking its roof? Which one will be better? The are many to choose from. There are images of bodies in the streets and of residential buildings twisted like twigs. There are fallen church towers and a barricade made of streetcars.

Or, perhaps the surviving statue of Friedrich Wilhelm III would be the best? The king on a horse, in full gear, stares at a yawning hole in a residential building on the other side of the street that is no more. The monarch has no reason to enjoy his survival. Soon, he and his horse will fall from the pedestal and will be sold for scrap.

Figure 8.6. Statue of Friedrich Wilhelm III. May 1945. Henryk Makarewicz / City Museum of Wrocław

In spring 1944, Adolf Hitler hit on the idea of designating certain cities as fortresses (*Festungen*) that would be symbols of German resolve and would delay the Red Army's march on Berlin. As *Festungen* he selected, among others, Mogilev, Babruysk, Vitebsk, Königsberg, Danzig, Oppeln, and Posen. In August, the Führer declared Breslau a fortress. In September, Johannes Krause became the first *Festungskommandant* of the city. He didn't do much for the future fortress. Although he drew up a plan for the evacuation of people, that plan was never announced. This was because Gauleiter Karl Hanke, a fanatical Nazi, didn't want to even hint that the greatness of the Reich might be threatened.

On January 20, 1945, everything changed. The First Ukrainian Front commanded by Marshal Ivan Konev was approaching Silesia. The temperature dropped to minus four degrees Fahrenheit. There were one million people in Breslau. Besides the residents, there were German refugees from the East, prisoners of war, prisoners of a branch of the Gross-Rosen concentration camp, and forced laborers.

At ten in the morning the loudspeakers called upon women and children to evacuate immediately. Panic broke out in Breslau. The train stations were swarming with crowds, so some people decided to flee on foot. Sixty thousand women and children headed toward the town of Kanth. Eighteen thousand of them would die on the way.

In the next few days, mothers with children would be followed by men unfit for military service. The authorities already knew that two-thirds of the population had to be evacuated. They couldn't imagine, however, that ninety thousand Breslau residents would die during the escape. Some refugees headed toward a Dresden that soon would be destroyed by carpet bombing.

On February 5 the Soviet army encircled the city. There were 65,000 German soldiers in Fortress Breslau, and, according to various estimates, 80,000–200,000 civilians. A week later the Soviets stormed the city.

The fighting didn't stop. Sometimes the Russians entered the suburbs, then they were forced out. In March the Germans introduced a new fighting tactic called *toten Räume*, or "dead space." They forced the suburbs' inhabitants to evacuate with only a few moments notice and then they burned down their homes. They destroyed churches and historic monuments. The Russians kept up with them. They incinerated every seized house to flush out hiding Germans and captured the buildings, floor by floor.

Airplanes delivered provisions for the city. In total, they would bring 1,638 tons of supplies, mostly ammunition. When the main city airport, in the nearby village of Gandau, was in danger, Gauleiter Hanke came up with the idea of building a new airstrip in the center of Breslau. He was backed by the new fortress commander, Hermann Niehoff. Part of one street with its university buildings, numerous edifices, and offices would be blown up, then leveled by civilians. Several thousand people, forced laborers and residents, including children, died during the construction of the new airfield.

The fighting continued through April. The Russians bombed the city from the air and opened heavy artillery fire. They captured Breslau step by step. So when on April 14, 1945, Bolesław Drobner's team arrived in

Wrocław from Kanth, they barely got to Hindenburgplatz. The Russians discouraged them from venturing any farther into the city.

On the last day of April 1945 Adolf Hitler committed suicide. On May 2 Berlin capitulated. Commander Hermann Niehoff surrendered Fortress Breslau four days later. At night, Karl Hanke, furious and frightened, confiscated a light aircraft and fled into the Sudeten Mountains. His plane was the only one that had ever taken off from the new airstrip in the city center.

APRIL AND MAY 1945

The photographer caught them when they moved. He called out to them to stop for a moment, and they appeared a bit blurred. They were standing on a pile of rubble that used to be Lehmgrubenstrasse, and soon would be Gliniana Street. There were incinerated buildings behind them. The barricade reached halfway up the ground floor.

It was on May 10, 1945, that Drobner had his first moments in this city. It must have gotten cooler because, despite the sun, they had their coats on and the mayor was wearing a hat. There were five members of the new City Council of Wrocław. The had gotten out of the car to ask for directions because the street they were driving on came to an end abruptly.

They were appalled by the magnitude of destruction, but they didn't know the numbers yet. They didn't know that out of 30,000 surviving buildings, 20,000 were seriously damaged. Of 186,000 apartments, over 53,000 had been completely destroyed. Of 422 public buildings, 48 were gone. Of 176 schools, 116 were severely damaged. Of 104 university places, 70 were in ruins. Sixty percent of the industrial structures had been totally destroyed. Three bridges on the Oder and a fair number of railway overpasses were severely damaged and impassable. Streetcars, tracks, and overhead cables hardly existed. Phones didn't work. There was no electricity, gas, or water.

Besides, Wrocław was still burning and new fires kept erupting. Some were set by Soviet soldiers who wanted to cover the traces of their plundering. Buildings were also accidentally set alight by looters who illuminated plundered basements with burning pieces of paper. The city was stuffed with exploding mines and projectiles.

Recruitment to the group of Wrocław pioneers continued through April. Almost every day Bolesław Drobner interviewed candidates personally.

Figure 8.7. Bolesław Drobner on Gliniana Street. Wrocław, May 10, 1945. Reproduced from *Dolny Śląsk. Collective work*. Edited by Kirył Sosnowski and Mieczysław Suchocki. Vol 1. Western Institute. Poznań. Wrocław 1948

These interviews were open to the public. The Wrocław mayor wished to assemble a team of people dedicated to the cause, like himself. Potential looters and freeloaders were dismissed. He would have preferred to hire only socialists from his own party. However, he was aware that this wouldn't always be possible. "Prewar supporters of Sanacja with their blemished résumés were willing to go to Wrocław. I had to make use of them, if they had administrative experience. One of them was Doctor Łach. In the past we had a bone to pick with him. . . . Sometimes those people had to be expelled from Wrocław," Drobner would recall, explaining his hiring followers of the prewar Polish government.

At Drobner's invitation, professor Stanisław Kulczyński, an expert on arachnids and the prewar rector of Jan Kazimierz University in Lvov, tried to assemble a group of scientists. Many declined his request. They preferred to remain in Krakow, move to Toruń or to Silesia. In the end, Kulczyński recruited twenty-seven people—university and polytechnic fellows and

experts on the preservation of historical treasures. That group was comple-
mented with students and assistants. They didn't know in what conditions
they would live and therefore decided not to take any women along. The
only exception was Zofia Gostomska, a librarian, who had walked across
Canada and was familiar with weapons. One of the first assignments of
this academic group, while they were still in Krakow, was to prepare pho-
tographic copies of the map of Wrocław.

The Wrocław gasworks was to be resurrected by Mieczysław Seifert,
the former director of the City Gasworks in Krakow. Mieczysław Rakisz,
a fire brigade captain, would be in charge of the Fire Department. Adam
Konopczyński, a Krakow labor inspector, would organize the Housing Department. The Department of Culture would be headed by Stefan Podgór-
ski, and the Health Department by Mieczysław Czarnecki, a community
worker. Maciej Łach, former district head of Nowy Sącz, would supervise
the Municipal Council. Drobner also invited his old friend, Adam Kabaja,
"a man of great ideas" from the technical staff of the Słowacki Theater in
Krakow.

Drobner, a nonbeliever himself, realized that in Wrocław he would need
Polish clergy. The Krakow Metropolitan Curia appointed canon Kazimierz
Lagosz to join the group. Before the war he had been a priest in the Lvov
Archdiocese, a religion instructor, and an activist in the People's Libraries
Society. Lagosz brought with him three Catholic priests and one Protestant.
In the Wrocław Municipal Administration, the engineer Kazimierz Kuli-
gowski, prewar director of the Syndicate of Polish Steel Casting Companies,
would be responsible for commerce and industry. Bolesław Drobner would
appoint him his deputy.

Józefa Filipowiczowa would be the second deputy mayor. Who was
that rather short and sturdy woman who, in every photograph, hugged
a large purse that made her look like Moominmamma, who resembled a
cartoon hippo? I found her only trace in a letter of Bolesław Drobner to
a PSP comrade. This letter was written in July 1945 when it had been a
month since Drobner had stopped being mayor of Wrocław. "Consider the
Filipowiczowa case. She is a fraud because she pinned on a bunch of medals
without being entitled to them. It turns out that she has never been a judge,
captain, or voivode. She was in Pawiak prison for nonpolitical reasons. She
should be removed immediately, but Mazur tells me that Wachniewski
[Drobner's successor as mayor] allowed her to oversee state property, that

is, the furniture from the villa. She came to Wrocław with a purse, and left with a truck . . . for her services to Wrocław."

Altogether, the group that would go to Wrocław with Bolesław Drobner was made up of 160 people. They would work in eight departments and in the Public Benefit Administration. They were later joined by cooks, a hairdresser, and a cleaning crew.

The department heads were meeting every day in Bolesław Drobner's apartment in Krakow. Packed and ready, they waited for the signal that Wrocław had surrendered. On May 7, Mayor Drobner received the message from Lieutenant Colonel Repin that the path was clear. A day later the pioneers loaded their belongings and equipment onto the trucks. It was May 8, 1945. That day the war ended.

"I didn't reprimand people for being so exhilarated. Wrocław is ours! They were singing, '100 years! 100 years, may they live!' They couldn't stop," Drobner reminisced after many years.

On May 9 at dawn, the first truck with the Supply Management Unit left Krakow, led by the academic researcher Antoni Kot. Their task was to find a night's lodging for the pioneers. The same day in the afternoon the remaining members of the Operational Unit of the Wrocław Municipal Administration left Krakow. They had stuck a white and red flag on the truck hood. They made a stop in Katowice. Miraculously, they found a table in the coffee shop near the train station and waited for a long time so the waitress could serve them lukewarm coffee. They spent a night in the District Office in Brzeg and in the early morning, after a potluck breakfast with butter, cold cuts, cheese, and canned food, they moved westward.

MAY 12, 1945

I like this photograph very much. It's private, random, and was taken as a souvenir, not for the needs of propaganda. Bolesław Drobner, standing between two police officers, doesn't pay any attention to the photographer. Turned aside, he is saying something to the smiling man in a flat cap, most likely the engineer Kuligowski. Two other figures on the right side of the photo, two bashful women soldiers in skirts and white socks, look like girls at a Scout meeting. The young women are wearing berets. They have rifles across their backs and small flags in their hands. They were assigned to direct traffic at the crossroads. They were probably bored on

Figure 8.8. Mayor Bolesław Drobner (second from left) with representatives of the Wrocław Municipal Administration, on their way to Żagań, Headquarters of the First Ukrainian Front. May 12, 1945. The signs show distances to various cities. Reproduced from *Trudne dni. Wrocław 1945 r. we wspomnieniach pionierów*. Zakład Narodowy im. Ossolińskich. Wrocław 1960

the temporarily empty road, so they were invited to the group photograph. They pose against a backdrop of road signs in Russian. From where they are standing, Breslau is 142 kilometers away, Berlin 164. The photo is taken by a photographer accompanying the Wrocław mayor's team on their way to Sagau (Żagań), where the headquarters of the First Ukrainian Front is stationed.

It was all very strange. The government in Warsaw was not interested in Bolesław Drobner. Nobody wanted any reports, nobody was curious how those Poles were doing in the ruined post-German city. No representative of the Ministry of Culture or Education showed up in Wrocław, not even for a day. As late as Bolesław Drobner's dismissal on June 9, 1945, the Ministry of Public Administration had never sent him any formal description of his powers. Only once did a representative of the Ministry of Industry drop by, but this representative claimed to have his own instructions regarding the industrial plants and didn't even contact the Municipal Administration.

It appeared that Mayor Drobner had a free hand in Wrocław, but he knew this could not be true. So he sent his people to Warsaw with questions about industry in Wrocław, assuming control over the factories and river transport on the Oder. "Warsaw remained silent," he recalled in the future. He asked for some people from the Ministry of Public Security. A small group of them arrived in Wrocław, but they didn't get in touch with the local authorities.

A police force was missing in the city and nothing indicated that it would be formed soon. So, on his own initiative, engineer Kuligowski created the Municipal Guard. He announced its recruitment and within a week assembled a unit of 150 men. He gave them weapons, swore them in, made a speech, and organized checkpoints. However, after two days, all the guards vanished without a trace, together with their rifles.

From mid-May, an Operational Unit of eleven people, sent by the Central Committee of the Polish Workers' Party, was active in Wrocław. Andrzej Żak, first secretary of the PWP City Committee, would reminisce: "Some activists from the Polish Socialist Party came with Drobner to Wrocław in May 1945. They also established their own party organization. At first, collaboration between our two parties was not smooth. Initially, we had no capacity to have an impact on the Municipal Administration." This would change soon and the next, post-Drobner mayor of Wrocław would be a communist.

In reality it was the Russians who governed the city and had the final say. Since his arrival, Bolesław Drobner sought an arrangement with the Soviet commander of Wrocław, Lieutenant Colonel Lyapunov. It was Lyapunov who issued passes for Poles that allowed them to move about the city, ordered members of the administration to wear white and red armbands, authorized them to govern in Wrocław, opened food depositories for them, and appointed Captain Burkunov as liaison officer. Burkunov's job was to rectify all potential misunderstandings with Soviet unit commanders, but by implication he was to spy on the Poles. It was Lyapunov who offered the pioneers the first lodgings in the surviving buildings at 23, 25, and 27 Blücherstrasse. A visit paid by Drobner in Żagań to the commanders of the First Ukrainian Front was of great significance. From there he brought a letter for Lyapunov, ordering him immediately to hand over all municipal plants, academic institutions, and factories to the Polish administration.

Truly, in his contacts with the Russians Drobner was balancing like an acrobat on a tightrope. He was aware that the Soviets had no inhibitions and treated Wrocław like their property. They looted, stole, drank, raped, set fires, fired in the air to celebrate, and they shot at people. So what if Lyapunov had promised to transfer Wrocław industry into Polish hands? Soon, there would be nothing left to transfer. Night and day, the Russians disassembled and removed anything they could from the factories. Mayor Drobner could see this, but couldn't talk about it. After all, whom should he complain to? Sometimes he tried to intervene. In the volume of his memoirs titled *Trudne dni* (Difficult days), published in 1960 (censored, to be sure), he would describe this diplomatically: "Workers informed the Municipal Administration that equipment from many factories in Wrocław was about to be shipped out. On May 18 I had to go to Legnica for the day to discuss this issue. Two days later I was visited by Colonel Repin and other officers, who claimed it was a misunderstanding, because the equipment that had been packed or that was to be packed remained the property of Poland."

The Russians lied to Drobner through their teeth. And most likely, he was aware of this. Although they would return some confiscated machines from the Linke-Hofmann Works to the Poles, they would be incomplete, missing important components that were hard to replace. They would keep on exporting more machines from other factories. According to the journalist Friedrich Jerrig's report from 1949, Bolesław Drobner was even slapped by one of the Russian generals for openly criticizing the increased looting by Russian soldiers.

The Poles were already in Wrocław. But the Potsdam Conference hadn't taken place yet. What if the Allies decided to leave Breslau in Germany? Just in case, the Soviet commander allowed a German administration to be formed.

The Germans divided Breslau into fifty-four blocks. Their administrators were in charge of registering the German residents (there were 200,000 of them in the entire city), sending them to work, allocating food, supervising local stores, and protecting their citizens. The Russians even allowed them to establish a police force, that, as in the Third Reich, was called the *Ordnungspolizei*. At the beginning of June, in Sępolno district, a curious announcement appeared calling for "all Jews, half-Jews, Poles, and citizens of any nationality" to report to the German Employment Office. Drobner intervened with the Soviet commander and the placards disappeared. Drobner received reports about passive resistance by the Germans, and even about military exercises by sabotage units like *Werwolf* in the woods outside Wrocław.

Germans, mostly socialists and communists, revealed themselves in the city, claiming that they hated Hitler and had always been against him. They joined together into groups. The most important was the Antifascist Freedom Movement also known as Antifa, led by Hermann Hartmann, and the German Union of Antifascists, headed by Paul Marzoll.

German antifascists offered support for the Soviet and Polish authorities in administering the city and in hunting for war criminals and Third Reich officials. The two German groups contended with each other, mainly by way of denunciations. As a result of this it would soon be clear that most members of the antifascist organizations in Wrocław not so long ago had belonged to the NSDAP (the Nazi Party).

The Soviet–Polish–German triumvirate in Wrocław would come to an end after the Potsdam Conference, and the German administration as well as the antifascist organizations would be dissolved on August 16, 1945.

MAY 1945

Here a photograph of Bolesław Drobner at work would be most appropriate. I have one, although it was not taken until early June and in my story it is still May. Drobner, lit by sunrays falling through the window, is sitting at a large desk. His right hand is resting on the desktop, and his left on the armrest. There is a flower in the pot in front of him. His hair, as always, is swept back and he is dressed in his eternal *gymnastyorka*, displaying equality with the workers. He has pinned a silver eagle, usually placed on soldiers' caps, to the left pocket of his shirt. He is smiling, but he is tense.

From the very first day their work had been grueling. As soon as they arrived and had hardly even gotten out of the trucks, they rushed to see whether anything was still standing in Wrocław. Among burning buildings, the priest Lagosz and other clergymen visited local churches and chapels. Lagosz wondered how to get planks, nails, and hammers to board up the ripped doors and windows. Tomorrow, the day after tomorrow at the latest,

Figure 8.9. Bolesław Drobner in his office. Standing: Maria Jeleniowa and Lieutenant Wiktor Orczewski. June 9, 1945. Reproduced from *Trudne dni. Wrocław 1945 r. we wspomnieniach pionierów*. Zakład Narodowy im. Ossolińskich. Wrocław 1960

the Russians would give him a yellow cart, one horse, and a bunch of planks. On the wall of each provisionally secured building he would post a sign: "No trespassing. Municipal Administration of Wrocław."

Professor Kulczyński, accompanied by his academic colleagues, forced his way through the rubble toward the university. The Department of Geology and Mineralogy had been destroyed, a skeleton of the building of the Department of Chemistry stuck out nearby, and on its ground floor one could only see squashed tables and instruments. The baroque main edifice had been split in two by a bomb. Access was blocked by a barricade made of wet and moldy books. In the building of Geology and Anthropology the Polish scientists found scattered animal bones and a stack of human skulls. Although the building of the Humanities Departments was missing windows and a roof, it was sound. The University Library was burning, but across the street, in the St. Anne University Church, they found 300,000 books carried there from the library. It was a real treasure. They didn't know that the next day someone would start a fire and the surviving collection would burn up. Further inspection of university property was disheartening. They could only see cinders, ruins, and fires. They went back low-spirited.

Mieczysław Rakisz, the Fire Brigade captain, could see that he would have a lot of work in the burning city, but how could he put out the fire without adequate equipment? Wandering around Wrocław he discovered the undamaged Museum of Firefighting. He then turned on the antique fire engines and with great effort stopped the fire in the city center.

Almost immediately, Adam Kabaja, from the Słowacki Theater, moved into the surviving, though damaged building of the Opera. Drobner would write about him: "He disappeared. He wouldn't come to dinner, wouldn't search for shoes or shirts. . . . He was making a record of stage props and costumes, patching holes in the roof, packing printed materials, and stopping small fires."

In the evenings, departmental heads and administrators attended a briefing in Mayor Drobner's apartment. They would continue to do so for many days, and then would move their meetings to the former school at Różana Street, because Drobner's apartment would turn out to be too small. They shared their impressions, studied city maps, and assigned tasks for the next day. This stubborn, argumentative, and resentful socialist, who was regarded as one of the worst local PSP activists, turned out to be—for the first and last time in his life—a natural leader in times of crisis. The month of his governing would later be known as the time of the "Drobner Republic." Bolesław Drobner later wrote: "What that first Operational Unit did in a few days was unbelievable. They were all possessed by zeal."

Drobner sketched plans for the future. Wrocław would remain a city with the status of a voivodeship. Administration employees would get the best apartments in the same neighborhood. Reportedly, his dream was that there wouldn't be any money circulating in the city and that workers would be getting coupons for food and clothing. What is certain is that, initially, there was no money in Wrocław. German currency was no longer valid and Polish currency didn't exist yet. And when the new currency finally came to the Western Territories, hardly anyone trusted it. Although the employees of the Municipal Administration had their salaries fixed at 100 zlotys per day, the actual payments were only made after a few months.

In spite of the fact that the mayor tried to pick the best people, some of them disappointed him from the very beginning. A foreman who was supposed to work on the renovations assigned by the administration, asked right away when he would be able to start his own business. Someone from the team plundered clothing, another stole some products for his drugstore in Łódź.

Michał Śliwa, the author of *Bolesław Drobner: Szkic o działalności polity-cznej* [Bolesław Drobner: Essays on political activity] recalled his own visit to Wrocław. The mayor would tell him, "You know, once again I started to believe in socialism! Some of my people don't take any salary at all!" And he mentioned a few of the names of prewar distributors of *Naprzód*, a socialist newspaper. "Doctor Drobner, this is not good!" Śliwa told him. And then he added in his memoirs: "Unfortunately, it came out very quickly that these demoralized drunkards had been doing 'exes' (expropriations), which in reality was plain robbery."

Perhaps Bolesław Drobner was not so naive as Michał Śliwa thought. A car bringing the wives of two engineers to Wrocław ran over a mine. The women died and their bodies, placed in coffins and loaded into a locked car, were to be sent back to Krakow. "With deep sorrow we were saying good-bye to our widowed comrades, but Doctor Drobner, a better authority on the human soul, insisted on opening the car. The key was missing. When we broke open the door, we noticed two coffins and two sacks of coffee next to them. It seems they were tossed in there to alleviate someone's grief," Stanisław Kulczyński would recall in the future.

Initially, all pioneers lived in several residential buildings assigned by the Russians on Blücherstrasse (later Pioneers Square). The mayor's apartment and the apartments of his close associates were located on the second floor of house number 27. The third floor was for the scientists. The fourth and fifth floors, as well as the other buildings, numbers 23 and 25, were divided among members of the administration, four people to one room. Shooting could be heard at night, a curfew was in force, and they all slept with rifles by their beds.

The Germans who used to live there had been thrown out. Only the owner of the bakery at number 27 was left. He baked free bread for the pioneers. The former residents had left fully equipped apartments. There were sheets on the beds, towels in the bathrooms, and tableware in the credenzas. One of the clergy who accompanied the priest Lagosz marveled at that luxury and believed that previously those apartments must have belonged to Germans who were officers, at the very least. Unfortunately, the buildings had no roofs. When after a few days it rained, all apartments were flooded down to the first floor.

From the very first day, on the square in front of the building, there had been a canteen for the pioneers. Three meals a day were offered at fixed times. Some people ate standing up because there were not enough seats for everyone. The canteen had no roof and occasionally raindrops would fall into the plates. Bean soup with bacon was a fixed item on the lunch menu, but actually finding food remained a serious problem. At first there were no shortages of flour, buckwheat, and sugar, but fresh meat, vegetables, and dairy products could only be dreamed of.

Zofia Gostomska would remember that the canteens were seriously concerned about "how to serve preserved meat, stinking and covered with maggots, in order that a customer could swallow it with the least possible revulsion. So the meat was first cleaned with a scrub brush and then rinsed with a disinfectant. The effects of consuming food treated this way were immediate . . . the lack of fatalities can only be explained as a stroke of luck. Flies that multiplied on dead bodies and horse carcasses during the siege of the city, preying on the reserves of salted . . . meat in the post-German depositories, were attacking even apartments in swarms, like bees, covering windows and equipment with their black, bustling multitude."

MAY 26, 1945

Two photographs. Each of them is missing something. Put together, they form one whole.

The first shows a raised platform in front of the ruins of the Hohenzollern Palace on Schlossplatz (from now on, Freedom Square). Ceremoniously decorated with white and red fabric and spruce branches, it supports dozens of people. Bolesław Drobner stands in the middle. The photographer caught him while he was giving a speech—the mayor's mouth is open as if he were singing. What is happening in front of the platform can't be seen.

The second photo shows a street and a parade. Three soldiers of the Polish Second Army, wearing their dress uniforms, are saluting in the direction of the platform, which is not visible. The orchestra is playing. But most important is what lies on the ground, under the soldiers' feet.

Figure 8.10. Mayor Drobner attending the parade on Freedom Square. Reproduced from *Trudne dni. Wrocław 1945 r. we wspomnieniach pionierów*. Zakład Narodowy im. Ossolińskich. Wrocław 1960

Figure 8.11. Parade on Freedom Square. Polish soldiers trampling German flags. May 26, 1945. Archive

The mayor of Wrocław not only worked for the city. He was also a host. In other words, he did what he liked best—delivering speeches, writing appeals, organizing meetings and rallies. A day after his arrival in the city, he visited former prisoners of the concentration camp in Buchwald, outside Wrocław. He was accompanied by a team from Polish Film Chronicle. On May 16 he attended the opening of the newly finished cemetery for Soviet soldiers. In his speech he promised that the city would never forget "those who died on Polish soil for your freedom and ours," quoting a traditional Polish slogan.

At the same time, he wrote an appeal to the Poles who were in Wrocław—residents of prewar Breslau, prisoners of war, and forced laborers. "Poles! Lower Silesia has returned to the Motherland! . . . You are not in a foreign country, but in your own, free, independent, and democratic Poland, in the lands of Bolesław I the Great and Bolesław III the Wry-Mouthed." At the end of May, he met representatives of the Wrocław Polish diaspora.

He was not fond of the monuments that had survived the battle of Fortress Breslau. Michał Śliwa wrote: "Because Doctor Drobner appreciated propaganda and liked historic gestures, I remember how once, using a thick rope, he was tugging the leg of some proud rider off his pedestal. It was some Fritz or Wilhelm. When the stubborn figure didn't fall, he ordered the hooves of the bronze courser to be sawed off." This Fritz on Wrocław's Market Square was a statue of King Friedrich Wilhelm III. In the future it would be replaced by a statue of the nineteenth-century Polish playwright Count Alexander Fredro.

Wilhelm I, made of bronze, and standing on the square in front of the Wertheim department store, was not to his taste, either. When in October 1945 the Municipal Administration decided to knock the figure down from the pedestal, Bolesław Drobner was invited to come and deliver a speech.

During the inspection of City Hall after the fire was extinguished, in the basement Drobner and his associates encountered several wooden chests and a coffer with metal fittings. In another room they found a storage place with flags bearing swastikas. The chests and flags were transported to the mayor's apartment. The engineer Kuligowski would recall that the coffer contained sixteen councillors' chains "made of silver-plated wooden links, with ornaments of guild insignias, Piast eagles, etc." The other chests were full of dozens of crystal glasses, cups, and jugs with engraved monograms of Friedrich Wilhelm.

Drobner convened a commission to take charge of the treasure. The chests ended up in the Municipal Administration Building. In 1948 they would fade away without a trace. The police and the Ministry of Public Security conducted a search and Drobner was interrogated, too, but to no avail.

When it came to the flags with swastikas, the mayor already had an idea how to use them.

Bolesław Drobner dreamed of a huge parade of Polish soldiers. Although Breslau was captured by the Russians, some units of the Polish Second Army participated in the initial battle for the fortress. They were later withdrawn and directed to the fighting behind the line of the Oder and Neisse. On May 10 the Russians held their victory parade, marching and saluting mostly to themselves and to the petrified Germans hiding in the basements.

Therefore, when, on May 22, 1945, the mayor received a message that one of the Polish Second Army divisions wanted to come to Wrocław, he announced preparations for a huge demonstration. Placards appeared all over the city: "Poles! Fulfill your national duty and come in great numbers to the place of celebration to pay tribute to our army returning with victory banners from Berlin, Dresden, and other German cities. City Mayor Doctor Bolesław Drobner."

Two days later the platform in front of the Hohenzollern Palace was ready. The crowd was quite large. Mayor Drobner delivered a speech: "I rub my eyes and can't believe that the Polish Army can stand on the former Schlossplatz, that we can sing our anthem 'Poland Has Not Yet Perished.'"

The units marched through the center of Wrocław and approached Freedom Square. Now it was time for a surprise. Drobner reminisced: "And at this moment, just before our riders showed up, some of our boys jumped out on the road and threw forty flags with swastikas under the hooves of Polish horses. Our horses trotted over the swastikas and trampled them. This demonstration made a huge impression."

JUNE 9, 1945

The farewell photograph. Today Bolesław Drobner is returning to Krakow. He has been mayor of Wrocław for thirty-six days. He doesn't want to leave

Figure 8.12. Farewell to Bolesław Drobner in front of the Municipal Administration building. June 9, 1945. City Museum of Wrocław

at all. The car door is open. Maria Jeleniowa, an employee of the Municipal Administration, taller than Drobner by a head, holds a bunch of roses. She is ready to throw them at the mayor as he gets into the car, but he halts to pose for the photo.

He doesn't feel tired at all. He has plenty of ideas.

So why did he resign? Was he forced out? Did Prime Minister Os-óbka-Morawski realize that this stubborn socialist was doing too well in Wrocław? They were certainly not so close as they used to be in Moscow. Actually, it looked as if they couldn't stand each other because, when alone with his friends, Drobner called Osóbka an imbecile.

Was it because Drobner didn't allow people from the Polish Workers' Party to have any influence on his ideas? The socialists predominated only in the Municipal Administration. Other organizations in the city had been taken over by members of the communist PWP. Drobner insisted on the separation of the PSP and the PWP. Even though officially he advocated collaboration with communists, he also demanded equal treatment for socialists. The Polish Socialist Party could not be treated like a younger brother! Was this the reason the Secret Police kept a file on Drobner (code name "Shaky") and investigated whether he was a fascist and a traitor to Poland?

Maybe it was about the mayor's hurt pride? How long could you put up with being ignored? After all, Ochab had promised him that he would govern Wrocław as a voivode, but at the end of May a new administrative division of Lower Silesia was announced, and Wrocław did not get the status of autonomous city. The true reason for Bolesław Drobner's resignation is not known.

The photographer triggers the shutter. The closest coworkers who have come to say good-bye to their mayor split up. Drobner gets into the car, shuts the door, and with roses on his lap departs for Krakow. The trunk is full of gifts from his pioneers: five liters of vodka, ten kilos of cottage cheese, thirty cans of food, two carpets, and some small appliances.

In 1955 he was not invited for the tenth anniversary of the liberation of Wrocław.

SEPTEMBER 1945

Attention! If you want something sweet, go to Gdańsk for your treat. Bison, a sweet beast, offers a feast. Gingerbread, cookies and candy, pudding, pepper, everything dandy. Bison Food products.

—*Dziennik Bałtycki*, Sept. 3, 1945

• • • • • • • • • • • • • •

Witnesses to the death of Józef Żabczyński in Żoliborz are kindly asked to provide more details to his parents. Grochów, 24 Igańska Street.

—*Życie Warszawy*, Sept. 4, 1945

• • • • • • • • • • • • • •

If you were employed in Warsaw after the Uprising and can point out the location where the bodies from the premises at 24 Wiktorska Street, Mokotów, are buried, please leave a message. Reward. Mokotów, Maryjna.

—*Życie Warszawy*, Sept. 4, 1945

• • • • • • • • • • • • • •

For family reasons I am looking for Viera Fedoronko, the wife of military chaplain Szymon Fedoronko. Whoever may have some information about her, please write to Rey Joseph Fedoronko, PO Box 763, Terryville, Conn., USA

—*Życie Warszawy*, Sept. 7, 1945

• • • • • • • • • • • • • •

Bedbugs! I will pay 1,000 zlotys to anyone who finds a live bedbug after pest control or disinfection performed by me with gases that don't damage any fabric or other objects. Licensed disinfection company,

Antoni Marcinkowski, Warsaw, 13 Leszno Street.

—*Życie Warszawy*, Sept. 8, 1945

• • • • • • • • • • • • • •

Attention, homeless! We are convening shareholders to collect the capital for purchasing a beautiful building in the center for 15% of its prewar value and renovating its apartments. Pacek.

—*Życie Warszawy*, Sept. 9, 1945

• • • • • • • • • • • • • •

I will sell copyrights for mystery stories and novels. 24 Poznańska Street.

—*Życie Warszawy*, Sept. 10, 1945

• • • • • • • • • • • • • •

Doctor Leon Yepifanov, gynecologist. All procedures. Eugenic, sexual, marital, and premarital consultation. Gdynia, 17 Starowiejska Street.

—*Dziennik Bałtycki*, Sept. 16, 1945

• • • • • • • • • • • • • •

Street and courtyard singers who, during the occupation, were singing or playing FORBIDDEN SONGS in the streets, courtyards, streetcars, and trains, please report to the Warsaw Branch of the Film Company on Monday, September 17, and Tuesday, September 18, between 3 p.m. and 6 p.m., 5 Belgijska Street. Telephone no. 756.

—*Życie Warszawy*, Sept. 16, 1945

• • • • • • • • • • • • • •

State Vehicle Office, 5 Narutowicz Square, will be hiring a number of former officers and NCOs with vehicle and repair expertise. They will be sent to vehicle units in the countryside, mainly in Upper and Lower Silesia, Western Pomerania, and East Prussia. We are looking for foremen, mechanics, fitters, electrical fitters, turners, locksmiths, and grinders.

—*Życie Warszawy*, Sept. 16, 1945

• • • • • • • • • • • • • • • • •

Esteemed doctors and surgeons. John of God Hospital, August 12–15, 1944. The last moments of Andrzej Sobolewski. I plead for any information. 10 Szuster Street.

—*Życie Warszawy*, Sept. 26, 1945

• • • • • • • • • • • • • • • • •

Soldiers of Batallion Parasol! I implore you for any information about Zofia Świeszcz, nom de guerre: "Zojda," medic, after the surrender sent to German camp. Leave message at 36 Mniszewska Street near Tarnowiecka Street, Grochów. Mrs. Świeszczowa.

—*Życie Warszawy*, Sept. 28, 1945

• • • • • • • • • • • • • • • • •

We will buy a large number of Polish keys for typewriters. Block Brun Agency, Gdynia, 37 February 10 Street.

—*Dziennik Bałtycki*, Sept. 29, 1945

• • • • • • • • • • • • • • • • •

Tractor drivers, drivers, mechanics. Apply for work on American tractors. Thousands of tractors received from the UNRRA [United Nations Relief and Rehabilitation Administration]. The Recovered Territories are awaiting you. They have to be plowed and planted with seeds. Polish society, devastated and malnourished during the occupation, cannot go hungry. Each of you will receive room and board, salary, and a bonus for good work. Apply to State Company of Tractors and Agricultural Equipment, Łódź, 46 Kościuszki Avenue.

—*Dziennik Bałtycki*, Sept. 29, 1945

• • • • • • • • • • • • • • • • •

You will make 1,000 zlotys or more in any city by selling top-quality goods in high demand. Brochures mailed by Florina, Krakow, 19 Chocimska Street.

—*Życie Warszawy*, Sept. 29, 1945

• • • • • • • • • • • • • • • • •

Belgians! Come back to your motherland! Information available at Mission Belge de Repatriement, Warsaw, Przyjaciół Avenue, and Polish Red Cross, Gdynia, Świętojańska Street.

—*Dziennik Bałtycki*, Sept. 30, 1945

• • • • • • • • • • • • • • • • •

September 1945, new publications by Czytelnik Publishers: Henryk Sienkiewicz, *Teutonic Knights*, 160 zlotys; Zofia Dróżdż and Władysław Milczarek, *In Love with Pomerania*, 26 zlotys; J. Zawicki and D. Walawski, *Collection of Special Rules against Nazi Criminals* and *Traitors to the Nation*, 45 zlotys.

—*Życie Warszawy*, Sept. 30, 1945

Edith and Władzia in Breslau / Wrocław

EDITH

"The Soviets hanged us," says a boy. "My mom, my sisters, and me."

Edith walks up to the attic to see her neighbors hanging in a row from the wooden ceiling.

"And you?" She turns to the boy. "You are surely alive."

"I slipped my hand under the noose when they left. I succeeded somehow," he replies.

The funeral of the hanged is brief. Edith's mother doesn't know where the cemetery is, so she asks some men to bury the bodies in the garden, next to the house with the attic.

This happens in January 1945 in the town of Oels, near Breslau. The Poles who will one day move to Oleśnica, the former Oels, near Wrocław, and take possession of the garden will never discover the German family buried under the flower beds.

Edith Schmidt was eleven years old. She had two younger brothers and her mother, Agnes. Her father, Franz, had been in the war for a few years fighting the enemy. That was what the adults said over the children's heads, because her mom didn't talk to Edith about the war. She considered her daughter too sensitive for this.

Until now Edith hadn't been able to imagine an enemy. But now she knew that he looked like a Soviet soldier.

Agnes protected Edith from the enemy. The first day the Soviets entered Oels, she hid her and her brothers in a large cauldron for boiling linen. She covered it with some rags.

Then every morning her mother disheveled Edith's hair, smeared ashes over her face, dressed her in rags, and told her to slouch. "You look like a grandma." Agnes smiled. Edith didn't understand why she had done this.

Agnes removed golden earrings from her daughter's ears. They were a present from her godfather, a jeweler in Breslau. Women in Oels were saying that Russians would pull out gold and ears together.

Edith took with her a doll with a porcelain face. She called her Andzia. It had been her birthday present a few years earlier. The doll had a few dresses, a coat, little shoes, and a pram in which she was wheeled about. At night Edith reminded Andzia in whispers what their life had been like in Breslau.

Her dad was a carpenter. People said he was highly skilled. He worked on the construction of Wertheim, now Renoma, the largest department store in Breslau. Mom took care of Edith's three-year-old brother. She and her other younger brother went to school. They lived in the center, at Brunnerstrasse, which led toward the main station. The children's room was full of toys. Their parents had their own bedroom. There was a kitchen and a large clothing closet.

On Sundays they would walk in the park together or they would go to the neighborhood of Hundsfeld, where their aunt and uncle had a large apartment house with a garden in which they could play all day.

Edith was the first to leave Breslau. She got sick from sitting in the school basement where classes were held because of the bombing. So in the fall of 1944 her mother applied to the local administration and Edith was placed with a nice childless couple in Ludwigsdorf near Oels. The older of Edith's two brothers, who also left the city, was not so lucky. The farmer's wife who took him told him to sleep in the barn.

When Edith's mother found out, she applied for social housing in an unfurnished attic in Oels. From her apartment at Brunnerstrasse Agnes took beds and chests, and loaded them onto a wagon. She tied up pots and pans with a rope, rolled up the bedsheets into a bundle, locked the door, and moved to Oels with her youngest. The two older children joined her there. The wardrobe was left in Breslau. The attic in Oels was too low for such tall furniture.

A farmer she knew in Oels was fleeing with his family to the West before the Russians showed up.

"I will take you on my wagon," he told Agnes. "But when the horses get tired, you will have to walk."

"Even in the fields, in the snow and freezing weather?" asked Agnes.

"Yes," answered the farmer.

"In that case, we are staying," she decided.

When the Russians came, Agnes Schmidt moved to the large farm nearby, where a dozen other German families were seeking shelter. She thought they would be safer there together. The Soviets ordered the women to work on the farm. Every day Edith's mother milked sixteen cows.

At night, people in Oels watched the glow above the burning "Fortress Breslau," as the Nazi propagandists called it. Agnes was worried about whether there would be anything to come back to.

WŁADZIA

She couldn't stand being in Rzeczniów. When the Russians liberated the village in January 1945, she went to her native Radom to see what was going on, and then traveled to Warsaw because she liked some action. She was twenty-four and claimed she represented "active youth." Her most striking characteristics were her pleasant nature and dainty body. Her name was Władysława Okrutna, Władzia.

In Warsaw she could see posters saying, "Young people are rebuilding Piast Silesia." She read that in Warsaw and Kielce there would be preparatory courses for future administrators in the Recovered Territories. She applied in Kielce because there she would be closer to her parents. In April 1945, at the first lecture, she met a hundred people like her. They studied history, administration, accounting, and management of human resources. The course would last until August.

Figure 9.1. Wrocław in ruins after the liberation. May 1945. PAP

Władzia's father had been a medic in the military. Drafted by the tsarist
army in 1905 he went East, leaving his wife and son in Radom. A few years
later she went to join him in Nizhny Novgorod by military train.

In 1920 the Okrutnys returned to Radom with four children, two chests
full of books printed in Cyrillic, and the father's screaming in his sleep in
Russian. Władzia was born in a newly independent Poland. She claimed
she had inherited a globe-trotting nature from her parents.

The bus was dilapidated. You could take a nap in it, and when you wanted
to pee at a stop along the road, it was ladies to the right, gentlemen to the
left. You could pick plums in the abandoned gardens because it was August
1945. The team of future administrators was traveling to the Recovered Territories. The man in charge was Stanisław Piaskowski, the former voivode
of the Kielce district, then government plenipotentiary for Lower Silesia,
and future voivode of the Wrocław district.

Figure 9.2. Wrocław in ruins after the liberation. May 1945. Reproduced by Kamil Kajko / Forum

They drove through ruined Wrocław without stopping because it was Lignica (future Legnica), spared from destruction, that was to be designated the capital of the voivodeship.

For the first three days they lived on the right bank of the Kaczawa River.

One of her colleagues wanted to scare Władzia. Standing by the window he said, "Look, three dead bodies are floating in the river." She shrugged. During the war she had completed first-aid training. She remembered pushing long meters of gray intestine into her friend's belly, before his funeral.

Then the Russians moved them to the other side of the river and a week later the plenipotentiary announced they were leaving for Wrocław.

EDITH

Agnes walked to Breslau to check on whether everything was in order in their old apartment on Brunnerstrasse. She took a friend with her. The more the merrier. They vowed not to speak German loudly, at the sight of Russian military vehicles they hid in the ditches, and not for all the world would they agree to a lift. There were thirty kilometers ahead of them.

"I will be gone for two days and one night," Agnes told her children. They cried.

This was July 1945.

At night, when Edith's mother was on her way to Breslau, young Soviet soldiers came to the farm. They raped all the women. But they steered clear of Edith. Was it because she was filthy and unkempt? When Agnes returned from Breslau, she was crying, because her apartment building had burned down. Only the charred window frames were left, and the wardrobe inside was half-burned, she told her children. On the same day all the women on the farm in Oels were weeping, too.

Three days later Agnes decided to leave for Germany. She packed three rucksacks, one for herself, two for her older children. She had a wooden wagon with a drawbar and she loaded it with packed clothes, a quilt, one pot, and her youngest son. The food was placed in Andzia the doll's pram that would be pushed by Edith.

They would walk to Breslau. Agnes thought that it would be easier to get to the West from there. On their way they stopped in the neighborhood called Hundsfeld to rest at their relatives.'

WŁADZIA

The villa was large and well cared for. It stood in Zalesie, a Wrocław neighborhood. The first floor was occupied by its owner, an angry yet terrified German woman. Władzia and her three friends would live on the second floor. "Only for a few days," they were told by a tall, red-haired captain at the housing center for administrators. "At that point, we will find you something in Sępolno."

The young women moved in to the second floor. They stroked the veneer of the furniture, lay down with sighs on the clean linen, and made faces in the crystal mirror. Each of them would take a souvenir from there, they decided. Władzia was fond of a box full of small drawers with thread, needles, and buttons. And a mandolin! "I will take it, too," she made up her mind.

Some noises coming from the first floor woke them up in the middle of the night. Someone knocked at the door. Through a crack in the curtain they could see four men speaking German. The owner let them in very quickly. In the morning, the German woman came upstairs and explained apologetically that she needed something from the wardrobe in the hall. Władzia could see that she was taking four pairs of men's shoes.

Władzia and the other future administrative workers of Wrocław didn't want to live there anymore. They were afraid.

Four days later the tall, red-haired captain picked them up. He held a bunch of keys, an apartment assignment printed in Russian, and some sheets of paper stamped with "A Pole lives here" that should be placed on the door.

EDITH

Agnes Schmidt and her children were tired when they reached Hundsfeld, now officially called Psie Pole. Their uncle was happy to see them. Their aunt and her two daughters were suffering from typhoid. All were hungry, because Germans who didn't work were not entitled to food.

"Stay with us," they begged Agnes. "Move into our apartment house. This is Breslau, so Franz will be looking for you here."

Edith's mom unpacked the pram of Andzia the doll. She fed her relatives, admitted they were right, and decided to stay in the city. After all, the sick aunt was Edith's godmother. Agnes felt that as a Catholic, she could not leave the needy.

Right after that her own daughter contracted typhoid. A Polish doctor told Agnes to light a blessed candle because the girl would soon die. A Russian doctor requested two liters of milk, lifted the girl's head, and poured the entire contents into her mouth. "She will live," he smiled, and walked out. Edith was sick for a long time, but the Russian had been right.

The building still belonged to her relatives but the city administered its apartments. Agnes and her children got a room with a kitchen on the second floor, but they didn't like it there because it was cramped.

Every evening Edith's mom and her children would kneel on the floor and pray for their father to return. Every day the children would write a letter to him, although he never received them. But he was alive and would return after two years.

Then, before they went to sleep, they would put a wooden plank between the door and the wardrobe. It happened sometimes that at night someone would knock at the door, and they could hear people speaking Russian, so they pretended they were not there.

WŁADZIA

There was no glass in the windows. They had shattered during the war when a projectile exploded in the garden. The bathtub was covered with rust and there was no water. Electricity was turned on occasionally but only for a moment. A door to one of the rooms was locked. There were no bedsheets, pots, or stove. There were a few pieces of furniture, including a wardrobe stuffed with luxurious lingerie.

On the first floor of the low building on Kreuzschnabelweg, Władzia had the first real apartment of her own. Urban planners had designed the entire neighborhood—Sępolno—to look from the air like an eagle. If she'd had wings, she could have flown over her neighborhood and seen that from above it looked like a gigantic bird and that she lived in its lower belly.

As soon as Władzia had moved in, someone knocked at the door. She opened.

There was a young woman with a child. "Ich wohne hier," she said, smiling timidly. "I live here." The woman was scared.

Władzia opened the door widely. "Please, come in, I live here now."

"Earlier I lived at Mathiasstrasse and had a lingerie store there," explained the German woman. "My husband was sent to the front, our house was bombed, and the administration sent me here. May I take my things from the wardrobe?"

"Of course," said Władzia.

The German woman came three times. Each time she packed articles into her bag. Lace panties, silk camisoles, and petticoats. On the last day she brought a bunch of chrysanthemums for Władzia and two pairs of leather gloves—fur-lined for winter and thin for fall. She threw in two camisoles and two pairs of panties.

"Thank you," she said. "I was so afraid because people say that the Poles aren't allowing anything to be taken from the apartments."

There was another German woman, a neighbor from the second floor. She said her name was Frau Erna Breuer and she lived with her daughter Kristina. "Is there anything you need?" she would ask Władzia.

"I'm glad we'll be neighbors," replied Władzia. "Where can I get some water?"

Frau Breuer run with a pail to fetch water from the artesian well. She brought some soup and delivered tableware. "I will gladly clean your place," she offered.

"My name is Władysława Okrutna," said Władzia.

"Frau von Okrutna," repeated the German.

"No, without von," the Pole corrected her. "Władysława will do."

"*Nein*, Władysława too difficult. Frau Okrutna," insisted Frau Breuer.

They became friends. Frau Breuer found a glazier for Frau Okrutna. He framed salvaged pieces of stained glass in the windows. Without being asked, Frau Breuer removed the rust from the bathtub and ironed the clothes because the electricity was on for a while. She was a tailor and made clothes for Władzia and her office friends. She introduced Władzia to Havranek, a Czech soldier and a kind man, who lived in the basement and still didn't believe the war was over. She found some people who pulled out a piano detected by Władzia in the rubble on the other side of the street.

Władzia shared her ten-kilo United Nations Relief and Rehabilitation Administration (UNRRA) parcels with Erna, found her daughter, Kristina, a job, and arranged for some documents that exempted Germans from compulsory departure from Wrocław.

They were friends, but Kristina didn't like it. She was sixteen.

"Hitler will show you your place," she shouted at Władzia. "You will finally understand what the German nation is like!"

A tall, stout, old, and furious German man appeared one afternoon. He screamed on the doorstep that he had his belongings and a bicycle in the locked room. "You may take them away," said Władzia softly, although she was afraid of him.

The German locked himself inside. He yelled again and ran out.

"Where are my teeth? I can't find them!"

"Please, look around more carefully. I have my own, very good," responded Władzia.

The man went back to his room and emerged after fifteen minutes.

"*Frau, Frau,*" he shoved a small box under her nose. "*Meine Zähne.* My teeth."

He took his bicycle, teeth, and some bundles, and he never came back.

In the fall of 1945 Voivode Piaskowski proposed white armbands for Germans. But Aleksander Wachniewski, the mayor of Wrocław and Bolesław Drobner's successor, protested. "I am against the introduction . . . of mandatory wearing of armbands by Germans. Because their number is four or five times larger than the number of Poles. As a result of this, an overwhelming preponderance of Germans would be visible, bestowing a German character on the city."

At that time, there were 200,000 Germans in Wrocław, and fewer than 20,000 Poles.

EDITH

Every morning a yellow puddle of piss would flow under the door into Agnes Schmidt's apartment. If you didn't wipe it fast enough, the odor of urine would prevail in the apartment all day.

In September 1945 some families, settlers from Lvov, moved into her uncle and aunt's apartment building in Hundsfeld. An apartment across from Edith's was occupied by a family with two sons. A mother with two children took a place on the first floor. People from Lvov also moved into the apartment above the Schmidts. They threw out a coal stove of steel and enamel that people used to call an "English lady," and replaced it with a huge tiled stove. "I have to sleep somewhere," said a woman from Lvov, when Edith looked greatly astonished.

Edith didn't play with the Polish children in the courtyard. They called her the little Hitler girl.

Agnes had heard that some Germans had good Polish neighbors.

"What a pity such people haven't ended up in this house," she sighed, wiping the wet spot under her door that had been pissed on by the Lvov children.

Germans had to be expelled from the city, but at the moment they were indispensable. They removed rubble, worked at demolition sites, operated machinery in the factories, delivered mail, and were streetcar conductors, amusing Poles with their funny accent: "On yourr tickets, pleece, on yourr tickets, pleece."

There were not enough Poles to replace the Germans. Those already there were low-skilled. Polish postal workers didn't know the city and got lost in the rubble, Polish workers didn't have proper expertise, and tram drivers were yet to be trained.

Germans had to vacate apartments when Poles moved in. To avoid this, they sometimes put black flags in the windows, claiming to have typhoid. Sometimes, however, before they moved West, they lived with Poles, so Germans and Poles often became neighbors. In Wrocław they said that every Pole had his German.

WŁADZIA

Władzia worked in the Department of Education, Culture, and Art. Her office was located on the Oder in a gigantic National Socialist German Workers' Party (NSDAP, the Nazi Party) edifice. It had been under construction for a decade; in fact construction was still going on during the siege of Fortress Breslau. It was damaged during the fighting but was still functional.

On her first day Władzia got lost on her way home from the office. She wandered through identical little streets in the eagle-shaped neighborhood of Sępolno, which hadn't been damaged very much. The young woman passed by two churches, a cemetery, a school, and some shops. Her street had to be somewhere there, but she couldn't find it for a long time. The next day Frau Erna gave her a piece of chalk, so that Władzia could mark her way with white crosses. That was a marvelous idea; she would never get lost again.

Seven people from her training class lived in Sępolno. They arranged to meet in the bakery of some German who always offered them free rolls. They never walked to work alone, which was too dangerous. Twice, on Grunwaldzki Square, Władzia and her friend had to duck down in the rubble, when Soviets and Poles were exchanging fire. When they left their hideout, they found a wounded Soviet soldier. They dressed his wounds and waited for help. Around the corner an unconscious Polish policeman was lying on the ground. They administered first aid.

Sępolno, although it was far from the center, was not safe. Every now and then, through her open window, Władzia could hear women screaming "*Hilfe!*" She ran outside, asking whether she could help, but people just shrugged. Once again someone had attacked a German woman living alone.

Most German residents of Sępolno were elderly women. Their husbands were dead. Their daughters and grandchildren had been evacuated from Breslau in January 1945.

A gun was lying in the grass. Władzia bent down instinctively, put the bit of metal into her purse, and caught up with her friend on the way to work. She didn't tell anyone about her find. She knew she could be in trouble for illegal possession of arms.

In the end she revealed her secret to Antek, a partisan from the Kielce region.

"Sell it to me," said Antek.

"All right, for 500 zlotys," replied Władzia after a moment's thought.

With the money from the sale she bought a pair of shoes at the shoemaker's on Kołłątaj Street. They were of the latest trend. They had soles of wood and their tops were maroon and gray. Their price was 180 zlotys. Władzia's friends were dying of envy.

At first, the administrators in Wrocław weren't receiving any money. They got their first salary payment in October 1945. But very little could be bought for this. However, the employees of the Municipal Administration did have their privileges. They didn't have to pay for streetcars, they dined for free in the local canteens, and once a quarter they received coupons for clothing.

Holding a coupon, Władzia entered a warehouse at the Municipal Administration. Shelves, hangers, boxes, baskets, and chests were filled with American civilian and military clothing, new and used, sent to Poland by the UNRRA. She needed winter boots but apparently American women had longer and narrower feet than Poles, because no shoes fit her. From a pile of clothes, she picked out a light leather jacket, some navy blue "battle dress," and a few sweaters. This would have to be enough when the winter came.

EDITH

Edith's mom worked in a kitchen for the Soviets stationed in Hundsfeld. She had found a hole in the fence and every day she sneaked out with a cup of soup for her children. She knew that taking food from the kitchen was strictly forbidden and punished by death.

Later, she found a job in gardening, and she was allowed to take some vegetables and fruit home.

Edith worked for Poles from Łódź who had taken over a butcher shop. She took care of two-year-old Leszek, a sickly and heavy child who had to be carried all the time. Skinny and weak from typhoid, Edith hardly managed. She didn't know Polish and didn't understand her mistress or the children. They beat her, pushed her around, and didn't feed her the entire day. At the end of the week, instead of money, Edith got scraps of sausage.

There was a feast every Friday at the Schmidts'.

The only good Poles that Edith knew came from Stanisławów. They had come by horse-drawn wagon with their cows and had taken over a formerly German farm. They were nice. Agnes bought their milk until the day she discovered that the Polish woman was adulterating it with water.

Coming back from work Edith would cry from exhaustion. Her arms and back hurt. She cuddled her doll Andzia. "She is so light," she sobbed. "And Leszek is so heavy."

Her mother sold whatever she could from the house. First, Andzia's pram disappeared. Some Polish man bought it for a few zlotys for his daughter.

Finally, Mom told Edith, "Dress Andzia nicely, so we can sell her. You are a big girl now." Edith picked the nicest dress for her doll and saw her off forever.

WŁADZIA

Władzia's first Christmas Eve in Wrocław had seven stages. All her friends prepared Christmas at their own places. Then the whole group walked from one house to another. At five in the morning they showed up at Janusz's.

Władysława Okrutna has stayed in Wrocław forever. She got married and her granddaughter became a poet.

Erna Breuer, who had to leave for Germany in 1946, would pay her a visit.

Władzia still lives in the apartment assigned by the tall, red-haired captain.

Figure 9.3. A Wrocław street, 1945. Emmanuil Yevzerikhin / ITAR / TASS / PAP

EDITH

Edith's father was on the Eastern Front and after the war he ended up in Germany. He managed to get across to the American occupation zone from the Soviet zone. In Hanover he found a job as a carpenter, but in 1947 he found his family in Breslau. He returned in September and immediately got a job on the project of reconstructing Renoma, formerly Wertheim, the largest department store in Wrocław. In November he fell from a scaffold. In the course of the investigation it was discovered that his ladder had been tampered with. The perpetrator was never found. Franz went on disability.

Edith's younger brother served in the Polish army and died in an accident. Her older brother moved to the German Democratic Republic.

Edith's parents have never left their native city, where they lived into their nineties. And Edith still lives in the apartment building in Hundsfeld that once belonged to her uncle and aunt.

In 1945 barely 30,000 Germans were expelled from Breslau and a year later 140,000. By the end of 1947 only 2,416 Germans would be left in Wrocław.

Some 250,000 Poles would settle in the capital of Lower Silesia by 1949.

OCTOBER 1945

Stella, Anna-Ruth, and Alina Kossoy, residing until 1942 in Warsaw, 15 Leszno Street, are sought by Edward and Bertha Kossoy, 13 Hayarden Street, Tel Aviv, Palestine.
—*Życie Warszawy*, Oct. 1, 1945

• • • • • • • • • • • • • • • • • •

The Municipal Administration in Gdańsk announces that the lists of people who signed a declaration to be faithful to the Polish Nation and the Polish State have been posted outside the Municipal Administration Building at May 3 Street. . . . If someone knows that any people on that register were placed in the 3rd or the 4th group on the German national list by their own will, or that the behavior of those people during the occupation was not compatible with Polish national distinctiveness, inform the authorities.
—*Dziennik Bałtycki*, Oct. 2, 1945

• • • • • • • • • • • • • • • • • •

The lady in whose arms my son, Zbyszek Dzierzgowski, allegedly died in August 1944 at Długa Street, is kindly requested to contact me. Irena Dzierzgowska, Warsaw, 25 Kamionkowska Street.
—*Życie Warszawy*, Oct. 5, 1945

• • • • • • • • • • • • • • • • • •

Anna Michalewska, née Grabowska, prisoner in Auschwitz, is alive and living in Sweden. Information: Engineer Anraszkiewicz, LOT, 48 Nowogrodzka Street.
—*Życie Warszawy*, Oct. 5, 1945

• • • • • • • • • • • • • • • • • •

Before you go West, come to Grylaż Candy Factory, Krakow-Podgórze, 7 Węgierska Street, and buy inexpensive but excellent candy that won't get sticky, even if you travel for a month.
—*Dziennik Polski*, Krakow, Oct. 10, 1945

• • • • • • • • • • • • • • • • • •

I will take a girl from intelligent, healthy parents, age 2–5, preferably unbaptized, as my own. Leave information at Dziennik Polski.
—*Dziennik Polski*, Krakow, Oct. 10, 1945

• • • • • • • • • • • • • • • • • •

Teacher, former prisoner of Oranienburg, will borrow a blanket, or accept it as a gift. Teacher, Krakow, 3 Lubicz Street, Shelter.
—*Dziennik Polski*, Krakow, Oct. 10, 1945

• • • • • • • • • • • • • • • • • •

I have assets and own a small company. I am single and seek a single female business partner. Włochy, 11 Bem Street.
—*Życie Warszawy*, Oct. 11, 1945

• • • • • • • • • • • • • • • • • •

I seek a person to work on the farm and milk one cow, near Warsaw. 17 Wiejska Street.
—*Życie Warszawy*, Oct. 11, 1945

• • • • • • • • • • • • • • • • • •

Exhumations and transportation of bodies managed by Eug. Majewski Funeral Home, Warsaw, 16 Krakowskie Przedmieście.
—*Życie Warszawy*, Oct. 11, 1945

• • • • • • • • • • • • • • • • • •

Please return Stefan Rajch, a two-year-old boy, kidnapped on Tuesday, October 9, from a courtyard at 75 Nowogrodzka Street. I warn you that formal action has been taken. 50 Górczewska Street, Maria Rajch.
—*Życie Warszawy*, Oct. 11, 1945

. . . .

Due to the unlawful use of national emblems placed on mechanical vehicles, I order them to be removed by November 1, 1945 . . . Police Chief, Major Konwizor.
—*Dziennik Bałtycki*, Oct. 12, 1945

. . . .

Ewa Szyfer, age 74, and Stefan Oldak, age 10, are requested to immediately appear at the French Embassy in Warsaw. Their French visas are ready and they will find there all necessary assistance to leave for France.
—*Życie Warszawy*, Oct. 15, 1945

. . . .

October 20—formal opening of the literary cabaret At Fogg's, 119 Marszałkowska Street. H. Brzezińska, M. Fogg, F. Szczepański. Humor! Nostalgia! Songs!
—*Życie Warszawy*, Oct. 19, 1945

. . . .

My darling Felicia! Come back, I beg you. I am heartbroken. Jan Filipak.
—*Dziennik Polski*, Krakow, Oct. 21, 1945

. . . .

I will give away a newborn boy into good hands. Krakow, 7 Bosacka Street.
—*Dziennik Polski*, Krakow, Oct. 21, 1945

. . . .

Sown land means bread for tomorrow!
—*Dziennik Bałtycki*, Oct. 24, 1945

. . . .

I will take an orphan girl, age 15, as my own. Brwinów, 10 Lewicka Street.
—*Życie Warszawy*, Oct. 25, 1945

. . . .

Attention residents of 12 Moniuszko Street! If you have questions regarding the mass exhumation, come to 42 Nowogrodzka Street, First Floor. Dr Słubicka.
—*Życie Warszawy*, Oct. 25, 1945

. . . .

Security Company Rounds is hiring honest people, age 25–45, as night guards. Applications accepted every day from 9 a.m. to 2 p.m. Krakow, 6 Dunajewski Street.
—*Dziennik Polski*, Krakow, Oct. 28, 1945

. . . .

Citizens of Radom. Will any of you offer some money to a destitute cripple to buy crutches or a prosthesis? Please, kindly donate to: Janina Krzemińska, 45 Wałowa Street, Radom.
—*Dziennik Powszechny*, Radom-Kielce, Oct. 28, 1945

. . . .

Seeking someone to lead square dances.
—*Życie Warszawy*, Oct. 28, 1945

. . . .

We install new Polish keys in German typewriters. Office Equipment Workshop. J. Bartoszuk. S. Latek. 26 Jerozolimskie Avenue.
—*Życie Warszawy*, Oct. 28, 1945

10

We Are Not Germans After All

1945

Życie Warszawy, August 10: "What should be done with the Germans who are still in Poland? There is only one radical solution. All Germans fit to work, men and women, have to be mobilized. We should create camps and labor battalions. They will be given bread and soup, and after working all day, they will rest in comfortable and sanitary barracks. We will not abuse them, nor will we burn them in crematoria—we are not Germans after all."

SUMMER 1945

It was the last day of August. As on every Friday morning, Klara Maxara baked five loaves of bread for the week. Then she looked through the kitchen window.

"Erika! Look! What's happening? Soldiers!" she called her eldest daughter.

It was a strange formation, and ragged. Their uniforms, of various armies, were held together with twine. One was armed with a pistol, another with a rifle, and someone else was aiming at Klara with a hunting rifle. They had dispersed all over the village and two of them entered her kitchen.

"Get ready. You have to be at the roadside in an hour. You are going to Berlin to your Hitler," one of them said.

So in an hour they were standing at the roadside, waiting: Klara and her four children—ten-year-old Erika, in-between Oswald, younger Ursula, five-week-old Monika—with five loaves of bread, like quintuplets, hidden under the blanket in a pram. Only Konrad, Klara's husband, was not there. He had gone to the war and hadn't come back yet.

Klara counted the neighbors from her village. All of them had come, several hundred frightened people. She recognized some of them and could see people she encountered every Sunday in church. The armed men searched their luggage, beat the disobedient, grabbed wedding rings from the women's fingers, and ripped off their earrings. But she didn't know the people on the other side of the road, who looked at them in silence. They sat on wagons among chests, quilts, and sacks of grain. Their children were unkempt. The women covered their heads with babushkas and the men made clicking sounds at their horses. Five trucks arrived and Klara, her children, and the other women got onto them. The men walked on foot. Those who were slow, old, or feeble were hit with rifle butts by the men in ragged uniforms.

Klara didn't know yet that the armed men were Polish police. Nor did she know that the silent people from the wagons were just now moving into her house, and the houses of her neighbors. They entered her kitchen, touched her warm stove, lay down on her embroidered pillows, and knocked down from the wall the photo of her in traditional Silesian costume.

She had no idea that they had been camping on some grassy land near Opole for weeks. They had been soaking in the rain and scorching in the sun. They were sick, hungry, and they were dying. There were thousands of them, expelled from their homes, too, because their native villages that used to be in Poland were now in the Soviet Union. Klara's native village that used to be called Ellguth-Hammer, near Oppeln in Germany, from now on would be called Kuźnica Ligocka, a place in Poland, fifty kilometers from Piast Opole.

They were on their way, but they didn't know where they were going. Children cried, someone sang a Polish religious song, "Under Your Protection, Father in Heaven," and a few women loudly said the rosary in Polish.

Their journey came to an end. They were in the village that a few months ago had been called Lamsdorf. Klara could see a few barracks surrounded by a barbed wire fence and a gate with an inscription in Polish,

Figure 10.1. Photos of Czesław Gęborski from one of his trial files. The text states that asked to identify the person in the photos, a witness recognizes the commandant of the Łambinowice camp in two of them. Reproduced by Michał Grocholski / Agencja Gazeta

"Labor Camp in Łambinowice." Some civilians sat at a table and registered everyone entering the camp. They seized their luggage. Someone snatched Klara's pram stuffed with bread and pushed her toward the entrance. Later, Erika Maxara would see camp guards kicking her mother's bread as if they were playing ball.

2014

Gęborski recorded his life on five hundred typed pages. He put the numbered sheets into two navy blue folders and handed them to Zbigniew Konowalczuk, esquire. Unfortunately, I'm not even allowed to glance at them. Gęborski's most recent lawyer says their time has not yet come. So I search for Czesław Gęborski's résumés, prepared for his employers, minutes from his interrogations, his commanders' declarations, and confidential notes by his superiors. These were snippets of life tailor-made for the era in which they were created.

Gęborski was conniving all his life. He was used to manipulating facts
and recanting what he had said earlier. Already in 1947 his superiors noticed,
"He is brave and incorruptible, but not always truthful."

He was a handsome, but rather short man with thick wavy hair brushed
back, straight nose, shapely eyebrows, and a moustache. After the war, in
Łambinowice, he grew sideburns (*die Koteletten* in German). The prisoners
called him Cutleten Fritz. At the end of the 1950s, in jail, he grew a beard,
following his doctor's orders, because shaving irritated his skin. He liked
to pose for photographs, either in a German private's uniform (at first, he
explained that this was a joke, and later, that it was a part of a wartime plot),
in a Security Service officer's uniform, or in a military fur cap and sheepskin
coat. In the photographs he resembled Polish movie stars.

He was a perfectionist and an aficionado of pretty objects. His daughter
inherited a collection of cigarette lighters, paintings, and two thousand
watches. She threw out most of them, presented a dozen to her friends,
and kept twenty-six items for herself. Journalists asked her whether in her
father's collection she had found the watches of his victims.

1924 OR 1925

He was born on June 5 in Dąbrowa Górnicza, but the year of his birth is
uncertain. In the future he would say either 1925 or 1924. He was the son of
Aleksander Gęborski, a carpenter, and Wiktoria, a housewife. "No party
affiliation," he would write about his parents for a questionnaire in 1946.
Thirteen years later he would write: "They were members of the Polish
Communist Party." He had an older brother, Eugeniusz, a watchmaker. In
2001 he told the court that he had two brothers.

After completing primary school, he entered a vocational school for
miners. When the war broke out, he was fourteen or fifteen. In February
1946, applying for a job in the Office of Public Security, he would write:
"In September I joinded [we preserve his way of writing] the Polish Army.
In the same month I was injured in my right leg and captured with others
by the Germans. They sent me to Saint Anna Hospital in Miechów. When
I healed, I was released home. In 1940 I begun to work in my brother's
workshop as a watchmaker." In his next résumé he would write that from
1939 to 1941 he worked in a glass factory and lived with his parents.

Taken to forced labor in Germany, he escaped from the transport and
hid until June 1941. Captured by the Gestapo, he was jailed in Sosnowiec,

Katowice, and Gliwice. Beaten, kicked, and tortured, "with sore sides, a suppurating left lung, and a severe headake," he was free to go home. "I was living corpse," he claimed. After seven months of recovery he ended up in the labor camp in Kochłowice. There he met Jan Sulczyński, nom de guerre "Wańka," from the People's Guard. In the camp Sulczyński had a radio and was planning to break out. He drew Gęborski into the conspiracy. In April 1943 they helped sixteen Soviet prisoners escape, and themselves fled to the woods near Olkusz. Three years later his commander, Sulczyński, would recall, "Taking part in battles with the German invaders, he proved brave and heroic. Despite his young age he was promoted to sergeant."

Gęborski's father was taken away to Germany. In December 1944 Gęborski once again was captured by the Gestapo and sent to the subcamp in Mysłowice. Sulczyński wrote: "During the transportation to Auschwitz he was rescued by the partisan unit led by 'Black.' He went into hiding since he was exhausted and sick, and for some time he couldn't bear the hardships of living in the woods. Right after the liberation he joined the police service, exterminating Germans in Silesia."

WINTER AND SPRING 1945

Actually, Czesław Gęborski would have liked to join the army. He even sent in the correct application, but was directed to the police. At the end of January 1945 he began his service. A year later he would write: "I was sent to Świętochłowice II, where until April 1945 I was police chief. After having arrested the most significant German degenerates, I volunteered to join a commando platoon beyond the Oder to clear the area of German army remnants."

Nazis, *Volksdeutsche*, enemies of the state, and suspicious people were locked in the Zgoda Camp in Świętochłowice that reported to the Office of Public Security. The camp had been set up on the premises of a former labor subcamp of Auschwitz at the end of February 1945. It was commanded by Colonel Salomon Morel who enjoyed tormenting the prisoners. They died of starvation, diseases, and torture. It is uncertain whether Czesław Gęborski knew Morel personally, but we can assume that he visited the camp when the transports with "German degenerates" arrived.

At the end of April 1945 Gęborski was promoted, and after training in Katowice he reported to Second Lieutenant Bugalski. There, for the first time after the war, he met Jan Sulczyński. They left for Niemodlin, liberated a month earlier. Bugalski became county police chief with Sul-czyński as his deputy. A year later Bugalski would write about Gęborski: "During his service he demonstrated a lot of energy and commitment. He was an obedient and disciplined police officer. He created one of the first Police Stations in Niemodlin, in the Recovered Territories, exhibiting his skills and dedication."

Did Bugalski write the truth? Nobody knows. In the future Gęborski would maintain that he was city police chief in Niemodlin, but witnesses at his trial in 1957 testified that he was merely the ranking officer of the commando and guard platoon.

In late spring 1945, Gęborski received a new assignment from his superiors. He had to build a labor camp for Germans at the County Police Station in Niemodlin. Bugalski reported: "He got down to work, bringing barracks from a different town. He set up the camp on his own, using the German labor force. The camp could house five hundred people."

1945

They joined the police force because they could get a uniform. If you had nothing to wear, a uniform, even from a different army, was more valuable than gold.

They joined the police force because they could get food. The police wouldn't receive their salaries for a long time. In any event, there was nothing to buy for the money. Barter transactions were in effect.

They joined the police because they got an official gun permit. Although you tripped over rifles, guns, and ammunition all the time, armed civilians were frowned upon.

They joined the police to escape their past. In Wyszków, for example, the police chief was a former prisoner, sentenced for murdering a woman resisting rape. Among the police were people who had spent the war in the woods and who had a track record of violent assault and of murdering hiding Jews.

They joined the police because they had been in underground organizations and they didn't want to be arrested by the new authorities. Home Army soldiers joined the ranks of the police throughout the country.

They joined the police because they didn't know what else to do after six years of war, with no skills, not even writing skills. Some police were illiterate, some made striking spelling errors.

They joined the police because they got power. And they abused it. In February 1946, members of the special commission formed by the Central Committee of the Polish Workers' Party wrote a secret report about the situation in Niemodlin. They described it as deplorable. "The entire county is governed by lawlessness. People have lost their belief in justice and their hope of redress of their grievances. No crime comes as a surprise. The police and, to some extent, Public Security, violate and plunder the population. Sometimes people flee in a frenzy when they see a police officer. Women, especially, run for it at the first sight of a policeman. An extremely high number of abuse and rape cases have taken place in this county, but it is very hard to collect any evidence. People are afraid to testify and local government officials cover for one another."

They deserted the police force with rifles in hand. Because the allocated food was miserable and there were not enough uniforms, boots, and warm underwear, because they could make more money looting than catching looters.

With all that said, officer Czesław Gęborski must have seemed a real treasure to his superiors.

SPRING 1945

Monika, Klara Maxara's daughter, hadn't been born yet. That was March and Klara's belly was barely visible under her apron. She was worried.

She could sense the war was ending. In the winter, armed Poles came to her village. They said they were heading west, to reach Berlin before the Soviets who were likely to arrive at Ellguth-Hammer very soon. The Poles seized pigs from pigsties and jars from pantries. They had horses harnessed, got into the sleighs, and moved on. So then Klara awaited the Russians.

The first Soviet tank entered the village on March 19. It crushed the small bridge over the Steinau River, smashed the gate, and showed up in the courtyard of the Thomall family. A few soldiers jumped out from the turret, ran into the Thomalls' house, and left quickly with armfuls of quilts. They squeezed them through the hatch and drove away. In the future, Robert Thomall would marry Erika Maxara, Klara's daughter.

Residents of Ellguth-Hammer would remember those days as the worst, especially, the women. "*Frau komm*," could be heard all over the village, "Woman, come." Women covered their faces with soot, slouched, and dressed in rags. Their families locked them in sheds and blocked the doors

Figure 10.2. Klara and Konrad Maxara, Erika's parents. Private archive

with wardrobes. They hid them in barns, but all to no avail. The eye of the Soviet soldier could recognize a young woman in a filthy granny. His experience told him to move the furniture away. Ana was raped by ten men. Another woman, whose husband was at the front, got pregnant. She delivered a boy, but her baby died three years later. Klara's daughters were too small, she herself was pregnant, so they were saved from rape. The soldiers grabbed only Erika's gold earrings and stole her white dress shoes from a chest. She had them ready for her communion in May.

Soon after, on a cold spring day, they expelled the entire village to nearby locations because the front would pass through Ellguth-Hammer. They returned after two weeks. There wouldn't be any front here after all.

At the end of May Erika went to receive her First Communion. She wore a white dress made by her uncle, a tailor from Berlin, and a wreath. She was barefoot.

SUMMER 1945

Someone informed the police in Niemodlin that a madwoman was running through the streets of Łambowice. Czesław Gęborski and his unit went to the spot. It was his first time there. He walked in silence among the barracks of one of the largest prisoner-of-war (POW) camps in the Third Reich. Historians have estimated that over 300,000 POWs passed through Lamsdorf. About 40,000 of them, mainly citizens of the Soviet Union, died there of starvation, disease, and exhausting labor.

Gęborski's people heard a voice and looked into the barracks. Gęborski would recall, "We found a woman terribly unkempt and filthy, who had lost her mind. We wrapped her in a blanket and brought her to Niemodlin. Unfortunately, we didn't know how to deal with her. We simply bathed her, cut her hair, and put her in bed. And after two days, she simply died. Judging by her cries, we came to the conclusion that she was a Polish woman from the Warsaw Uprising."

The decision to create detention centers for Germans in the Śląsko-Dąbrowski voivodeship was made in June by the voivode, Major General Aleksander Zawadzki. The Niemodlin County chief administrator, Władysław Wędzicha, issued an order to translate words into actions. He recommended Czesław Gęborski, an experienced and estimable police officer, as the detention center commandant. In mid-July Gęborski came to the former POW camp in Łambinowice for the second time. His assignment was to organize a camp for expelled Germans. Gęborski had two weeks to set the camp in motion.

JULY 1945

Gęborski picked an area a few kilometers away from the POW camp complex. It was a small place, 300 meters long and 150 meters wide, where barracks, utility buildings, and the Wehrmacht Officers' Club used to stand. That place was very close to the village, so it was easier to bring water, which didn't exist in the camp. And the proximity of the village gave a sense of security. "The camp is disconnected from the outer world. There are no phones or electricity. It is situated among a hundred abandoned barracks and surrounded by enormous forests. The nearest police station is eight kilometers away, in Fyrland," Gęborski's friend, Mieczysław Paciorek from

Figure 10.3. POW camp Stalag 318 VIII F Lamsdorf. Wartime photo. Archive of the Central Museum of the POWs in Łambinowice—Opole

the Voivodeship Information and Propaganda Office, would write in his follow-up report about Łambinowice.

There was one more thing. POW Camp Lamsdorf, stretching out for kilometers, filled Gęborski with extreme fear. In the part of the camp designed for Soviet prisoners, dead bodies in uniform were lying on plank beds. A doctor he knew would explain that their bodies hadn't decomposed, but had undergone mummification due to the lack of fat in the tissue. The prisoners died of starvation. Nearby there was a shoemaker's workshop filled with shoes, soles, thousands of steel heel taps, and nails. Another building was the camp office with hundreds of prisoners' IDs, photographs, piles of books, ammunition boxes, and chests with projectiles. A deathly stink lingered in the air. When the camp began to operate, Gęborski would order his people to find the source of the foul smell. "I told them to take a few Germans, two guards, and the equipment, that is, shovels and spades, and to bury the dead horses or cows producing this odor. After a while one of the guards came and said that it was a huge cemetery of murdered people."

The new commandant worked fast and efficiently. The Łambinowice Labor Camp was set up in a dozen days. The chosen barracks were surrounded by barbed wire. Some would serve as workshops and garages. Straw mattresses and blankets were found on the spot. Other necessary items were brought from the section designed for British prisoners. Those barracks were in better condition with no dead bodies on the plank beds, so there was no danger of an epidemic. The police assigned a dozen guards to organize the camp, as well as forty men who, for various reasons, had been arrested by Public Security in Niemodlin. In the end there would be eighty of them.

Gęborski wanted his guards to look neat. "In the southern part of the camp we found a pile of British uniforms, obviously worn out. Some had bloodstains. I ordered those uniforms to be taken apart, then stitched together again. I made uniforms for my entire crew," he would testify many years later.

The guards were selected at random. He offered jobs to people he met in the streets of Niemodlin, looked for them at the police station when they ran their errands, and asked them to inform their relatives that there were jobs in the Recovered Territories. He notified his friends from Dąbrowa Górnicza. Not one of the guards had completed high school, but almost everyone had lost someone close during the war, had been in a concentration camp, or had been taken to forced labor, and felt a victim of the Germans. They were usually young; some were not even eighteen. Commandant Gęborski himself was twenty (or twenty-one). He appointed Ignacy "Ignac" Szypuła, age eighteen, to be his aide-de-camp. Szypuła spoke fluent German. Gęborski didn't. Gęborski made up the camp rules. His superiors merely advised him, "You are familiar with the German camps. You were in them, so you know."

At the end of July, all residents driven out from the village of Bielice ended up in Łambinowice. The village of Łambinowice would be one of the last to be emptied out, in February 1946. Overall, people from 150 locations would pass through the camp and the number of inmates, on average, would fluctuate between 600 and 1,200. Apart from the expelled, the camp would hold people suspected of belonging to Nazi organizations; German army soldiers, mostly Silesians, returning from captivity; the guards of the Lamsdorf POW camp; and people suspected of crimes against the Polish nation. This was supposed to be a resettlement camp, but it would become a place of repression.

On the last day of August 1945, Klara Maxara from Ellguth-Hammer, her four children, her neighbors, her friends, and people she encountered every Sunday in church, would arrive at the camp.

AUGUST 1945

Camps for Germans were emerging all over the country. It is certain that there were at least a few hundred, but later some historians held that the figure was 1,300. The camps reported to various institutions: the NKVD, the Soviet military authorities, the Main Information Office of the Polish Army, the Ministry of Public Security, and the voivodeship, county, and sometimes municipal authorities. They were located in former Nazi concentration camps, for example, in parts of Auschwitz, in former POW camps, where the Warsaw ghetto had been, or were built from scratch. The best-known camps were in Świętochłowice, Toszek, Łambinowice, Jaworzno, and Potulice.

In June 1945 journalists from *Życie Warszawy* visited the Central Labor Camp in Warsaw. It was set up on the premises of the former *Konzentrationslager Warschau*, situated in the Jewish ghetto. Today this is the site of the Museum of the History of Polish Jews. The reporters were delighted. Here, they reported, Germans lived in better conditions than anyone else in Warsaw. They had a garden at their disposal, "full of green plants, bushes, and trees." In place of the huge pit in which the bodies of murdered Poles had been buried during the war, the camp authorities created a flower-bed in the shape of the Polish coat of arms. An area from which twenty-four bodies were exhumed was now a vegetable garden. The German women lived in clean, whitewashed buildings. In one of the bedrooms the journalists spotted a vase with flowers. "We ask one of the prisoners about food and other details of camp life. She is satisfied. Sure, there is nothing like home, but she understands that she has to pay for her mistakes." The men lived in similar conditions. The bedridden were taken to the hospital, and later they recuperated in the camp park. "It is forbidden to beat prisoners. This will be severely punished. In addition, the inmates cannot be denigrated or reviled."

Did the journalists fall for the propaganda of the camp authorities, who showed them what they wanted, or did they write this article on their own, inventing what they couldn't see? Nobody knows. But it is a fact that in June, four hundred dead German prisoners were buried on camp territory. A report written in September by a journalist from *Życie Warszawy* about the Wrocław camp seems more realistic: "Long black barracks stand in a southern suburb of Wrocław. Behind the fence of barbed wire, there are thousands of cadaverous creatures. These are the people who wanted to tie up all of humanity with such wire. Here the members of the invincible army await their well-deserved fate."

1959 AND 2000

Years later, at his two separate trials, Czesław Gęborski denied everything the former prisoners of the Łambowice camp stated before the public prosecutor's office and the court in Opole. He said, "This is reactionary nonsense and slander!"

FALL 1945

Guards were screaming at six in the morning and Klara Maxara opened her eyes. She slept at the bottom of a bunk bed. Erika, Ursula, and Oswald slept above. Monika, the youngest, used to sleep with her. But she was not here anymore. "My five-week-old daughter died. Of starvation," Klara would testify in the future.

This was common in the barracks inhabited by several hundred mothers with children. One woman lost three children. Infants and small children didn't get separate rations. Prisoner Jan Wancke testified, "My wife died in this camp of hunger and emaciation. She had our children with her and wanted to feed them. The food was bad, and scarce, so she had to deny herself food."

What they had for drinking was tea made from the grass growing in the camp, but it was the end of September and the tiniest plants had been picked to the bare ground, so what was left was boiling water. Klara's relative from a different village—who hadn't ended up in the camp—brought them sour rye soup in a metal container, which the guard would occasionally pass to Klara. Usually it was the guards who ate it, like the food from the parcels brought for other prisoners.

Klara checked whether a rusty tin can that served as a basin was still hidden under the straw mattress. On the first day in the camp all their personal items were taken away, including silverware. Later there was a story about a man who had hidden a spoon and a fork in his pocket. He was shot immediately. Klara's children dug this can out from somewhere. It was probably a relic of the prisoners of the Lamsdorf camp but now the can was the Maxaras' treasure.

There was a lot of yelling. Klara got up from her plank bed and looked at her children. Lice were crawling all over them and pus was oozing from their scratched wounds. Bedbugs squashed at night had left bloody spots on their faces.

"Erika, come with me to the latrine," Klara shook the arm of her oldest daughter.

It was better to go together. Sometimes guards shot at women running to the toilet, for fun. It was said later that a pregnant woman, sitting on the latrine seat, had confessed to the stranger next to her that she was about to give birth because she felt the baby move. She died from a single shot, in mid-sentence, with her skirt pulled up and her underwear down. Klara hoped the guards would take pity on a mother and her child going to the toilet.

At night they peed into a bucket because nobody was allowed to leave the barracks. According to camp rules, anyone outside could be shot. Sometimes in the dark they heard single shots. Occasionally, the drunken guards aimed at the thin barracks walls and bullets would go through the planks. You could die in your sleep.

Klara Maxara tried to leave the barracks as little as possible, but sometimes she had to leave for the morning roll call.

"Sing, Hitler bitches!" screamed the guards.

Children and their mothers sang the mourning song of the German armed forces, "Ich hatte einen Kameraden." Later, Klara Maxara would find out that song was sung by the men from the male barracks and the young women from the female barracks at the same time.

"March, Krauts!"

Klara, her daughters and son, her neighbors, and strangers took long steps.

"Dresses up!" Sometimes the guards felt like joking, so skirts and dresses were pulled up.

The roll call was over. Then it was better just to sit on the plank bed and wait until evening. Once in a while the guards forced the women from the family barracks to clean the camp. When they returned, they watched the life outside through a filthy window.

Nobody took a bath there because water was only for drinking. Nobody did laundry because the same clothes were worn all the time and airing out the clothes was impossible because there were no clotheslines. Hanging clothes on the barbed wire fence was strictly prohibited and punished by death. Everyone knew what had happened in early September to Marta Preussner, the Maxaras' relative from Ellguth-Hammer.

Getruda Kuboń testified later, "Marta left the barracks and went outside. She came back a bit later and stopped in the doorway. I noticed that she had been shot. Blood was trickling from her chest. She told her daughter, 'Anna, Ignac shot me. He wants to kill me because I hung my rags on the barbed wire.'"

Anna Wieczorek, Marta's daughter, added to this testimony, "At this moment I heard, 'Come back, bitch!' My mother turned around and went back, and I returned to the barracks. I heard a shot. After ten minutes Ignac returned to the barracks and asked, 'Are there any relatives here of this woman who was shot? They should go and pray.' My two aunts and I went outside. We were severely beaten by Ignac, Antek, and other guards. Later, I found out that my mother had been shot in the head for the second time."

1945

Yet Klara couldn't see everything from her barracks window. Perhaps she didn't know that water was brought from the village in the barrel used for liquid manure or that bread and potatoes for the prisoners were delivered by a wagon pulled by human beings. Only the commandant could use the horses. Or that the fields around Łambinowice were cultivated by prisoners who whipped other prisoners tied to ploughs and harrows, as if they were oxen. Or that some prisoners fixed shoes, others mended clothing, and still others repaired broken tractors and cars that later were exchanged for food.

A funeral procession passed through the camp every day. "Not always, but often we saw eight or twelve gravediggers. They were taking murdered and starved people, and those who died of diseases, on two-wheel carts to the mass graves in the camp cemetery," Lothar Goerlich, one of the detainees, would recall years later.

It didn't even cross Klara's mind that Cutleten Fritz had sent dozens of German women to the mass graves of the prisoners from the Lamsdorf

Figure 10.4. Prisoners working on exhumations of Soviet POWs. Łambinowice, 1945. Archive of
the Central Museum of the POWs in Łambinowice—Opole

camp, discovered in July. Those women were forced to exhume the bodies
with their bare hands and without face masks. The male bodies, stacked
up in layers, were decomposed, so the female prisoners were plunging their
hands in the slime and sinking in it up to their knees. The invited journalists watched them work. In August 1945 the weekly *Przekrój* published
photos of the German women exhuming the bodies. "When they started to
uncover the graves, cynical smiles of disbelief froze on their German faces.
Each spade that hit the ground found bodies and bones of prisoners starved
to death by the German criminals," said the captions under the photos.
The exhumations, observed by a Soviet commission, would be resumed in
autumn and would last until winter. This time they would be performed
by male detainees. Czesław Gęborski admitted, "It happened sometimes
that a prisoner would accidentally fall into a grave. Since the bodies had
decomposed and turned into revolting slime, he would drown."

From her window Klara couldn't see Ignac, the commandant's right-
hand man, chasing two old men from a neighboring village across the
camp yard. "He was hitting their backs with a chain wrapped around his
right hand. Soon after that they both died," Anna Mike, a detainee, would

affirm. But actually Ignac preferred to lash people with a leather whip found in the German camp. Klara didn't know about the basement under the kitchen where, every day, men suspected of belonging to the SS or the Nazi Party were executed without trial. She didn't know that after the escape of one prisoner, ten other inmates, picked at random, were killed. That after the evening roll call some men never came back to their barracks. Those who were the last to leave the yard were murdered for being sluggish.

Klara wouldn't believe the story about a live man whose leg was cut off with a saw by the commandant and his aide-de-camp or that the guards were visiting the barracks of young, childless women at night, but later she would learn that Ignac told one prisoner to lie down in the road, and then ran over him with his carriage pulled by a gray horse. That someone saw a few men chased up a tree, and others ordered to cut the tree down. That when the deputy commandant's rabbit was killed, a little boy was found responsible.

"Ignac wanted to know who killed his rabbit. If nobody confessed, he would shoot all the women who gathered there in a line. In fact, about six meters right in front of us, there was a rifle on the ground and its barrel was directed at us. A little boy, age nine, ran up to him and said that he knew who had done it. Then Ignac told the women to return to the barracks, but a guard, whom I didn't know, grabbed the boy by his neck and pants, and repeatedly hit him on the ground," Paulina Wancke, a prisoner, would recall.

1945, ALSO

The commandant fell in love. His fiancée, Jadwiga Gęborys, looked pretty. She had a chubby face and curly hair. Before the war her father was a worker, but now he was managing a restaurant in Niemodlin. She was a year, or two, younger than Czesław, and came from Warsaw. She finished primary school, at the age of sixteen got married, and didn't take part in the Warsaw Uprising. After the war she and her parents left for the Recovered Territories.

Gęborski divided his life between love and duties. He administered the camp during the day, participated in expulsions, acquired food for the prisoners, and organized their transport to Germany, but his evenings were devoted to Jadwiga. He never spent a night at the camp. After work Ignacy Szypuła would take him to Niemodlin in his cart and pick him up in the morning. They were afraid some marauders from the German army might attack them, so they changed their route every day.

Did Czesław tell Jadwiga about camp life? Did he try to amuse her by telling her about the female prisoners who stood in the roll-call yard with their skirts up? About putting military helmets on German peasants' heads and beating them with sticks so that blood trickled down their faces? About sons forced to sing and trample their fathers, so they died? About kicking the prisoners with spurred boots, which was so tiring that they finally had to be shot?

Or perhaps he protected her by saying nothing. Perhaps he didn't want her to hear what drunken guards, on leave and in her father's restaurant, said about him. Was that why he sent her away to Dąbrowa Górnicza? Jadwiga moved in with his parents and waited for him, arranging a divorce from her first husband. She married Czesław on July 22, 1954.

They didn't have any children, but they adopted a girl from a German orphanage. Occasionally, Gęborski claimed that she was his wife's daughter. This was a bit strange because Czesław Gęborski was filled with pure and profound hatred of Germans. In this hatred he was not alone. This was a time when the word *Germans* was often written in lowercase. Polish office workers, railwaymen, journalists, teachers, children, old people, and guards in the Łambinowice Labor Camp loathed everything Germanic.

After the commandant was arrested, Mieczysław Paciorek from the Voivodeship Office of Information and Propaganda would write in November 1945, "I hereby testify that citizen Sergeant Gęborski is worthy of respect as a Pole and as a patriot. I witnessed the arrival of his father, already an old man, with his arms and legs broken by germans. Whoever has never personally experienced the effects of german civilization, may not approve how harshly Sergeant Gęborski treated germans. I am the first to curse them because in Warsaw they shot my brother-in-law, they took my sister and her daughter to the camp in Hamburg, they executed my younger brother, and they transported my other brother, his wife, and his children to the unknown. There are miljons [*sic*] of such families in Poland."

A few years later Gęborski explained, "I had only one purpose, namely, revenge on the Germans. I became familiar with a German prison when I was sixteen. There are also German crimes against civilians and captured soldiers. After the liberation I secretly continued my activity from the time of occupation, and my only motive was revenge on the Germans."

Gęborski encouraged his subordinates to beat the prisoners. The detainees nicknamed him Morderling, but most of all they were afraid of Ignacy Szypuła, Antek, and Jan Furman. Roman Rydzyński, a former guard in Łambinowice, would testify, "According to Gęborski, the best guards were those who treated people with cruelty and killed them."

Ignacy Szypuła declared, "I admit I beat prisoners sometimes and kicked them with my boots. I only did it to men. In this way I was avenging Auschwitz. One district official called me an eagle and told me to teach Germans a lesson for their oppression of Poles during the occupation. At the same time Paciorek promised to promote me to platoon leader if I did the right thing. I understood that I was supposed to beat the camp prisoners. In order to be promoted I indeed beat people with a whip, my hand, or the rifle barrel."

In 1958 Szypuła would still believe his actions were justified by the times. He wrote: "There is a statute of limitations for the postwar period and for that phase of hatred toward fascism."

Czesław Gęborski invited Wilhelm Nowak, a barber from Niemodlin who served in the town's Volunteer Fire Brigade, to the camp and allowed him to abuse the prisoners. Yet not all guards were cruel to the prisoners. The detainees from the Łambinowice Labor Camp remembered some of them as decent.

1959 AND 2000

Twice, the prosecutors had no doubts. At least forty-eight prisoners had died as a consequence of the fire.

OCTOBER 4, 1945

The Voivodeship Office of Public Security in Katowice, Department of Internal Affairs: "On October 4, 1945, between 2:00 and 3:00 p.m., in the Łambinowice Labor Camp, Germans set the uninhabited barracks on fire. A fireman, Wilhelm Nowak, had arrived at the camp in order to take a water pump. As he was about to leave, alarmed camp guards told him there was a fire. He immediately started to try to put it out. The camp commandant ordered all prisoners to help. The guards were instructed to surround the camp and place their rifles in the places where the barbed wire had been cut by the prisoners (Germans). Gęborski was trying to force the prisoners to extinguish the fire, but some of them disobeyed his orders. To suppress the revolt, he ordered a round of shooting in the air. However, some Germans made a run for it, toward the cut wire. The camp guards had no choice but to use the rifles to shoot the fleeing Germans. In consequence, forty-eight Germans were killed."

Władysław Szlabski, a guard: "Drzemalski, a deputy commandant, told me that Gęborski, Ignac, Antek, and a fireman from Niemodlin whose name I didn't know colluded to deliberately start a fire in order to take revenge on the people in this camp."

Czesław Gęborski: "I remember very well that on the day of the fire I was not in the camp. I was in Niemodlin together with Wędzich, a district head."

Jan Furman, a guard: "Two men barged into the camp. One of them was wearing a fireman's uniform. They beat anybody who was in their way. Both of them were drunk."

Józef Malorny, a prisoner: "On the day of the fire, Nowak, a barber from Niemodlin, was beating the prisoners one hour before the fire."

Wilhelm Nowak, a fireman and barber: "As supply officer of the Volunteer Fire Brigade in Niemodlin I applied to the local Security Office, asking for assistance in finding uniforms for the fire brigade. I was directed to the Łambinowice Camp where the uniforms of the former POWs were stockpiled. That's why I went to the camp. When the uniforms were loaded onto the wagon and we were about to leave, the fire broke out. One of the barracks was burning. I went there immediately to coordinate the firefighting on my own."

Ignacy Szypuła, a guard: "When the fire started, I was in the barracks of the camp administration."

Jan Furman, a guard: "The women told me they had seen Ignac leaving the barracks right before it started to burn."

Józef Malorny, a prisoner: "The guards told us to put out that fire with water and sand. I took a bucket with sand and I went. Following the guards' instructions, I entered the barracks, but when I emptied the bucket and wanted to leave, I was shot in the hand. After that I couldn't participate in fighting the fire any longer. Since the wounded were being killed, in order to conceal that I was wounded, I hid in the pit from which sand was being taken to put out the fire. I could see Gęborski, who was standing about ten meters from me. His rifle was hanging over his shoulder. In his right hand he was holding a gun. He shot a few times toward the people putting out the fire. All the guards were shooting and dead bodies were falling down."

Franciszek Smołka, a prisoner: "I was told that one of the guards ordered my wife to dance by the fire. When she refused, he hit her with the rifle barrel and shot her in the back of her head, killing her instantly."

Anna Mike, a prisoner: "I couldn't see everything by looking through the window. There was a lot of smoke around the burning building. However, I saw people fighting the fire, my father-in-law, Paweł Mike, among them. At one point, the guards started shooting at them and I lost sight of my father-in-law. After the fire was extinguished, I found out that he had been killed. My mother-in-law, Maria Mike, was near the burning building. She was suddenly stopped by one of the guards, who hit her with his rifle barrel, and then shot her in the back of her head, killing her right away."

Hildegarda Łukaszek, a prisoner: "I participated in putting out the fire. I personally saw one of the guards pushing Franciszek Walczyk and Paweł Hoffman into the burning barracks. Both of them died in the flames."

Ewa Żyła, a prisoner: "Ignac killed the largest number of people. He had guns in both hands. I saw live people being pushed into the fire. All of a sudden, Edek, the guard, pushed me into the fire, too. Some woman pulled me out. My hands were burned and my sweater was ablaze."

Klara Szlechter, a prisoner: "Anna Tyrke's daughter told me that she had seen her mother pushed into the fire by the guards. She tried to get out, crying that she wanted to go back to her children. As far as I know, she had five children, who were also in the camp. A guard shoved her three times, and finally shot her with a rifle. Her body remained in the flames."

Jan Furman, a guard: "People didn't try to run away at all. There wasn't any prisoners' revolt. I know nothing about holes cut in the barbed wire fence through which the prisoners were allegedly trying to escape."

Emanuel Schmolke, a prisoner: "During the fire I saw commandant Gęborski shooting with his rifle at the people who were trying to put it out. After it was extinguished, I personally was burying dead bodies. On the day of the fire there was no revolt, and I didn't see the camp prisoners trying to take flight."

Władysław Szlabski, a guard: "With my own eyes I saw Ignac Szypuła shooting a few people unknown to me. At the same time, I saw Czesław Gęborski killing a man unknown to me with his gun."

Ignacy Szypuła, a guard: "The Germans were herded to fight the fire. Those who didn't want to participate in the rescue operation were shot.

Gęborski and the district head arrived at the camp after the shooting. During the fire all possible kinds of weapons were used for the shooting that lasted no more than fifteen minutes. Only those who were running away and didn't want to fight the fire were shot. The fire was extinguished with sand and dirt. Each guard was shooting on his own. I was shooting at those taking off toward the fence. I didn't see anyone falling to the ground."

Czesław Gęborski, the camp commandant: "When I arrived at the camp, I got reports about the fire and the escape of the Germans. I didn't take part in stopping them fleeing. When I arrived at the camp, the order to use firearms had been already issued. While I was there, firearms were no longer being used. After my arrival, I inspected the cut wire through which a few Germans had run off. It was impossible for the guards to shoot toward the burning barracks. In this situation they would be shooting at one another. It was I who ordered the use of firearms to control the situation. My order to use firearms was issued according to the rules. I had made these rules myself. I admit the rules were very harsh and, in fact, I overstepped my authority."

OCTOBER 1945

A Czechoslovak newspaper published an article titled "The Łambinowice Camp Smolders with Death." General Zawadzki, the voivode, sent his aide-de-camp, Major Leon Foicik, to Łambinowice and ordered him to arrest Czesław Gęborski. The former commandant was detained in the Office of Public Security in Niemodlin. However, he was not locked in a cell, but held in a room between two offices. His case was taken over by Department IX of the Voivodship Office of Public Security in Katowice (Internal Affairs). In mid-month he was fired from the police. Nevertheless, he was still in touch with his wartime commander and friend, Second Lieutenant Jan Sulczyński, the deputy police chief in Niemodlin.

NOVEMBER 1945

At the end of October 1945, Konrad Maxara, Klara's husband, returned from captivity. He discovered that his native village was now called Kuźnica Ligocka, his house was empty and plundered, and his family was in the camp. Although a German, he learned that if he signed a declaration to be faithful to the Polish nation and the Polish state, his close relatives would be released. So in the beginning of November he showed up in the administrative office of the Łambinowice Labor Camp. He held documents claiming that the Poles named Maksara had been imprisoned there by accident. To get these certificates in a local office, he had paid 25 zlotys per person.

The Thomall family, from now on Tomal, got out of the camp the same way. Silesians and Germans who didn't want to become Polish were expelled to across the Oder. At the end of the year a verification commission arrived at the camp. It discovered that among the prisoners were some who from the first had been declaring their Polishness. They were released and went home. In autumn 1946 the Łambinowice Labor Camp ceased to exist.

NOVEMBER 1945

"To Whom It May Concern. Citizen Czesław Gęborski, former camp commandant, was exceptionally kind and courteous to the prisoners. He cared about their well-being, appearance, and health. Knowing how germans had dealt with Poles, I was surprised how benivolint he was to german former prison guards, but I interpreted this as an indication of the gudness in our Polish hearts that don't hold grudge. I was internally proud of the fact that we, Poles, never forget how to be human. District Commander of Fire Brigade in Niemodlin, [Illegible signature]."

"I hereby testify that citizen Sergeant Gęborski is worthy of respect as a Pole and a patriot. So I am distressed and heartbroken that he, one of the many persecuted by the germans, is now arrested because of them. I do hope that Sergeant Gęborski, as an innocent and true Pole, will be returned to Polish society. District Department of Information and Propaganda in Niemodlin. Paciorek."

NOVEMBER 1945

The Polish-Soviet Commission for German War Crimes arrived at Łambinowice. It was headed by Doctor Dmitry Kudryavtsev, who had already investigated the Auschwitz camp, and whose findings were expected in Nuremberg. Nobody knew the Lamsdorf POW camp complex better than Gęborski. By Kudryavtsev's order he was released from jail and became a permanent camp guide. Allegedly, he also interrogated prisoners detained in the Łambinowice labor camp by Public Security.

DECEMBER 1945

The Ministry of Public Security was upset. The Voivodeship Office of Public Security in Katowice asked, "Why is the investigation of Gęborski moving so slowly? Please speed it up. In case Gęborski turns out to be innocent, release him! Just in case, we enclose a prepared motion for case dismissal. Simply sign it."

JANUARY 1946

"A certificate. It is hereby certified that Comrade Czesław Gęborski, while working in our district, was an active member of the Polish Workers' Party. He organized a party cell in his workplace. He is a sincere Pole and democrat. District Committee of the PWP, [Illegible signature]."

"As camp commandant the aforementioned turned out to be a hundred-percent democrat who performed his duties diligently and impeccably. This certificate is issued for the appropriate authorities. Head of the District Office of Public Security in Niemodlin, [Illegible signature]."

In January 1946 Gęborski was released from jail and, at the behest of General Zawadzki, left for Katowice.

After two years the case against Gęborski would be definitively dismissed by the District Military Prosecutor's Office in Katowice. "He followed existing law, so he is not guilty of killing forty-eight germans who tried to escape. Military Prosecutor Marek Szauber."

FEBRUARY 1946

"To the Head of the Voivodeship Office of Public Security [VOPS]. I request to be accepted as an officer of the VOPS in Katowice. I ask for favorable consideration of my application. Sergeant Czesław Gęborski."

1959 AND 1976

Czesław Gęborski, major in the Security Service, BA in economics, enthusiastic reader of books on religion, secret agent who infiltrated the National Party, lecturer in the School of Public Security in Katowice, would be tried twice. He would be charged with brutal treatment of detainees in the Łambinowice camp, beating, torture, murder, and complicity in starting the fire that killed at least forty-eight people.

Figure 10.5. Bilingual obelisk commemorating deaths of Germans and Poles in the Lambinowice Camp in 1945–46. Rafał Mielnik / Agencja Gazeta

In 1958–59 he would be charged together with Ignacy Szypuła. Gęborski and Szypuła would never plead guilty. At first, they would be found innocent. In 1976 Ignacy Szypuła fell from a balcony during a coughing fit and died instantaneously. He had advanced TB. Czesław Gęborski died in June 2006 before the end of his second trial. Just before his death he asked the doctors for euthanasia, because the dying deserved mercy.

2014

In the spring, I visited Erika and Robert Thomall in Kuźnica Ligocka. They had returned to their German-sounding name. Klara Maxara, Erika's mother, lived for many years after the war. She died of Alzheimer's. Her photo in traditional Silesian costume, which once had been knocked to the ground, was hanging on the wall of the Thomalls' living room.

NOVEMBER 1945

Vitamins. Sauerkraut—wholesale. Information at 16 Wilcza Street.

—*Życie Warszawy*, Nov. 1, 1945

• • • • • • • • • • • • • • •

I thank Doctor Hauser and Mrs. Żabianka for effective treatment of my nerves. Helena Sewerniak.

—*Dziennik Polski*, Krakow, Nov. 7, 1945

• • • • • • • • • • • • • • •

I request that whoever took a dead body in early April from the corner of Oboźna and Tamka Streets provide their address. This is very important. 1 May Avenue, Łódź. Zuchowicz.

—*Życie Warszawy*, Nov. 7, 1945

• • • • • • • • • • • • • • •

I have returned from Germany and am looking for my children, son Władysław Wiśniewski and daughter Jadwiga Wiśniewska. 7 Dobrowoj Street.

—*Życie Warszawy*, Nov. 8, 1945

• • • • • • • • • • • • • • •

To Mr. Feliks Nowakowski from Żoliborz. Please come to pick up a letter from America. 10 Noakowski Street.

—*Życie Warszawy*, Nov. 8, 1945

• • • • • • • • • • • • • • •

Mrs. Julia Brodowska-Hickman who in July 1945 was looking for her husband, British pilot Goeffrey Patrick Hickman, is kindly requested to appear immediately at the British Embassy.

Hotel Polonia, room 415. Office of the Air Attaché.

—*Życie Warszawy*, Nov. 9, 1945

• • • • • • • • • • • • • • •

I am looking for my husband, Jan Madera. I am without a job and destitute. Leave a message for Kazimiera Madera, Polish Red Cross.

—*Dziennik Polski*, Krakow, Nov. 11, 1945

• • • • • • • • • • • • • • •

I will rent a Bechstein piano to honest people. 75 Starowiślna Street, Krakow.

—*Dziennik Polski*, Krakow, Nov. 11, 1945

• • • • • • • • • • • • • • •

We are destitute. We will give away our 10-week-old boy. Offers: Dziennik Polski.

—*Dziennik Polski*, Krakow, Nov. 11, 1945

• • • • • • • • • • • • • • •

Like the Phoenix out of the ashes, Kamea is rising out of the cinders in the form of cosmetic products of prewar quality. 11 Grodzieńska Street, Praga. Adamczewski.

—*Życie Warszawy*, Nov. 11, 1945

• • • • • • • • • • • • • • •

I appeal to your conscience. On November 6 my apartment at 5 Rakowiecka Street was robbed. Please return letters and photographs since they are most precious to me. Reward. Please name the location.

—*Życie Warszawy*, Nov. 11, 1945

• • • • • • • • • • • • • • •

Columnist and writer looking for editorial job. Offers: Warsaw 1, PO Box 12.

—*Życie Warszawy*, Nov. 11, 1945

• • • • • • • • • • • • • • • • • • •

Jan Kielman. Footwear since 1883. Currently at 6 Chmielna Street.

—*Życie Warszawy*, Nov. 12, 1945

• • • • • • • • • • • • • • • • • • •

Please return the portrait of Virgin Mary that was in the suitcase stolen from the car on November 6 to St. Vincent Palotti Church at Skaryszewska Street.

—*Życie Warszawy*, Nov. 14, 1945

• • • • • • • • • • • • • • • • • •

Mister Pickpocket from streetcar No. 9 on November 9. Return the documents, and for the rest, we will celebrate with a drink! Major Dobrowolski, 10 Litewska Street.

—*Życie Warszawy*, Nov. 14, 1945

• • • • • • • • • • • • • • • • • • •

Goat found. If you can prove its ownership, appear at 3 Ludna Street.

—*Życie Warszawy*, Nov. 14, 1945

• • • • • • • • • • • • • • • • • •

Dr. Grodzki. Plastic surgery. 40 Przejazd Street, Łódź.

—*Życie Warszawy*, Nov. 15, 1945

• • • • • • • • • • • • • • • • • •

Experienced percussionist (jazz). She would like to join a band. 15 Inżynierska Street, Orłowo.

—*Dziennik Bałtycki*, Nov. 19, 1945

• • • • • • • • • • • • • • • • • •

This year's leeches, fresh, for medical purposes. 6 Dmochowski Street, Bielska.

—*Życie Warszawy*, Nov. 19, 1945

• • • • • • • • • • • • • • • • • •

An elderly settler from the East, honest, healthy, energetic, and a good cook is looking for a job as a housekeeper for two people. Live-out. No carrying of coal. Apply in person at 3 Wróblewski Street, Krakow.

—*Dziennik Polski*, Krakow, Nov. 22, 1945

• • • • • • • • • • • • • • • • • • •

Eustachy Barański, age 38, who has been in Russia since 1940, is being looked for by his mother, wife, and brother. Leave a message at 4 Mazowiecka Street, Krakow. Mrs. Barańska.

—*Dziennik Polski*, Krakow, Nov. 22, 1945

• • • • • • • • • • • • • • • • • •

Lost. Certificate no. 1408 confirming membership in the Home Army, issued by the Office of Public Security in Kielce, as well as the birth certificate of Stanisław Karasiński, residing at 21 May 1 Street, Radom. Misuse punishable by law.

—*Dziennik Powszechny*, Radom-Kielce, Nov. 27, 1945

11

Sanok

GOOD FORTUNE, 1945

They arrived in Sanok with their children and down quilts. Those who had horses, came with horses. Those who had a cow, pulled it by a halter. Did they have anything to eat? Perhaps some bread, the last loaf baked before the stove burned down together with their house? Perhaps cottage cheese wrapped in a clean cloth? I guess not. When your house is on fire, first, you check to see where your children are. Then you run to untie the cow in the barn, chase the horse away from the backyard, and afterward you hurry back into the fire to save the quilts. Why quilts? I don't know, but in the memoirs of the victims of conflagration, mothers always rushed back to save their quilts in the last moments.

And then they walked to the town to find shelter and help. Those were Poles from villages burned by Ukrainians. Ukrainians from villages burned by Poles stayed in the fire-devastated area. It was estimated that those who arrived in Sanok brought one thousand head of cattle. They took over vacated buildings on Cerkiewna, Jagiellońska, and Zamkowa Streets. Before the war some of these had belonged to Sanok's Jews. The animals were also taken to the apartment buildings.

Bolesław Gorączko, the deputy mayor of Sanok, wrote: "They have placed their cattle in the apartments, the cellars, the basements, even on the upper floors. Because of that, communal lavatories deteriorate. The cattle lie on dirt or parquet floors without any straw bedding while liquid manure trickles down the rotting walls, spreads all over the courtyards, and defiles entire properties."

JAROSŁAW CHOLEWKA

"Before the war a photographer would come to our village. He spread a sheet and anybody could be photographed. One guy from the village had bought a bicycle and his picture was taken while he was riding it on the road. That road was in front of our house, so the house was captured, too. I have a memento of it. I asked a painter to copy my photographed house onto canvas. Look at it, there was a little room with windows, a kitchen—also with windows—then a closet, a hallway, a court for threshing grain, and a separate shed for agricultural tools. The house was burned down by Poles in the spring of 1946."

"My name is Jarosław Cholewka. In Ukrainian it is Kholyalka, but it was polonized after the war. I was born in 1930 in Ulucz, thirty kilometers from Sanok. Our village was large—about five hundred houses, two Eastern churches, a Catholic church, and a synagogue. Poles constituted 10 percent of the population, Jews also 10 percent, and the rest were Ukrainians. Poles used to say that we were Ruthenians, but this was just drivel.

"My mother, Katarzyna, had five children, four boys and a girl. My father, Michał, owned 3.5 hectares. He was a weaver. He produced canvas and did a bit of shoe repairing. He was an elder in the Eastern church that stood on the hill behind our house. He had keys to the church where all important holidays were celebrated.

"For two years before the war I attended a Polish-Ukrainian primary school. We wrote with a stylus on tablets and everybody had a piece of cloth for wiping. My teacher was Polish, but the principal was Doda, a Ukrainian.

"And then the war broke out [in September 1939]. I remember the beautiful weather just after the harvest when the Germans arrived. They disappeared after three weeks, but then the Russkis came from the direction of Przemyśl. They had long rifles and greatcoats and looked like Uzbeks. It was almost impossible to understand their speech. They announced that the

Figure 11.1. Andrzej Polański riding a bicycle in Ulucz with Jarosław Cholewka's family house in the background. www.ulucz.pl, Jarosław Cholewka's archive

border with Germany would be on the San River. They said we would be free and no longer oppressed by Polish lords, that the land would be ours, everything would be ours. And they told us to join the collective farm, the kolkhoz. We had to cover the windows and tie up the dogs. Pigeon breeding

Figure 11.2. Painting of Jarosław Cholewka's house. www.ulucz.pl, Jarosław Cholewka's archive

was forbidden, so the birds wouldn't carry messages to the other side of the river. At first people in Ulucz said that Russkis were people like us, with our language and religion, but it wasn't true. They despised Ukrainians.

"It was like that until June 22, 1941. It was Sunday when they announced that Germany had declared war on Russia. Soon Germans returned to Ulucz and introduced their rules. They branded the cattle and demanded the millstones. People were taken away for forced labor, but not the Jews. One day the Germans took all of them at once. Jews were sad and before they left they told us, 'We will be fermented, they will turn you into sourdough.' You don't understand? When you make bread, you start with the fermentation of dough, then you add more flour and finally get sourdough.

"In 1944 the front passed through our village. And then came the real fear. Your year 1945 lasted here until 1947. Afterward we were all forcibly resettled in Operation Vistula."

Figure 11.3. Ukrainian Insurgent Army soldiers on a mountaintop. From the left: Nazariy Dani-
luk (known as Pierebijnis), Vasyl Kuziv (Baz), member of Petro Melnyk's personal security team,
Petro Melnyk (Khmara), commander of unit TW-21 Hutsul'shchyna, and sotnik, or captain,
Ivan Kulik (Siriy) with binoculars. Sotnik Dmytro Bilinchuk looking at the camera. 1940s, Kosiv
region, Eastern Carpathians. Collection of the KARTA Center

"They say the Ukrainian Insurgent Army [UPA in its Ukrainian acronym, led by Stepan Bandera] had its base in Ulucz. This isn't true. These Banderite nationalists didn't visit us very often, but if someone came hungry, we had to feed him. How could you not feed a hungry man? Wouldn't you? While they were eating, the Banderites kept saying they were waiting for World War III, which was supposed to happen soon. That Ukraine would be free. That they would defend us. We listened but we didn't say anything. We stayed away from politics.

"Polish Home Army soldiers didn't come to Ulucz. They just passed by a few times. The UPA partisans were protecting us from them.

"A number of men volunteered to join the UPA. It was better than going to war in a German or Soviet uniform. Later, when the UPA was fighting the Polish army and was sustaining losses, villagers were forcibly drafted and they couldn't refuse. So we can't say that all UPA members were volunteers.

"Poles from Ulucz, about eight of them, who had mixed families, were told to move to the other bank of the San, where the Polish villages were. The UPA told them, 'We won't hurt you, but we won't be responsible for you. Others will come and kill you.' So Polish men left Ulucz. Were they really Poles? They couldn't even speak Polish correctly. You could recognize Poles in Ulucz because they were more daring. Our people were more restrained."

"How was it in 1945? The Banderites in the forest were pursued by the Polish army. Some soldiers came and said nothing. Others were arresting people for having a son supposedly serving in the UPA. Sometimes the Poles would lend horses, so people could plow, because there were no horses left in the village. And later, the Poles would plunder again.

"Their army was accompanied by Poles from the neighboring villages. They came to loot. They showed up at our house, too, but my aunt, my father's sister, who married a Pole and lived in a Polish village, followed them. She saw my mother crying because some Polish shithead was untying our cow. She knew him and chased him away. He still lives in Sanok and I have revealed his name in the book I wrote in Ukrainian. They grabbed chickens and ducks. Anything. They stole all the cows in the village. Only ours was left.

"We didn't rob Polish villages. The UPA didn't steal. You say the UPA had an even worse reputation? Listen, would a Pole write a negative history of his own country? The truth is that we were afraid of both sides, the Polish army during the day and the Banderites at dusk. After the war we had a Polish village head. He was killed by the UPA because he had allegedly denounced some Ukrainians to the NKVD. Right afterward, a Ukrainian village head was elected. He was shot, too, but I don't know why. Later on, there was no longer any village head. Once, the Banderite gendarmes cut off my cousin's beautiful hair and administered twenty-five lashes to her friend for talking to the Polish soldiers. A neighbor had denounced them, but what could the girls do? The soldiers were passing through the village, asked for something, and they had to respond.

"Our house burned down in the spring of 1946. But first, a Polish lieutenant on horseback entered our village. He was holding a sack. The soldiers who followed him were shooting chickens and putting them into this sack. At the same time, a Banderite unit—a *sotnya*—from Przemyśl had been camping nearby. They surrounded the village, took the lieutenant away, and killed two people. Soon after, the Polish army retaliated. They were chasing one another in the village, shooting incendiary bullets. . . . Many houses went up in smoke, including ours. We moved into the basement and in the winter we walked to another village from which Ukrainians had been forcibly resettled into the Soviet Union.

"You ask me if in 1945 I was fortunate. My reply: I was fortunate because that year nobody from my family died."

ZOFIA CHOLEWKA

"Those who were fortunate, were fortunate. In 1945 I was not. In 1941 my father, Vasil, was taken by the Russkis to the war. He never came back. I was left with my mom and my older brother. Our second tragedy was hunger. We were eating pigweed. And later, Poles burned down our house.

"My name is Zofia Cholewka. I was born in Ulucz in 1935 and I'm Jarosław's wife. I remember when I was ten, standing in the backyard with my brother. My mom showed up, followed by two uniformed men. That scene is stuck inside in my head, like a photograph. One soldier made a protracted gesture with his hand and lit a match. He tossed it on the straw roof. My mom only managed to save a quilt. My aunt's house was burned down, too.

"After that, in 1946, our village was burned down twice more. The most vengeful were Poles from Volhynia. They were familiar with our language and religion. They were telling us to cross ourselves and they immediately knew who was from the Eastern Church and who was from the Catholic Church.

"This wasn't the end of our misfortune. My mom contracted typhoid and died. At that time people were dying in Ulucz. Sometimes several people in one house.

"In the spring of 1947 we were given two hours to leave the village. And they took us to Prussia. My husband and I returned in the 1960s, but our Ulucz is no more. Only our Eastern church, the oldest in Poland, is still standing on the hill behind my husband's house. We live near Sanok."

REPORTS FROM THE POLICE STATIONS

April

"Unknown perpetrators were firing at the village of Ratnawica for half an hour. There were no victims. Someone says this was not done by the Banderites, because Ratnawica is a Ruthenian village."

May

"Banderites hanged Józef Nisiewicz, a forest ranger, and his wife. They shot Katarzyna Demkowicz, Marian Popiel, Zygmunt Progorowicz, and the Karczynkis."

"Two unknown perpetrators attacked Michał Ciepły, the head of a dairy factory in Jaćmierz. He was heading to Sanok in a horse-wagon filled with butter and cheese. The perpetrators stole forty-two kilograms of butter. They wore civilian clothing and spoke Polish."

"The Ukrainian National Self-Defense [UNSD] sentenced Wasil Homyk, of Ukrainian nationality, to death by hanging. Before the sentence was carried out, representatives of the UNSD had severely beaten the village head Teodor Dziaba, Jan Swyrycz, Fena Milan, and Andrij Łakomy with an iron bar. They were told they 'had been beaten for informing the NKVD and the Polish police about everything.'"

THE TOWN

Sanok, entered by the Red Army in August 1944, was in a difficult situation. Fleeing Germans blew up the battery factory, three hundred buildings were burned down or destroyed by shells, windows had no glass, and the town power plant was not working. In 1945 Sanok County was one of the most devastated places in Rzeszów Voivodeship.

The Soviets treated the town as their own property. They made decisions regarding local administrative posts and totally controlled the County Security Office. According to the agreement of September 1944 between the Polish Committee of National Liberation and the republics of Belarus, Lithuania, and Ukraine, they started to resettle Ukrainians to the Soviet Union. The resettlement was theoretically voluntary, but it resembled roundups. People who didn't manage to hide in the forest were captured in the villages and taken to the train station. After days of waiting, they would leave for the Soviet Union. Their homes were taken over by Polish settlers from the East, but not for very long. The villages with the newly arrived Poles were often burned by the UPA.

In addition, the Russians made a terrible mess. In February 1945, fearing an epidemic, the county doctor Kazimierz Niedzielski warned the authorities that buildings housing Soviet soldiers were surrounded by filth. The courtyard of the building at 5 Market Square "was covered with waste, bandages, animal bones, and slops that were overflowing into Łazienna Street." The courtyard of the boarding school was flooded with human waste and rotten potatoes, and the square in front of the barracks was covered with garbage thrown from the windows. There was a similar situation at the hospital located in the regional court building and at the quarters at 120 Jagiellońska Street. Cleaning up after Red Army soldiers was futile because after a few days everything was the same.

ALICJA WOLWOWICZ

"The end of the war was our good fortune. Probably for everyone. Because nobody would be in danger or be shot at. When we began to understand what was going to happen next, our joy vanished. But at first we were happy.

"My name is Alicja Wolwowicz. I was born in 1928 in Sanok. I had two older brothers. My father, Wiktor, worked in the petroleum industry and my mom, Tekla, at school. We lived in Boryslav because that was the center of oil drilling. When the Russians arrived, they wanted to send my father to Baku since they needed specialists. Thanks to his friends my father moved instead to the nearby Gorgany mountains. We went with him. He was in charge of two oil wells, five kilometers from the nearest village. It could be reached only by a narrow-gauge railroad. When the Ukrainian attacks on Poles began, two of my father's assistants were killed. One was shot, the other had his throat slit. In February 1944 my father brought us to Sanok. He went back because the Germans who were in charge there told him to. Ukrainians attacked my father, too, but they didn't hurt him. They gave him just three days to leave. After that they would come back to kill him. They claimed to have shown him mercy only because he was kind to his Ukrainian workers. He managed to join us in May 1944.

"I remember that by the end of the war Sanok had become overpopulated. The town was a shelter for Poles from the Poznań and Łódź regions, residents of Warsaw after the Uprising, people from the Eastern Borderlands, and victims from nearby burned-down villages. The middle and high schools were already open in October 1944 and the students were of various ages. The turnover was high. People were going home as soon as the Germans left their areas.

"When the Polish Scouting Association was founded in Sanok, I became a Girl Scout. We organized assistance for the settlers coming by trains from the East. We worked in the monastery kitchen, making soup. Then we would take the soup in pots to the station. We would distribute it with ladles among the people. Sometimes we would dress a wound or explain to someone how to get to the town center.

"As a Girl Scout I organized short trips outside of town. One Sunday I went with my group to White Mountain on the bank of the San. We made camp near the forest. One unit was preparing lunch in the field kitchen. We were exercising and playing hare and hounds. Suddenly, a man appeared from the forest. He was wearing boots, military pants, a civilian jacket, and a military cap. He was carrying a rifle on his shoulder. At first, I didn't know whether he was Polish or Ukrainian, but from close up I noticed a Polish eagle on his cap. He asked me who was there with us. I didn't understand his question. He wanted to know who the most senior person was. I said I was because I was team leader. He ordered us to collect everything and go away. I tried to convince him we were not going into the forest. He advised us to leave. We had no choice, but to take off. We made camp on the San. Was that man sent by Żubryd, a National Armed Forces unit commander? I don't know. I think there were many more partisan units out there.

"One day, a rumor spread in our school that Poles arrested by the NKVD

Figure 11.4. Rally in Sanok celebrating the end of World War II. On the podium is mayor Stanisław Lisowski (Polish Socialist Party) or Dr. Jan Świerzowicz. Both were delivering speeches that day. May 9, 1945. Michał Smulski / Historical Museum of Sanok

were being held in the basement of the local bank. People said they were being tortured. At that time, basement windows had no glass panes, only three bars separating them from the street. Walking on the sidewalk anyone could surreptitiously drop something in. During school recesses my friends and I were trying to drop in some sandwiches. Ordinary sandwiches made for school. We worked in pairs in order not to attract any attention. One day, a ball of paper was thrown from the little window. We opened it and saw a letter in Ukrainian!

"We were aware of what Ukrainians were doing in Volhynia, we knew that in the Bieszczady mountains they were burning Polish villages. I remember that with other Girl Scouts I organized a festival for children. All profits were donated to victims of the fires. There were many Ukrainians in the town. My guess is they had lived in Sanok before the war. They were doctors and lawyers. They sent their children to Polish schools since there were no other schools around. They couldn't pretend they were not Ukrainians since everyone knew them, but they were quiet as mice. They didn't talk in the streets and never participated in the life of the town. Did we like Ukrainians? Of course not. We threw that ball of paper into the garbage and that was the end of our help."

REPORTS FROM THE POLICE STATIONS

May

"Because of the continual attacks and murders of the Polish population by the Ukrainians, the Poles from the incinerated villages of Borownica, Kuźmina, Tyrawa Wołoska, and other places moved to Mrzygłód. Right now this settlement is overcrowded with the newly arrived and their livestock. There are shortages of food and fodder."

June

"Thirty armed men burned down the house of Jan Dzusło, a Ukrainian. They ran off with his cow and two sheep. They stole one horse, one heifer, and four sheep from Onufry Chomuk. When they were leaving, they broke all his windows and took his clothes. They walked away toward the village of Lubatowa."

"On June 23, 1945, at 9.30 a.m., Michał Płatek, age thirty, from Besko, threw himself under the freight train to Sanok. The motive for his suicide was love. Michał Płatek was of Ukrainian nationality. He was in love with a Polish woman residing in Besko."

WŁADYSŁAW SZUL

"Hroszówka. That was the name of the village where I was born in 1928. I am a love child. My mom died when I was eight months old. I was raised by my grandma and aunts. At home we only spoke Ukrainian, but I have known Polish since I was a child. Our village was so close to Ulucz that it almost merged with it. But Hroszówka is no more. It was burned down. On January 13, 1946, our New Year's Eve, the Polish army arrived and burned it down. This was in the morning. They came from the forest. People couldn't run away. The soldiers took all the horses and set the village on fire.

"Poles and Ukrainians were burning one another in revenge. Poles incinerated Hroszówka and Ulucz. Ukrainians burned down Tremeszów and Witryłów. Every action had its reaction. However, the UPA never initiated

Figure 11.5. Buildings in the village of Bircza (Bieszczady Mountains) burned down by the Ukrainian Insurgent Army. January 6, 1945. Archive of the Military History Institute

violence, never murdered anyone just for the sake of murdering. Only in retaliation. They used to say the Banderites were killing people. This is not true. After the war, the most frightening shout you could hear in the place we lived was: 'The Poles are coming!' What was left of Hroszówka was a roadside shrine of Saint John. It had been erected in 1848 to commemorate the abolition of serfdom. We still take care of it. Look, I had it painted on canvas. Isn't it beautiful?

"My name is Władysław Szul. My wife is called Katarzyna. She was born in 1936 in Werchrata, Lubaczów County. There were sixteen households in Werchrata and only one Polish woman, whose husband was Ukrainian. Katarzyna remembers the Home Army attacking her village. They were looting everything they could lay their hands on. Katarzyna's mom wrapped her silverware in a cloth and tied it around Katarzyna's waist, just to save a few forks and spoons. Katarzyna's father was arguing with a Polish partisan about the last pot. They were pulling each other's ears in an altercation. 'I won't give it to you,' Katarzyna's father was shouting. 'How will I make dinner for

Figure 11.6. Polish Infantry Unit 9 in Bircha, a village burned down by the Ukrainian Insurgent Army. January 6, 1945. Archive of the Military History Institute

my children?!' 'I'll kill you if you don't give it to me,' the partisan screamed. 'Kill me, I don't care. I'll be dead, but right now I have to feed my children!'

"In 1945 I never went to Sanok. I had gone there on foot a few times when the Germans were in charge, but not when the Poles came, because I was scared. If we wanted to buy kerosene, matches, and salt we had to get to Przemyśl. You say it is seventy kilometers from here? Yes, but we would walk through Ukrainian villages. None of us would go to Sanok because it was mostly Polish villages that were along the way. It was dangerous. Poles didn't visit us, either. They stayed on the other bank of the San. Of course, we had known one another before. And suddenly we stopped trusting one another. Let me tell you, whoever survived 1945 was fortunate."

REPORTS FROM THE POLICE STATIONS

July

"On July 18, 1945, Michał Budzik, a platoon leader in the Polish army, Michał Kabierski and Marian Kabierski, all residing in Żohatyn, appeared at the police station in Dynowo and reported that Ukrainians from neighboring villages had told them to leave. Otherwise, they would all be slaughtered like people in Borownica. . . . Poles are leaving in panic."

October

"Someone left a handwritten note on a chestnut tree by the church in Bukowsko: 'From the Polish Partisans of the Home Army. Lieutenant Rogacz: I instruct all residents of Bukowsko not to turn over a single kilogram of your grain quota. . . . So, Mister Village Head, do your best for Bukowsko, otherwise you will share the fate of village head Mazur. Attention! Police! Stop collecting the quota! Otherwise, you will all be executed together with your commander and village head. Down with the Polish Workers' Party.'"

JAN KOBIELA

"In 1945 this was a real circus! Earlier, in the summer of 1944, Russkis came to our village with horse-wagons. They let the horses run free on the stubble. The animals ate the chaff and died soon after. A Russian soldier with a bullet in his jaw burst into the village. The bullet was sticking out and one of the peasants had to pull it out with pliers. '*Nichevo*, that's nothing,' the soldier was shouting. These Russkis did what they pleased. They slapped my face many times, for nothing. Once I was walking on the road and saw a drunken Russki coming from the opposite direction. '*Sobaka*, you dog,' he said and smacked my mug. I told my brother. He found the Russki and beat him up.

"My name is Jan Kobiela, born in 1929 in the village of Płowce near Sanok. I have lived there all my life. Before the war we and the Ukrainians lived in peace, but, really, some were Ukrainians and some were Old Ruthenians. The latter were much better and living with them was great. And then everything broke down. This was the Russkis' doing. They set them against us. Night after night in 1945 and 1946 everything around Sanok was on fire. Cows were mooing, horses were neighing, and people were shooting. I was watching when Nowosielce, the train station, Nowotaniec, and Bukowsko were burning. Damn it! Daily massacres.

"In our Płowce the Ukrainians didn't burn anything. Once we received a warning from another village: 'Be careful, the Banderites will come and burn you down.' But the entire forest nearby was swarming with Home Army soldiers. They were protecting us. You say that it was not only the

Figure 11.7. Ukrainian Insurgent Army partisans captured by the Polish Army. January 6, 1945. Bircza in the Bieszczady Mountains. PAP

Home Army that was hiding in the forests? Other Poles, too? I know it very well. Those were partisans, armed units, and Antek Żubryd's unit. I had known him from wartime. He was short and agile; I was sixteen and taller. On Christmas Day in 1943 he came to Płowce. He organized dance parties and there was no shortage of moonshine. I would play the accordion.

"Only once did the Ukrainian insurgents come to our house. It was the beginning of 1946. It was night. It was the end of my watch, when I heard my dog barking. I wondered why he was barking so much. You are asking, what watch? I had joined the Volunteer Reserve Police. I participated in many actions. Once we got a report that the UPA was in the neighboring village. So we went there, but they had fled toward Baligród. I have a veteran's card. It says I was strengthening the people's power. The people's power? We were fighting for our lives! Should I have let the Banderites kill me? I was thinking: before they kill me, I will finish off ten of them. They would pay a high price to get me.

Figure 11.8. Ukrainian Insurgent Army partisans captured by the Polish Army. January 6, 1945. Bircza in the Bieszczady Mountains. PAP

"So I heard my dog barking. I entered my house and before I took off my cap, they started pounding on the windows. 'Open up, Polish army, tie up the dog!' We opened the door. It was freezing. I realized they were Ukrainians, Banderites with tridents on their caps. Sons of bitches. They got in and started plundering. My brother, who was in the Polish army and had reached Bologna in Italy, sent us military boots, uniforms, and sweaters. These Ukrainians were stealing everything. Suddenly, my brother's wife, who was Ukrainian, said that our father once had helped release a Ukrainian friend from prison. In the end they didn't hurt us. They just robbed us and walked away, though they could have killed us.

"At these times life was worth nothing. People were shooting other people like rabbits, but our own people didn't steal from us. Only once, in 1945, Stanisław Kossakowski, who spent a brief period with Żubryd, visited my aunt. My uncle was not at home. He was in the camp in Jaworzno, having been arrested for his activity in the Home Army. Suddenly, Kossakowski seized my aunt's pig! My brother showed up and shouted, 'Kossakowski, leave it! How can you steal from a Polish soldier?! Kossakowski replied, 'What am I supposed to eat?' My brother said, 'I don't give a damn. Go and steal from the Ukrainians.' Kossakowski didn't listen and ran away with the pig.

"I will tell you more about my good fortune. First, Ukrainians were deported to the Soviet Union as early as 1945. I felt sorry for neighbors from nearby villages. I had known them from my childhood. I helped Adam and Józek carry their belongings to the train station, then I went back to say good-bye, but right after the Ukrainians had left the village of Stróże near Płowce, I checked their houses. I found a lot of weapons, rifles under the roofs or grenades in the storage areas. On my back I carried a long projectile home. It was a *katyusha* [a Russian rocket launcher]. My brother followed me with a wheelbarrow filled with grenades. My father asked, 'Why do you need so many weapons?!' 'To shoot rabbits, Dad,' we laughed. Let me tell you, this was really our good fortune."

DECEMBER 1945

Joseph Gruss, New York, Broadway, is looking for his daughter Joanna, age 8, and his mother Mrs. Żelaźnikowa, and will be grateful for any information about them. Until May 1944 both were in Belsen.
—*Życie Warszawy*, Dec. 2, 1945

Central Baths. 16/18 Krakowskie Przedmieście Street, near the Copernicus monument. Baths and tubs are operating.
—*Życie Warszawy*, Dec. 2, 1945

The Center for Fighting Epidemics in Krakow will hire 6 experienced disinfectors immediately. Apply in person at the Center, 20 Straszewski Street, Krakow.
—*Dziennik Polski*, Krakow, Dec. 4, 1945

We would like to thank Mr. Frydrychowicz, owner of the bakery, for comporting himself like a citizen during the German occupation and the Uprising, and for his help with providing coal, flour, and bread for the sick, elderly people, and orphans in our Institution. May God Bless You. The Charitable Institution of the Albertine Sisters, 42 Kawęczyńska Street.
—*Życie Warszawy*, Dec. 5, 1945

Anyone who uses electrical energy by bypassing the meter is a thief.
—*Życie Warszawy*, Dec. 7, 1945

Powered by the all-Slavic alliance, we are creating a powerful and democratic Poland.
—*Dziennik Rzeszowski*, Dec. 8, 1945

Aware citizens do not only think about themselves. By turning their heaters off in the evening, they allow electricity for someone else.
—*Życie Warszawy*, Dec. 9, 1945

Christmas toys, wide selection, cheap. American Bazaar, 21 Poznańska Street.
—*Życie Warszawy*, Dec. 10, 1945

A former store owner from the East, 20 years of practice, is looking for a position as a store manager. May be a butcher's shop. She is familiar with the coupon system.
—*Dziennik Polski*, Krakow, Dec. 14, 1945

If someone noticed a person carrying the sewing machine legs that were stolen on December 12 between 7 p.m. and 9 p.m., please leave a message at 3 Św. Jan Street, Krakow. Reward.
—*Dziennik Polski*, Krakow, Dec. 14, 1945

American Information Bureau, Warsaw, corner of Zielna and Próżna Streets, announces that it handles parcels up to 30 kilos, with new and used clothing, shoes, food, medicine, and other items of daily use, shipped by relatives and friends from the USA. We also help establish business relations between American and local companies.

—*Życie Warszawy*, Dec. 14, 1945

· · · · · · · · · · · · · · · · · · ·

Dentist, single, age 31, cultured, handsome, with successful practice is looking for a female dentist for future collaboration. Please send applications to Future, Świdnica, Lower Silesia. PO Box 18.

—*Życie Warszawy*, Dec. 16, 1945

· · · · · · · · · · · · · · · · · · ·

The nicest Christmas gift—the new book by Stefan Wiech, *Wiadomo—Stolica*.

—*Życie Warszawy*, Dec. 18, 1945

· · · · · · · · · · · · · · · · · · ·

I am not responsible for the debts of my wife Janina Orman, née Chom. Engineer Marian Orman. 12 Smolka Street, Krakow.

—*Dziennik Polski*, Krakow, Dec. 21, 1945

· · · · · · · · · · · · · · · · · · ·

I will hire a young woman or man to work in a pastry shop. Room and board guaranteed. Orphans have priority. Send your offer to Dziennik Polski.

—*Dziennik Polski*, Krakow, Dec. 21, 1945

· · · · · · · · · · · · · · · · · · ·

A merchant, experienced, intelligent, persecuted by the Germans, reliable, hardworking, and full of energy, is looking for a job.

—*Życie Warszawy*, Dec. 23, 1945

· · · · · · · · · · · · · · · · · · ·

The story of a gigantic death machine. Seweryna Szmaglewska, *Smoke over Birkenau*,

Czytelnik Publishing Cooperative. Price: 140 zlotys.

—*Dziennik Bałtycki*, Dec. 27, 1945

· · · · · · · · · · · · · · · · · · ·

Nurse, with Lvov State Certificate, 12 years of experience, prisoner of Ravensbrück, is looking for a job at the Baltic Coast. 15 Warszawska Street, Końskie, Łódź Voivodeship. Kołodziejczykówna.

—*Dziennik Bałtycki*, Dec. 27, 1945

· · · · · · · · · · · · · · · · · · ·

New Year's Eve party in Wierzynek's Restaurant and its rooms on the second floor. Reservations accepted by Kazimierz Książek, 16 Main Square. M. Kałuża, Chef.

—*Dziennik Polski*, Krakow, Dec. 31, 1945

· · · · · · · · · · · · · · · · · · ·

The first issue of the women's magazine *Fashion and Practical Life* is now available. Recent fashion designs from Paris. Dresses, coats, jackets, hats, and hairstyles. Also, the latest fashion trends created in Poland. Price: 20 zlotys.

—*Życie Warszawy*, Dec. 31, 1945

12

Red Birthmark

On the evening of January 30, 1945, at about 10:00 p.m., Lucie Rybandt and her son fell from the German cruise ship *Wilhelm Gustloff* into the Baltic Sea. Ten minutes earlier a crowd had pushed her out onto the deck. She looked around. Emergency lamps illuminated the night. To the right, a dark mass of people milled about. They tried to get into the lifeboats wearing their winter coats and furs, with their suitcases and quilts wrapped into bundles, with jewelry stitched into their linings. Women screamed and trampled one another, lost children cried, and men stepped on the fallen. They crushed fingers and noses with their heels and pulled the hands of others off the railings. Sailors armed with hatchets cut the frozen ropes holding the boats.

The temperature was below zero Fahrenheit. Lucie had forgotten to take a cap from the cabin but she didn't feel cold. She checked whether Hans Jürgen was securely tied to her with three scarves. He was quiet and didn't cry. Lucie didn't want to push into the boat. She walked on the icy planks, passing people jumping into the water and others praying loudly. She saw her neighbor from Gdynia, but she didn't recognize Lucie. The neighbor stood still, gazing at the sea. She cuddled her younger son in her arms. The older son, a nine-year-old, who revolved around her, crying, was unwittingly pushed away. Lucie felt the ship tilt more and more. She made the decision to jump into the water, but it was already too steep for the railings to be reachable. She asked some sailors who rushed by for help. They pushed her to the edge. She stood there and looked down. Thousands of people swarmed in the black waters dozens of meters below. She didn't know how to jump. Someone pushed her over.

ŁUCJA, 1998. WE KINDLY ASK YOU . . .

In the morning the postman dropped a letter into a bent and scratched mailbox painted an ugly yellow. The envelope was ordinary and white with the Polish Red Cross logo. It was August 18, 1998, and Łucja Bagińska was seventy-five. Around noon she came back from her doctor's. On the ground floor she took the letter out from her mailbox. Walking up four flights, she wondered what was inside. She thought it was another offer of assistance from the Red Cross. They had asked her before whether she might need a nurse. When she got to her apartment she put the keys on the shelf above the heater, put on her slippers, and sat down at the table in the blue kitchen. She opened the envelope impatiently and looked for her reading glasses. The letter was typewritten. Below the signature of the director of the Bureau of Information and Searches, there were two stamps, one with a larch tree, for 45 groszy, and the other with Sagittarius, for 2 zlotys. Łucja Bagińska read the letter. It had 11 lines, 4 long sentences, 110 words.

Summary of the letter: "Our Bureau was contacted by Hans Jürgen Rybandt, who asked us to search for his mother, Lucie Rybandt. According to the information provided, on the night of January 30, 1945, his mother had been on the ship *Wilhelm Gustloff* before it was sunk. Therefore, we kindly ask you whether the above search is in regard to you."

LUSIA. 36 DEUTSCHMARKS

Łucja Raczkowska was born on February 22, 1923, in Grudziądz. She had eight siblings and was only ten when her mother died. One of her older sisters promised to take care of the four youngest children as well as her father. This sister went to Gdynia looking for a job. In Oksywie, near the naval base, she opened a laundry for the foreign ships. Soon, her family joined her. In Gdynia, Lusia (as Łucja was called in the family) finished primary school and enrolled in vocational school. She wanted to be a salesperson. When the war broke out, she was sixteen. In September 1939 the Germans took her for forced labor. She had only two dresses in her cardboard suitcase, a woolen dress for cool days, a silk one for warm ones. The Germans assured her that she would be away just three days. In Darłowo, at the market for hired hands, Łucja was bought by a German farmer's daughter for 36 deutschmarks. Her duties included feeding the pigs, milking the cows, and cleaning the household. The farmers were kind to her. They treated her as their own daughter, saying, "Lucie, du bist unsere," or "Lucie, you're one of ours." For Christmas she was given a camera and an apron with an embroidery kit. Łucja's German got much better. She learned German in the lavatory from the newspaper clippings hanging there instead of toilet paper.

In spring Łucja returned to Gdynia. The Germans forced her family to sign the *Reichsdeutsch* list of prewar German citizens. They found some documents affirming that Łucja's father had lived in the Reich before World War I, got married, and had some children there. Signing the list meant no more slave labor for them, as they were now officially Germans.

Lusia found a job in a shop with dresses, buttons, Christmas decorations, and elastic bands for underwear. She made 60 deutschmarks a month. The elastic bands were *nur für Deutsche*, only for Germans, and even then only for those with special coupons, but Lusia sold it under the counter to anyone in need.

LUCIE. LONG GOWNS REQUIRED

The Raczkowskis lived in a residential building across from a military barracks. Łucja, a nice looking nineteen-year-old, often sunbathed in one of her windows. She would pile up her thick dark hair in the current fashion. She exposed her bare arms to the sun. The soldiers, bored in their barracks, played with their mirrors, casting reflected sunlight onto the girl. She pretended she didn't care, but she put her hat on and started to watch them from beneath the brim.

A few months later, on Easter in 1942, Lusia became engaged to one of them, the German Georg Rybandt from Puck. They would write letters to each other and a year later they got married. The groom, age twenty-one, was granted furlough and at his wedding appeared in uniform. The bride, age twenty, had her dress made of lace and white fabric for which she had swapped her cigarette coupons. She never smoked herself. Food and wedding rings were provided by Lucie's former employers from Darłowo. The wedding took place in the church in Gdynia, and the party in a rented room. Łucja's family didn't show up. The groom's mother announced to the Raczkowski sisters that despite the war her son's wedding had to be elegant and that long gowns were required. Lusia's sisters didn't have long gowns.

After the wedding the groom was sent to Yugoslavia to fight the partisans. The bride was left alone in the rented thirty-two-square-meter room. In order not to feel lonely she asked her mother-in-law to move in with her. Lucie was pregnant. On September 26, 1943, she delivered a son, Hans Jürgen Rybandt. She spoke to him only in German. For speaking Polish, she would have ended up with the Gestapo.

ŁUCJA, 1998. *AUF WIEDERHÖREN, MUTTI*

"Maybe we should call him, Mom," her youngest daughter told Łucja Bagińska.

The woman shook her head. Not today. It was August 18, 1998. Her head was spinning, her heart was beating faster, and tears were coming from her eyes, although she tried to stop them. Hans Jürgen had survived. She couldn't believe it. She wouldn't be able to talk to him today. She was sitting with two daughters, grandchildren, and husband. All of them had read the letter from the Polish Red Cross. They found the number of Hans Jürgen in a German phone book.

"I'm calling," the youngest daughter decided. She dialed the number and passed the receiver to her mother.

"Are you really my son?" Łucja Bagińska asked the man at the other end.

"Yes." He was saved by one of the sailors and sent to an orphanage in Germany. After a few years his grandmother and his father found him there. They took him to East Germany.

"When will we see each other?" his mother asked.

"What for?" He didn't want any contact. He only asked for a formal document stating that Łucja Bagińska was Lucie Rybandt, his mother, and that as a one-and-a-half-year-old-boy he had been on board with her. He had applied for the compensation for the *Gustloff* victims. He needed that certificate to receive the money. *Auf Wiederhören, Mutti.* Talk to you later, Mommy.

LUCIE. YOU KNOW WHAT RUSSIANS DO WITH WOMEN LIKE YOU

Lucie wasn't fond of her mother-in-law. She complained about her to Georg. She didn't like it when her mother-in-law brought a married man to the room they rented in common. Georg scolded his mother in the letter.

When Hans Jürgen was eighteen months old, Lucie went to see her husband in Yugoslavia. The train station in Vienna was bombed. She didn't run away like other train passengers, but hid under a bench. Those who ran away were killed. Lucie was only covered with debris. In Yugoslavia she saw Georg for the last time in her life. He had never seen his son. After Lucie left, he was sent to the Eastern Front. His letters stopped coming.

In January 1945 everybody knew Germany was going to lose the war. Germans were being evacuated from East Prussia. Germans from Gdańsk, Sopot, and Gdynia were getting ready to flee, too. The landlady from whom Lucie rented a room had received a ticket on the *Wilhelm Gustloff* sent by her policeman husband. She had a cabin for five people at her disposal. She planned to flee with her two sons. There were two free spaces left.

She tried to convince Lucie, "Your husband is German. You know what the Russians do with women like you. They rape and murder them. Come with me. We'll wait out the end of the war at my friends' in a village outside Hanover. Then we'll return."

Lucie Rybandt would rather go to her husband's family in Puck, but she wanted to break away from her mother-in-law. She made the decision to board the ship.

THE *GUSTLOFF*. THE YOUNG LADIES SLEEP IN THE SWIMMING POOL

The ship *Wilhelm Gustloff* was the pride of Kraft durch Freude, Strength through Joy, a Nazi organization that provided regimented leisure opportunities for German workers, including, among other things, ocean cruises. During the war the ship didn't sail anywhere. At the end of September 1939 it had sailed from its native port of Hamburg first to Gdańsk, then to Gdynia where it was docked for the entire war. The cruises were to be resumed after the victory of the Third Reich. First, the ship was turned into a naval hospital, then a military barracks. It housed several units of young men who after a brief training period would serve on U-boats. A bit later several hundred young women from the naval auxiliary service were quartered there, too. Nevertheless, many cabins that had been occupied by 1,436 tourists and 417 crew members, before the war, now stood empty. Vacant cabins began to be occupied by refugees only in January 1945.

By January 28, when the ship's office was still working efficiently, there were 6,000 people registered on the *Gustloff*, including 1,000 U-boat

Figure 12.1. *Wilhelm Gustloff*, the flagship of the Nazi organization Kraft durch Freude, incorporated into the German navy during the war. 1938. AKG Images / BE&W

trainees, 370 young women from the naval auxiliary service, and a few dozen Croatian military volunteers who filled in for the ship's crew. The civilian refugees were three times as numerous. The luxurious cabins designed for Hitler and Robert Ley, president of the Nazi labor organization, were appropriated by Nazi dignitaries from Prussia and their families. Other spaces were filled by refugees from Elbląg, Olsztyn, Malbork, and Kwidzyn, as well as a few hundred Gdańsk residents. Despite freezing temperatures the crowd at the dock kept growing. The newly arrived who had special passes continued to board the ship, which was about to get under way. It was impossible to count them all. The naval print shop issued about 3,000 food coupons. There were undocumented passengers who had paid bribes or who had been smuggled in by those already inside. The refugees took every nook and cranny on the ship's nine decks. The last group to embark legally—young women from the auxiliary service and wounded soldiers—had to be lodged in the emptied swimming pool on deck E. In total, there were about 8,000 or 9,000 people on the ship, half of them children.

Figure 12.2. Passengers entering the cruise ship *Wilhelm Gustloff* in the port of Hamburg. 1938.
AKG Images / BE&W

LUCIE. THE FOURTH DECK FROM THE TOP

Lucie and her neighbor decided to board ship in the morning of January 29. The night before she couldn't sleep. Out of a thick woolen blanket, she made a jacket with a hood for her little son. She packed his toys and coveralls. Before she left, she had put on her husband's underpants and suit pants. She put a wallet with a prayer in German into her pocket. This was supposed to save her from war calamities. She added a novena to Saint Anthony and her own photograph. Over everything Lucie pulled on a woolen dress and tucked it into her pants. She also put on a sweater and a suit jacket. Three warm scarves were packed in a bag.

She lived on Gdynia's main street, Świętojańska. People had to walk in tunnels dug through the snow that had covered the street and reached the second-story windows. Lucie, holding her son, and her neighbor, with two boys, struggled to get to the port several hundred meters away. The *Wilhelm Gustloff* was docked at Oksywie quay. They reached the ship by tugboat. The sea was freezing and the tug had to avoid the ice floes. Lucie, her neighbor, and the children boarded the ship with no problem. They had tickets for a designated cabin on the fourth deck from the top. Its portholes were at sea level.

The ship was so overloaded that on January 29 it couldn't leave the harbor. They made an attempt a day later, using more powerful tugboats.

THE GUSTLOFF. HITLER ADDRESSES EVERYONE

This was on Tuesday, January 30. The temperature reached just below zero Fahrenheit and thick snow was falling from early morning. The wind was level 6 on the Beaufort scale: strong breezes. The *Gustloff* left the harbor accompanied by another cruise ship, the *Hanza*, overloaded with refugees beyond measure. They were escorted by two warships. Soon after, the *Hanza* broke down and had to stay behind with one of the *Kriegsmarine* ships. The passengers were crying and lamenting, jealous of those from the *Gustloff.* Two days later, the *Hanza* was repaired and sailed safely to Kiel.

Near Hel Peninsula, the *Gustloff* encountered the steamship *Reval*, carrying refugees from Piława. The situation on the *Reval* was dramatic. Not all its passengers had been able to get to heated compartments. Those on the upper deck were freezing to death, drenched by spray from icy waves. The *Gustloff* stopped to take on its passengers. They occupied the warm staircases and overcrowded hallways. In the evening everyone listened to the broadcast of Hitler's speech celebrating the twelfth anniversary of his coming to power.

LUCIE. WHAT WILL HAPPEN IF WE ARE BLOWN UP?

Dinner was porridge cooked with canned milk. Lucie Rybandt was hungry because only dry rations had been served for lunch. Now she ate her portion and tried to feed her son. He didn't want to eat so she passed some food from mouth to mouth. Lucie's neighbor didn't eat, either. She was nervous. She worried all the time that the ship would sail onto a mine. When after dinner they came back to the cabin, she asked Lucie, "What will happen if we are blown up?" Lucie shrugged her shoulders. She wasn't afraid of any disaster. After all they were accompanied by another ship. If need be, it would take on the passengers. Lucie put Hans Jürgen to bed and the boy immediately fell asleep. She talked to her neighbor for a while and took off her winter boots. Just before nine o'clock a sailor knocked at the cabin door. He was checking that the passengers had their life jackets put on properly. Lucie's was tied up around her waist. The sailor joked that if she had to jump into the water, she wouldn't drown, but she would swim upside down. He helped her put on the life jacket correctly and advised her to put the jacket on her sleeping son. Lucie didn't follow his instructions. The jacket was too big for Hans and he couldn't sleep in it. Besides, wearing one herself, she wouldn't be able to hold him in her arms.

THE *GUSTLOFF*. MARINESKO SAILS TOWARD HEL PENINSULA

The captain of Soviet submarine S-13, Alexander Marinesko, was in a tight spot. For weeks he had been on the lookout for German ships near besieged Klaipeda, but not a single target for his torpedoes had showed up on the horizon. He couldn't return to his naval base unsuccessful. The NKVD was waiting for him there. Just a month earlier he had miraculously survived the nightmare of his first interrogations.

At the end of December, the entire secret police force from the occupied Finnish port of Turku had been looking for him while he was getting drunk with his Finnish lover day after day. Contact with the defeated Finns was punishable by death without trial. Leaving his military unit for a few days guaranteed severe punishment. Marinesko was saved by his supervisor, Captain Oriel, the commander of the submarine fleet. Oriel needed experienced officers. He showed Stalin's order to launch an offensive at all costs to the

Figure 12.3. Alexander Marinesko, the captain of Soviet submarine S-13 that sank *Wilhelm Gustloff*. Photo from September 1944. RIA Novosti / AFP / East News

NKVD commander, and tried to pull Marinesko out of jail. It was unheard of in the Soviet military, but all forty-seven submarine crew members stood up for their captain. The NKVD officer released Marinesko on parole, but just for one voyage. After his return, the investigation against him would continue.

Marinesko, lying in wait near Klaipeda, was dreaming about some spectacular success that would erase his faults. On the morning of January 30 he heard on the radio that the city had surrendered, but he had no intention of returning to base with nothing. Without informing anyone, he ordered submarine S-13 to be turned toward Hel Peninsula.

THE *GUSTLOFF*. FOUR TORPEDOES

Eight thousand or maybe even nine thousand people were herded together on the *Wilhelm Gustloff*. They were counting the hours left to Kiel. The engines worked steadily, but the ship sailed slowly. Captain Friedrich Petersen, an experienced Merchant Marine officer, set the speed for 12 knots although the *Gustloff* could move faster. The ship's engines hadn't been used for years and he didn't want to risk a breakdown. He ignored the danger of being spotted and sailed with the nautical lights on. He also rejected his second-in-command's suggestion to sail in the shallow waters along the coast where no submarine would dare go. He didn't agree to sail in a zigzag pattern.

All those navigational mistakes were being watched through a periscope with astonishment by Marinesko. On January 30 he was already near Hel Peninsula. Marinesko followed the illuminated *Gustloff* and its escorting torpedo boat, the *Löwe*. He looked for a suitable position for the attack. Hidden by dark night and snowstorm, his submarine surfaced, moved behind the afterdecks of the German vessels, and appeared on the left side of the cruise ship. Captain Marinesko earmarked four torpedoes for the *Gustloff*. His sailors, bored in the harbor, had scribbled on them "For Motherland," "For Stalin," "For the Soviet nation," and "For Leningrad." At 11:16 p.m. Moscow time—so two hours earlier for the Germans—Marinesko gave the order, "Fire!" Three torpedoes whooshed toward the cruiser. The fourth, "For Stalin," got stuck in the torpedo tube. The Soviet crew was in lethal danger, but fortunately for them they managed to disarm it. The first torpedo hit the *Gustloff*'s bow deep under the water line where the crew's quarters were located; everyone there was killed. The second one exploded under the swimming pool on deck E. Shattered tiles killed sleeping women from the auxiliary service and wounded soldiers. Hardly anyone survived. The third torpedo exploded in the engine room. All engines stopped, as did the radiotelegraph. Only the torpedo boat *Löwe* could send a dispatch: "*Gustloff* sinking, hit by three torpedoes."

Figure 12.4. Swimming pool on *Wilhelm Gustloff*. AKG Images / BE&W

LUCIE. WE ARE GETTING OFF!

Right after the first torpedo hit the ship, Lucie's neighbor ran from the cabin with her children. The strong tremor woke Hans Jürgen up. He was so scared he didn't even cry. The light was still on. Lucie put on her boots, unpacked the scarves from her bag, and tied the boy to her body. She could hear the shouts coming from the passageway, "We're getting off!" Then, there was a second strike and the lights went out. Yet Lucie was not afraid. She thought the ship had hit a mine. She knew she had to get to the upper deck where the lifeboats were. After the third explosion she went out to the passageway. Sailors were running with flashlights. Shots were fired in a nearby cabin. A Nazi dignitary's wife shot her children and herself. People with suitcases and bundles pushed forward, hitting one another on the head. Screaming and lamenting. Lucie and her child, pushed by others, slowly reached the staircase. It was full of dead children and older people trampled by those who went upstairs. Weak, wounded soldiers crawled on the floor toward the exit. In a dozen minutes Lucie Rybandt got upstairs and the crowd pushed her to the deck.

LUCIE. YOU CAN'T FALL ASLEEP

The ship stayed afloat for about an hour. The mechanisms releasing the life-boats stopped working. Their pulleys and cogs were covered with ice. The large lifeboats were missing since they had been used to place smokescreens during air raids. The available lifeboats were dropped into the water with great effort. They were swinging and many people fell off. Those who fell into the freezing waters could survive only two minutes.

After jumping into the sea, Lucie Rybandt surfaced very quickly. Her son was not with her. He must have untangled himself from the scarves when she was jumping or when she was under the water. There were thousands of people swimming around. Those who were drowning grabbed Lucie's legs, pulled off her boots, and seized her feet. A six-person inflatable raft carrying sixteen survivors passed by. Lucie gripped its edge and pulled the raft down. Desperate people aboard tried to pry open her stiffened fingers. When they failed, they helped her get aboard. They drifted for five and a half hours, falling asleep one by one. Lucie was lying next to a man.

"Please keep talking to me," he asked her. "You can't fall asleep."

At two thirty in the morning sailors from the minesweeper TS2, which had been called for a rescue, were on their way to the port with the survivors. Fortuitously, they noticed the raft. One of them went down to see if anyone was alive.

"Two people are alive," he shouted. "A man and a woman. The others have frozen to death."

Lucie Rybandt was taken to the engine room of TS2.

In total, about 1,200 passengers of the *Wilhelm Gustloff* survived the disaster. It is not clear exactly how many died. Estimates vary between 6,600 and 9,600 (1,523 people died on the *Titanic*). Captain Petersen and his top officers survived.

Captain Marinesko, thanks to his "torpedo attack of the century," avoided NKVD arrest, but he didn't become a hero. After the war he was discharged from the navy and he lost his captain's license in the merchant marine. He committed minor fraud and was sent to Siberia, where he commanded a river tugboat pushing timber rafts.

ŁUCJA, 1998. BLOOD TYPE

After she got the letter in 1998, Łucja Bagińska couldn't sleep for months. Every night she wondered if the man claiming to be Hans Jürgen Rybandt was really her son. Every evening she asked him the same questions in her head: What orphanage was he sent to? What clothes was he wearing? How is it possible that he survived without a life jacket, but with a heavy water-soaked coat? How did he know what his name was? How was he recognized by his grandmother and his father? Why was he silent for so many years? Why doesn't he want to see her? Why did he seek her, and now reject her?

Perhaps he was an ordinary con man. She fell asleep in the morning.

Łucja read Heinz Schön's book *Die Gustloff Katastrophe*. She found out that only one little boy like her son had survived the shipwreck. However, that one had been taken directly to a lifeboat. He had been wrapped in a blanket the entire time. Łucja stared at the photo of the boy. He didn't look like Hans Jürgen. And besides, his history had been written up. The boy had been adopted by a family from West Germany.

Łucja checked her blood type, to compare it with the blood type of that man. She was told that DNA tests were very important. She decided she would try to convince him to undergo genetic testing. She sent him a Christmas card with a note at the bottom: "When will we see each other?" He called twice and asked whether Mutti had sent the documents confirming that he was her son. He didn't want to meet.

LUCIE, LUSIA, ŁUCJA. A PHOTOGRAPH

Year 1945. Lucie Rybandt left the hospital where she had been since the shipwreck. She went to a village near Hanover, the same one she had planned to go to with her neighbor from Gdynia. After the liberation she could go back to Gdynia by sea or with the Red Army returning to the Soviet Union. She chose the latter. She was incorporated into auxiliary service. She was sent to Ukraine but managed to escape.

Year 1946. Łucja Rybandt appeared at her sister's apartment in Gdynia. Her photograph with its black crepe was hanging in the dining room. The entire family was sure that Lusia was dead. Lusia went to Puck to visit her husband's family. Nobody knew what had happened to him. She was legally declared a widow.

Year 1950. Łucja Rybandt married Wacław Bagiński, a Polish sailor. Soon afterward she received the message that her husband, Georg Rybandt, was alive. He had been sent from the Eastern Front to Siberia. He was living with his mother, Lucie's mother-in-law, in East Germany. Georg sent Lucie divorce papers. He didn't want to see her and didn't leave any address.

Year 1951. Łucja Bagińska's former mother-in-law sent her a letter with a little boy's photo. She informed Łucja that she had found Hans Jürgen in one of the German orphanages. The photo was the size of a postcard. The boy looked more or less as old as Hans when he had disappeared. His hair was blond, but his eyes seemed too large. Hans's eyes were like little chinks. The shape of his skull looked different, too. After all, Łucja would have recognized her own child. She was sure it was not Hans Jürgen, but she wanted to meet the boy and see for herself. Unfortunately, the mother-in-law didn't leave her address and the photograph was somehow misplaced.

Year 1955. Łucja Bagińska's former mother-in-law visited her in Gdynia. She entered the kitchen and asked Łucja in Polish, "Are you happy?" "Yes," Łucja answered. Her mother-in-law turned around and left. They never saw each other again.

Year 1998. The postman dropped a letter in an ordinary envelope with the Red Cross logo into a mailbox.

Year 2002. Günter Grass published the book *Crabwalk* in which he presented the story of a fictional family who survived the sinking of the *Gustloff*. The story was very similar to Łucja's experience. She didn't know about the book.

HANS JÜRGEN, 2003. TOMORROW MORNING

I was on my way to meet Hans Jürgen Rybandt in Lüdenscheid, a small town in North Rhine-Westphalia. I had only his address. I hadn't called him earlier to make an appointment. I was afraid he would refuse to meet me. I didn't know what kind of person he was, what he looked like, what he did, and whether I would find him at home.

On Tuesday, June 3, 2003, at 9:00 a.m. I rang the buzzer next to the name Rybandt. He lived in a four-family house located on a clean and very quiet street. Nobody opened the door. So I asked a neighbor where I could find Mr. Rybandt. She told me he worked in a home improvement store, in the electric appliances department. I went there. Hans Jürgen was just leaning over the drills. He was an elderly man with a round face and thinning hair. He was badly shaved and a little stooped. There was a wedding ring on his finger. He wasn't speaking clearly; rather, he was muttering under his breath. He was surprised by my visit but agreed to meet me the next day at 9:00 a.m.

HANS JÜRGEN, 2003. NO

It was Wednesday, June 4. I arrived ten minutes early. At first, again, nobody answered the door, but after a moment Hans Jürgen left the house with a canvas bag in his hand. He was surprised to see me. I figured he was planning to make off but I caught him. He waved his hand with annoyance. He didn't want to talk about the *Gustloff* anymore. The night before he had discussed the situation with his wife, and she didn't like it, either. I stood in front of him. I shouted, "Why don't you want to meet your mother? Perhaps you are not Hans Jürgen Rybandt, but a common con man?"

He turned around vehemently and started shouting at me. From his short, broken, and inarticulate sentences I heard the story of an unfortunate child. He was saved from the sea by a sailor. Nobody knew who he was, so he was sent to an orphanage in the GDR. When he was ten, his photos were published in the newspapers, since after the war many families were seeking their relatives. He was recognized by his grandmother, who had been living with his father. She came to the orphanage and checked to see whether he had a red birthmark, as her missing grandson did. He did. So he was Hans Jürgen. For years he was told by his grandmother and his father that his mother was dead. Then, accidentally, he found out this was not true, but they told him his mother had never loved him and deliberately threw him into the sea. So why would he look for her? Yet he thought about her all his life. Ten years earlier he had left East Germany and settled in Lüdenscheid. His grandmother and father were dead. When he got the opportunity to receive the special compensation for the *Gustloff* victims, he found his mother, because he didn't have any documents confirming that he had been on the ship.

He was standing there, crumpling his bag. His forehead was covered with sweat. He didn't want to talk anymore. He didn't want to see his mother or have any DNA tests. He was Hans Jürgen Rybandt and that was the end of it. I asked him to stand still while I took a picture for his mother. He walked away slightly hunched down.

On my return to Poland, I called Łucja Bagińska.

"Did your son have a red birthmark on his back?"

"No."

ACKNOWLEDGMENTS

In researching *1945* I met people in all walks of life, farmers and intellectuals, people from many parts of Poland, people who called themselves Poles, Germans, Jews, Kashubs, Silesians, and Ukrainians.

I am sorry that I couldn't write down all the stories of 1945 that I heard. I am grateful to all who shared with me their own experiences and those of their close relatives, first of all, Hildegard Bober, Czesław Morawski, Iścisław Karabon, and Agnieszka Urbańska-Ciszek, as well as her wonderful family.

A reporter's job means first and foremost talking to people and using source materials. In the case of *Poland 1945: War and Peace*, I assumed from the very beginning that I would be searching for witnesses of that year who were still alive. Soon I realized that I would not find anyone who was an adult at that time and that I would have to write a book from the point of view of people who were children in 1945.

I can hardly recall the number of my interlocutors but I think there were about two hundred of them. A first group included academics, historians, reporters, staff personnel of archives and museums, local activists, and librarians who helped me approach the heroes of my future book and explained to me the nuances of Polish, European, and world history at the end of World War II. These people don't appear in my work but without their kindness I wouldn't have gotten anywhere on my own.

Certainly, the most important are the heroes of my stories. Some didn't agree to reveal their names, such as Niusia the looter of chapter 2, whom I found thanks to her granddaughter, or "Edith Schmidt" (not her real name) of chapter 9, a German who stayed in Polish Wrocław with her family after the war. I can't name all of them because I might leave out someone. And they are all very valuable.

I am asked quite often which story had the greatest effect on me. I have one simple answer: all of them. Both the story of Jewish children in the Otwock Children's Home and the story of Stanisław Szroeder, the Kashub boy who deserted from the German army in the last moments of the war. How can we not be moved by the story of Werner Henseleit, the boy who was touched profoundly by sinister fate?

The stories of some I talked to have remained in my archives. I hope they don't resent me and that in the stories of others they will find their own. Maybe the purpose of my work was to remind us what our grandfathers and our grandmothers were not able to tell us? Or that we were not able to listen to them to the very end?

I am thankful for the support and assistance I received (in alphabetical order) from Karolina Babicz, Robert Bańkosz, Barbara Bednarczyk, Mariusz Burchart, Barbara Engelking-Boni, Paweł Goźliński, Marcin Hamkało, Ryszard Herman, Dagmara Jakułowicz, Renata Kobylarz-Buła, Ewa Kosior-Szwan, Hanna Krall, Katarzyna Kubicka, Iwona Kuźma-Ebel, Daniel Lis, Mirosław Maciorowski, Jerzy S. Majewski, Cezary Obracht-Prondzyński, Ewa Prussak, Eugeniusz Pryczkowski, Andrzej Romaniak, Danuta Sabała, Małgorzata Skowrońska, Elżbieta Skowrońska-Herman, Filip Springer, Rafał Szczepankowski, Małgorzata Szejnert, Jaromir Szroeder, Tomasz Szwan, Agnieszka Wolny-Hamkało, Renata Zajączkowska, and Mira and Jacek Zaremba. And, as always, I would like to thank Robert and Tosia. Without all of you, nothing would be successful. Chapter 2 was coauthored with Karolina Oponowicz and chapter 12 with Bogusław Kunach.

I profoundly thank all who made this book possible.

SOURCES

While working on *1945*, I never parted with the book by Marcin Zaremba, *Wielka trwoga: Polska 1944–1947: Ludowa reakcja na kryzys* (Krakow: Znak, 2012). It has helped me understand that we cannot apply any modern norms and standards to these events from the past. I have realized that we will never be able to completely understand our parents and grandparents who happened to live through 1945.

Two other books were equally important to me: Keith Lowe's *Savage Continent: Europe in the Aftermath of World War II* (New York: St. Martin's Press, 2012) and Ian Buruma's *Year Zero: A History of 1945* (New York: Penguin Books, 2013). After reading these works, I got rid of the naive stereotype unconsciously embedded in me that 1945 was a year of happiness.

Yet what was most important were conversations with people. I supplemented these conversations with published and unpublished memoirs, contemporary newspapers, archival documents, and historical monographs and dissertations. For a list of written sources for each chapter, I refer readers mostly to the Polish originals.

CHAPTER TWO: JUNK, OR LOOT

Cichy, Michał. "1945: Koniec i początek." *Magazyn Gazety Wyborczej* (21), in *Gazeta Wyborcza*, no. 121, May 26, 1995.

Konopińska, Joanna. *Tamten wrocławski rok 1945–1946: Dziennik.* Wrocław: Wydawnictwo Dolnośląskie, 1987.

Maciejewska, Beata. "Szaber w majestacie prawa." *Ale Historia*, no. 234, October 7, 2013.

Maciejewska, Beata. "Szaber Ziem Odzyskanych." *Ale Historia*, no. 228, September 30, 2013.

Thum, Gregor. *Uprooted: How Breslau Became Wrocław during the Century of Expulsions.* Princeton, NJ: Princeton University Press, 2011.

Życie Warszawy. Various issues, 1945.

CHAPTER THREE: ICE

Kieser, Egbert. *Zatoka Gdańska 1945: Dokumentacja dramatu*. Gdańsk: Oskar, 2014.

CHAPTER FOUR: WHY DID YOU COME HERE?

Dulczewski, Zygmunt, ed. *Drugie pokolenie: Wspomnienia mieszkańców zachodnich i północnych ziem Polski* [Second generation: Memoirs of the settlers of the Recovered Territories]. Poznań: Wydawnictwo Poznańskie, 1978.

Kalicki, Włodzimierz. *Ostatni jeniec wielkiej wojny: Polacy i Niemcy po 1945 roku*. Warsaw: W.A.B, 2002.

Koniusz, Janusz, ed. *Mój dom nad Odrą: Pamiętniki i wspomnienia mieszkańców Ziemi Lubuskiej*. Zielona Góra: Lubuskie Towarzystwo Kultury, 1971.

Maciorowski, Mirosław. *Sami swoi i obcy: Z kresów na kresy*. Warsaw: Agora SA., 2011

Maciorowski, Mirosław. "Szli na zachód osadnicy." *Gazeta Wyborcza*, December 20, 2013.

Melcer, Wanda. *Wyprawa na Ziemie Odzyskane*. Warsaw: Biblioteka Społeczno-Naukowa, 1945.

Osmańczyk, Edmund. *Był rok 1945. . . .* Warsaw: Państwowy Instytut Wydawniczy, 1977.

Przekrój. Various issues, 1945.

Życie Warszawy. 1945, various issues.

CHAPTER FIVE: DESERTER

Borchers, Roland, and Katarzyna Madoń-Mitzner. *Wojna na Kaszubach: Pamięć polskich i niemieckich świadków*. Gdańsk: Muzeum II Wojny Światowej, 2014.

Bykowska, Sylvia. *Rehabilitacja i weryfikacja narodowościowa ludności polskiej w województwie gdańskim po II wojnie światowej*. Gdańsk: Instytut Kaszubski w Gdańsku, 2012.

Dąbrowa-Januszewski, Jerzy, ed. *Opowieść o rodzinie: Szrederowie*. Słupsk: Zrzeszenie Kaszubsko-Pomorskie, 2006.

Szczepuła-Ponikowska, Barbara. *Dziadek w Wehrmachcie*. Gdańsk: słowo/obraz terytoria, 2007.

CHAPTER SIX: FIRST, REVIVING WARSAW

Ajewski, Eugeniusz. *Polska Walcząca: Na moim podwórku: Pamiętnik z lat 1939–1947.* Warsaw: self-published, 1995.

Archives of Warsaw Reconstruction Office. Warsaw, 2011.

Berezowska, Małgorzata, Emilia Borecka, and Józef Kazimierski, eds. *Exodus Warszawy: Ludzie i miasto po Powstaniu 1944.* Vols. 1–4. Warsaw: Państwowy Instytut Wydawniczy, 1992.

Fedorowicz, Andrzej. "Jak warszawianki chowały powstańców." *Polityka,* October 28, 2013. http://www.polityka.pl/tygodnikpolityka/historia/1559551,1,jak-warszawianki-chowaly-powstancow.read.

Górski, Jan, ed. *Pamięć warszawskiej odbudowy 1945–1949: Antologia.* Warsaw: Państwowy Instytut Wydawniczy, 1972.

Maciej, Robert, Jerzy Majewski, Jarosław Stachowicz, Grzegorz Sołtysik, and Krzysztof Wójcik. *Warszawa: Ballada o okaleczonym mieście.* Warsaw: Wydawnictwo Baobab, 2006.

Sigalin, Józef. *Nad Wisłą wstaje warszawski dzień (szkice).* Warsaw: Iskry, 1963.

Sigalin, Józef. *Warszawa 1944–1980: Z archiwum architekta.* Warsaw: Państwowy Instytut Wydawniczy, 1986.

Tarasiewicz, Kordian. *Cały wiek w Warszawie.* Warsaw: Agencja Wydawnicza Veda, 2005.

Tereszczenko, Jan B. *Wspomnienia warszawiaka egocentrysty: "Ja."* Warsaw: Muzeum Historyczne m. st. Warszawy, 2012.

Żeromska, Monika. *Wspomnień ciąg dalszy.* Warsaw: Czytelnik, 1994.

Życie Warszawy. Various issues, 1945.

CHAPTER SEVEN: I'M NOT A SHIKSA, I'M A JEW

I found Franciszka Oliwa's memoirs and some information about the Otwock Children's Home in the archives of the Jewish Historical Institute in Warsaw.

Buergenthal, Thomas. *A Lucky Child*: *A Memoir of Surviving Auschwitz as a Young Boy.* New York: Little, Brown, 2009.

Janicka, Elżbieta, and Joanna Tokarska-Bakir. "Sublokatorka po latach." An interview with Hanna Krall, 2015. https://ispan.waw.pl/journals/index.php/slh/article/download/slh . . . /161.

Kornblum, Władysław. *Ostatnia latorośl: Wspomnienia małego chłopca z getta warszawskiego*. Warsaw: Ypsylon, 2002.

Krall, Hanna. *The Subtenant*. Evanston, IL: Northwestern University Press, 1992.

Leder, Andrzej. *Prześniona rewolucja: Ćwiczenia z logiki historycznej*. Warsaw: Wydawnictwo Krytyki Politycznej, 2014.

Nałkowska, Zofia. *Dzienniki*. Vol. 6. [Introduction by Hanna Kirchner]. Warsaw: Czytelnik, 2000.

Zawada, Bartosz. "Żydowski Dom Dziecka w Otwocku 1945–1948." *Kwartalnik Historii Żydów* (1), March 2005.

Zielińska, Hanna. "Bo tam jednak było życie: Powojenny żydowski Dom Dziecka w Otwocku. Próba monografii." Master's thesis, Institute of Philosophy and Sociology, Polish Academy of Sciences. In the author's archive, 2006.

CHAPTER EIGHT: THE THIRTY-SIX DAYS OF BOLESŁAW THE FIRST

Davies, Norman, and Roger Moorhouse. *Microcosm: Portrait of a Central European City*. London: Jonathan Cape, 2002.

Drobner, Bolesław. *Bezustanna walka*. Warsaw: Polski Instytut Wydawniczy, 1965.

Drobner, Bolesław. *Moje cztery procesy*. Warsaw: Książka i Wiedza, 1962.

Drobner, Bolesław. *Wspominki*. . . . Krakow: Wydawnictwo Literackie, 1965.

Grynberg, Henryk. *Memorbuch*. Warsaw: W.A.B., 2000

Konopińska, Joanna. *Tamten wrocławski rok 1945–1946: Dziennik*. Wrocław: Wydawnictwo Dolnośląskie, 1987.

Markowski, Mieczysław, ed. *Trudne dni: Wrocław 1945 r. We wspomnieniach pionierów* [Difficult days: Wrocław 1945 in the memoirs of the settlers]. Vol. 1. Wrocław: Zakład Narodowy im. Ossolińskich, 1960.

Śliwa, Michał. *Bolesław Drobner: Szkice o działalności politycznej*. Krakow: Wydawnictwo Literackie, 1984.

Thum, Gregor. *Uprooted: How Breslau Became Wrocław during the Century of Expulsions*. Princeton, NJ: Princeton University Press, 2011.

CHAPTER NINE: EDITH AND WŁADZIA IN BRESLAU/WROCŁAW

Davies, Norman, and Roger Moorhouse. *Microcosm: Portrait of a Central European City*. London: Jonathan Cape, 2002.

Jakubek, Ewa Maria. *Marzenia spełniają się inaczej: Retrospekcje Ślązaczki.* Wrocław: Niemieckie Towarzystwo Kulturalno-Społeczne, 2010.

Thum, Gregor. *Uprooted: How Breslau Became Wrocław during the Century of Expulsions.* Princeton, NJ: Princeton University Press, 2011.

Wróbel, Stefania. *Jestem Niemką w Polsce: Fragment mojego życia.* Wrocław: Niemieckie Towarzystwo Kulturalno-Społeczne, 2013.

CHAPTER TEN: WE ARE NOT GERMANS AFTER ALL

I found much information about Czesław Gęborski's life in his records stored in the archives of the Opole District Court.

Nowak, Edmund. *Cień Łambinowic.* Opole: Centralne Muzeum Jeńców Wojennych w Łambinowicach, 1991.

Nowak, Edmund, and Roman Ciasnocha, eds. *Obozy w Lamsdorf / Łambinowicach (1870–1946).* Opole: Centralne Muzeum Jeńców Wojennych w Łambinowicach, 2006.

CHAPTER ELEVEN: SANOK

Kaczmarski, Krzysztof, and Andrzej Romaniak, eds. *Powiat sanocki w latach 1944–1956.* Rzeszów-Sanok: Muzeum Historyczne w Sanoku and Instytut Pamięci Narodowej Oddział w Rzeszowie, 2007.

Motyka, Grzegorz. *Od rzezi wołyńskiej do akcji "Wisła": Konflikt polsko--ukraiński 1943–1947.* Krakow: Wydawnictwo Literackie, 2011.

CHAPTER TWELVE: RED BIRTHMARK

Grass, Günter. *Crabwalk.* New York: Harcourt, 2002.

INDEX

Note: Page numbers in *italics* refer to figures.

52, 217, 263; Agnes working for, 250–51; in Breslau, 217–18, 232, 239–41; Drobner and, 208–9; Germans and, 41, 217–18, 239–41; in Koszalin, 80; looting and destruction by, 20–24, 292–93; in Poland, 213–14; Poles *vs.*, 249; POWs and, 264, *272*; *Wilhelm Gustloff* sunk by, 45–47. *See also* Russians

Soviet Union: gaining Eastern Borderlands, 92–93; Poland's territory and, 72, 100; Ukrainians and, 292, 302

Spychalski, Marian, 152

Stachuriski,Władysław, 85–86

Stalewo, 75–76

Stalin, Joseph, 42, 101, 209; Poland and, 100, 151–52

State National Council (SNC), 152, 210–12

State Repatriation Office (SRO), 77, 92, 94–96

Steinhaus, Hugo, 27

Stepnica-Staś, 86–89

Stykgold, Helena Kazimiera, 169–70, 172, 180

Stykgold, Włozimierz, 182, 189

Sulczyński, Jan, 261, 278

Szaberplac. *See* Looters' Square

Szczecin, 101

Szczerbiński, Stefan, 155–56

Szereszewska, Izabella, 181

Szkolniak, Kazimierz, 81, 83

Szlabski, Władysław, 276

Szmigiel, Eugeniusz, 86–89

Szpilman, Władysław, 78

Szroeder, Stanisław, *113*, 122; desertion of, 117–18, 120–21; military service of, 115–18

Sztarkman, Andzia, 170–71

Sztarkman, Linka, 184–85, 193–94

Szternes, Eda, 170–71, 191–95, *192*

Sztykgold Włodek, 184, 195, 261–62

Szul, Władysław, 296–98

Szwagierek, Jan, 75–76

Szwagierek, Krystyna, 75–76

Szyndler, Ryszard Janusz, 79–82

Szypuła, Ignacy "Ignac," 267, 271–73, 275–77, 281

Teheran Conference, 101

Tereszczenko, Jan, 136, 149

theater, resumption of, 33

Thomall family, 278, 281

Tołwińsky, Stanisław, 155

Tosia, 96

train stations, settlers living in, 94–95

transportation, 112, 143; collapse of, 80, 97; for repatriates, 94–96

treasure, looters finding, 12

Trylowska, Wilhelmina, 97–98

Tuwim, Julian, 182, 184

Tworzowaka, Bronisława, 105–8

Ukraine, 101

Ukrainian Insurgent Army, *289*, *300–301*

Ukrainians, 288, 292, 302; Poles *vs.*, 285–86, 290–98. *See also* Banderas